Personality as an Affect-Processing System

Toward an Integrative Theory

Personality as an Affect-Processing System

Toward an Integrative Theory

Jack Block

University of California, Berkeley

LAWRENCE ERLBAUM ASSOCIATES, PUBLISHERS

2002   Mahwah, New Jersey   London

Lawrence Erlbaum Associates, Inc., Publishers
10 Industrial Avenue
Mahwah, NJ 07430

Cover design by Kathryn Houghtaling Lacey

Library of Congress Cataloging-in-Publication Data

Block, Jack, 1924–
Personality as an affect-processing system : toward an
   integrative theory / Jack Block.
      p. cm.
   Includes bibliographical references and index.
   ISBN 0-8058-3912-7 (alk. paper)
   1. Personality.   I. Title
   BF698 .B545   2002
   155.2—dc21   2001040377
                                                       CIP

Books published by Lawrence Erlbaum Associates are printed
on acid-free paper, and their bindings are chosen for strength
and durability.

Printed in the United States of America
10 9 8 7 6 5 4 3 2 1

My life and work has been aimed at one goal only:
to infer or guess how the mental apparatus is constructed
and what forces interplay and counteract in it
—Sigmund Freud

Se no e vero ma e ben trovato
[It may not be true but it is well contrived]
—Giordano Bruno

Contents

    Conjecture   152
Some Diverse Observations and Asides   154

10 **Connections to Theoretical Alternatives**   **156**
The Five-Factor Approach of Costa and McCrae   156
    A Short History of a Still-Unsettled Approach   156
    Unresolved Issues   158
    Some Recent Five-Factor Findings   159
    Higher-Order Factor Analysis of the Five Factors   161
    The Five-Factor Model as the Five-Factor Theory   163
    Evaluative Remarks   163
Mischel's Approach, Past and Present, to Understanding
    Personality   164
    Some History and Orienting Remarks   164
    Mischel's Current View Regarding the Status of Personality
        Consistency   168
    Mischel's Current Theoretical Conceptualization   168
    Mischel's Hot–Cool System Proposal   172
    Evaluative Remarks   173

11 **Prescript: Developmental Aspects of Ego Control**   **180**
    and Ego-Resiliency
General Considerations   180
    The Conception of Regulation   180
    Regarding Genetics and Personality   181
    The Basic Dilemma of Ego Development   183
    Ego Functioning Structures   184
    The Beginning Neonate   185
    Gender Differences in Ego Control and Ego-
        Resiliency   188
Molding Psychological Development   189
    Regarding Compliance   193
    Regarding Aggression and Prosocial Behavior   196
    Regarding Imitation–Modeling   198

    References   **201**

    Author Index   **225**

    Subject Index   **233**

Preface

The field of personality psychology continues inchoate in this new millennium. It is lively, conceptually multilingual, empirically prolific, contentious, ambitious, and unsatisfying. The reasons are many, most recently having to do primarily with the different paths by which psychologists attempt to explore the domain of personality psychology. Inevitably, rather different cartographies of the field have been offered up as guides to the terrain. Correspondences among these various maps are difficult to establish: Borders are differently placed by the different surveyors, mountains according to one topographer are valleys or no more than hillocks to another, the place-names or routes accorded by one mapmaker arouse anathema in other assayers of the personality field.

Quite separately, and dating back to at least Hippocrates, various speculations have been offered regarding personality-manifesting behavior. However, the theoretical underpinnings of personality, their origin, and their development over time are largely ignored systematically; much is insufficiently recognized or acknowledged; crucial areas continue unexplored.

In the busy marketplace of personality research, alternative, disparate, and competing visions and versions of the field continue to be actively promulgated by appeal, selectively, to subjectively resonant speculation, particular bodies of empiricism, or seemingly paramount methodological approaches. Scientific fragmentation remains.

However, it also has become increasingly clear that large congruencies exist, or seem to exist, among different construals of the field and its necessary constructs. I believe more order and conceptual equivalence is present than is now apparent. This book represents my own personal thoughts and efforts at some form of integration. My remarks on various issues are by no means fully considered, as I am painfully aware. However, I am a longtime observer and worker in the field. In the course of my involvement, I have inevitably become opinionated and rash in the way I conceive of personality psychology. But certainly no more so than my peers in the field.

In my view, the study of personality lies at the apex of the field of psychology because it is concerned with the adaptations of the individual in a world not entirely clear and logical, a world that is both threatening and appealing (e.g., J. Block, 1982; J. Block & Kremen, 1996). It subsumes the fields of learning and cognition, which are concerned with adaptations of a certain kind, when affective considerations usually are not especially regnant or are present in evolutionarily unrecognized or unacknowledged ways. It subsumes developmental psychology, which is concerned with how adaptations are constructed and evolve. It subsumes social psychology, which attempts to specify the interpersonal context and influences within which adaptational efforts must so often take place. And it subsumes clinical psychology, which is concerned with adaptational efforts that subjectively (intrapersonally) or objectively (societally) are judged as having failed. It acknowledges the normatively shaping role of evolutionarily ingrained adaptational modes but recognizes that, within these biological constraints, the enormously facile mental processes available to the individual can generate a remarkable variety of adaptive modes and solutions to existential problems. I would contend that there is little in the field of psychology that does not fall under the rubric of personality.

Within this overarching, admittedly ideological, intellectual framework, I view personality psychology as more specifically concerned with the ways individuals perceive, respond to, and understand their respective worlds as they seek to establish adaptive life modes. Personality psychology is concerned with conceptual and empirical inquiry regarding interpersonal functioning and intrapersonal experience, the personality and motivational structures underlying such functioning and experience, and the developmental basis—temperamental and environmental—studied over the life span that may explain both the similarities among people and the reliable differences among them that are so evident behaviorally. Personality psychology is concerned with the dynamics of intra-individual functioning and the coherence and thematic unity of particular lives. Personality psychology recognizes the shapings of human nature as a function of evolutionary pulls and pushes and the further shapings of perceptions and behaviors as a function of the cultural contexts in which lives are led. So much for the scaffolding within which I attempt a view of the personality qua system.

It should be noted that my conceptual offering takes a different tack than is usual or dominant in current, by now traditional, psychology. Cognitive emphases seem to be de rigueur everywhere. As Kellogg (1995) has remarked, "cognitive psychology has evolved over the past 40 years to become the dominant approach to virtually all aspects of human psychology" (p. xix). In a special issue of the *European Journal of Personality* that focused on personality and cognition, the opening editorial notes that "many ... consider cognitive structures and processes to be at the very heart of any reasoned attempt to understand personality" (McCann & Endler, 2000, p. 371). The dominant *Journal of Personality and Social Psychology* is replete with studies seeking to demonstrate myriad ways cognitive mechanisms influence social behaviors. But how should the notion of cognitive mechanisms be viewed?

Withal, the term *cognition* for too many refers only and vaguely to the mental process of knowing. Usage of such a broad and enveloping term as cognition may, in its catholicity, be convenient or tempting to invoke but all that is usually meant is that important processing occurs in the head. I prefer to use a term such as *mentation* for such unspecified mind functioning; the word *cognition*, should not be so readily used as to lose any specific meaning.

Alternatively, but not especially helpfully, some have reserved a very definite sense of cognition, that cognition means "intelligence" or some version of rationality (in an economic or utility sense). The conceptual difficulty here is that there are certain forms of intelligent behavior that are not rational and certain forms of rational behavior that are not intelligent.

Rather than awarding preeminence to cognition in the omnibus sense, or to cognition with a severely restricted and vulnerable meaning, I believe that cognition, however conceived, should be viewed as only one way of responding to affective imbalances. Affect is *not* in the service of cognition; instead I look at cognition, variously interpreted, as a way—often marvelous and constructive to behold—of reacting and responding to affect.

It should be remembered, as Izard (1993) has aptly remarked:

> The emotion system preceded the cognitive system in evolution and outpaces it in ontogeny. It is highly adaptive for animals to be able to feel before they think, as in the case where pain elicits withdrawal or pain-induced anger motivates defensive actions. It is equally adaptive for the preverbal infant (as young as 3 weeks) to smile at caregivers and begin establishing attachment bonds that greatly increase the chances of survival. (p. 73)

See also the similar arguments of Zajonc (1980; 1982). My own effort here takes affective considerations as paramount and cognition as an extraordinary (but not exclusive) way of adapting to affective imbalance.

Some early remarks by Simon (1954) are also pertinent here:

> Non-rational aspects can be imbedded in the model as the limiting conditions that "bound" the area of rational adjustment .... Improvement in the model of rational behavior will come primarily through careful attention to the boundaries of the area of rationality. (p. 394)

I suggest the psychology of personality must include but conceptually extend beyond the boundaries of commonly opined rational behavior.

In my writing herein, I am aware of (and occasionally somewhat troubled by) repetition of my arguments or superfluity of explanation. But redundancy has its benefits in delivering a message, and, moreover, some of my chapters perhaps should stand alone. So, I have not been insistently perturbed by this problem, however it may be adjudged. I also acknowledge a certain occasional unevenness in presentation; the press of my circumstances prevented a bettering.

I have many intellectual debts to acknowledge because many persons have contributed, knowingly or not, to my conceptual thinking and effort. Foremost among them is my late wife, Jeanne Humphrey Block, with whom there were countless, exciting, ramifying, mutually interrupting, theoretical discussions. We complemented, supplemented, and potentiated each other affectively as well as intellectually. More recently, I have benefited much from thoughtful interchanges with my research colleague, Adam M. Kremen, and the advice of David C. Funder. And I have received background and gained much from the writings of countless others personally unknown to me, partially referring to many in the text. Doubtless, I have forgotten many of the sources of my various thoughts and ideas; I apologize for these failures of mention. Of course, I absolve them all for any of my misconstruals of their words and suggestions.

In the immediate present, I am especially appreciative of the efforts of Susan Milmoe and Larry Erlbaum for their frustration tolerance before my various justified and unjustified delays in contributing a minimally sufficient manuscript. I know I am a difficult author to manage.

Finally, I remember well the various kinds of sustained affective support unreservedly tendered me by Gayle Roberts as I struggled for a tolerable manuscript.

—Jack Block

Chapter 1

Introduction and Orientation

INTENTION OF THIS BOOK

The purpose of this book is to bring forward a limited but presumably useful theory of personality functioning and motivation. It is limited, as all theories are, in that certain critical features of experience and of behavior are not expressed in the present terms of the model. On the other hand, a usefulness is claimed on the ground that some central concerns of what a proper personality theory must consider do appear to be encompassed by the constructs, defined system goals, and consequently generated relations of the present formulation. A grand sufficiency is not pretended. As Meyer Schapiro, the art historian, remarked in a somewhat different context, "Perfection, completeness, strict consistency are more likely in small works than in large."

This first chapter is largely devoted to a spelling out of the special emphases and interests that have guided the choice and definitions of subsequent concepts. Chapter 2 presents a variety of opinions on psychological matters that broadly condition the present theoretical effort. The third chapter considers some presystematic matters, to indicate the orientation and the ground rules within which the theoretical game is to be played. Chapters 4 through 8 present the concepts and their posited interrelations that, together, form a theoretical system. Chapter 9 sets the theory down in a variety of personality and clinical contexts to see how well it corresponds to or maps into the behavioral and experiential realities it has been designed to relevantly abstract or speak to. Chapter 10 analyzes and compares the possibilities inherent in two major alternatives to the theory espoused herein. And finally, in chapter 11, I seek to state the developmental process by which the structural variables of the theory evolve.

PHENOMENA STIMULATING THE THEORY

Theories are intended to order observations, to encompass in a reasonably unified and simple scheme what otherwise would appear as a heterogeneous and unwieldy aggregation of facts. As G. E. P. Box, the significant statistician has remarked, "all models are wrong but some are useful." A limited usefulness is all to which one can aspire.

What are the phenomena that have prompted the present theoretical formulation, and what aspects of experience and behavior is the theory interested in explaining?

The domain of personality functioning I am concerned with in this book may be conveyed by listing, with no especial ordering of importance, the kinds of behaviors, relations, and recognitions that have stimulated the present theoretical essay. The theory will presumably have, in its turn, something useful to contribute toward understanding the systematics of the observations from which it arose.

A second reason for indicating some phenomena for which the present formulation is designed to have relevance is to permit the reader, by gauging the intent, to gauge also prospective interest in the present effort.

1. Under certain circumstances, individuals develop feelings or manifest behavior that psychologists have tried to understand in terms of a vague construct labeled "anxiety." People experience "anxiety states"; they employ coping strategies or defense mechanisms to prevent the emergence of anxiety; they are held back from many forms of pleasure by the anxiety they anticipate will follow gratification; they are made anxious by special contexts of surprise or novelty.

For most well-ordered lives, anxiety may not be present in massive or chronic amounts, but it is presumed by perhaps all conceptualizations of personality that its potential is always present—no one goes untouched by anxiety or by its nominal surrogates. As Freud (1963) remarked, "one thing is certain, that the problem of anxiety is a nodal point, linking up all kinds of most important questions; a riddle, of which the solution must cast a flood of light upon our whole mental life" (p. 401).

In its more general terms, the formulation to be developed is an attempt to model the several ways in which anxiety comes about in an individual and the several ways by which anxiety is reduced. Especially to be noted is the contention, incorporated into the theory, that anxiety is a function of the specific relation existing among several intrapersonal variables. It further follows that anxiety may be managed within the personality system by changes in variables other than those initially involved in the anxiety rise.

2. In facing and reacting to a complex world, individuals may show a variety of behaviors. There is the phenomenon of *curiosity*, the relaxed, seemingly purposeless meandering through an unknown and unthreatening environment. The casual quality of curiosity may be converted by certain conditions into something more urgent and focused that may be labeled, after Bartlett (1932), "effort after meaning," the attempt to perceive pattern and coherence in what begins as uncomprehended complexity. In turn, this "effort after meaning" may, under certain circumstances, grade into what has been called an "intolerance of ambiguity" (Frenkel-Brunswik, 1949), wherein meaning is established by procrustean measures in a brittle effort to stave off a personal panic. These behaviors and the conditions of their change and conversion are a second special concern of the present theory.

3. To illustrate a developmentally crucial aspect of behavior, consider a simple game one can play with children. Let an adult dare a 4 year old *not* to laugh when the count—one, two, three!—is slowly and portentously made. Perhaps invariably, the child will impulsively burst into paroxysms of laughter or dissolve into giggles before the slow count is completed. With an 8 year old, sobriety is sometimes maintained and sometimes not. With an adolescent, the game is never won. Alternatively, consider the game of "Simon Says," wherein a child is supposed to restate verbatim a spoken command rather than respond to the imperative in that spoken command. Young children tend to make the contextual error of saying their name when the command is issued, "What is your name?" With increasing age, the child becomes less susceptible to this kind of error. We wish to be able to explain these developmental differences in the ability to control impulse, inhibit spontaneity, maintain directed attention for sustained periods of time, and the like. Especially in recent decades, much psychological conceptual and research attention has been directed toward understanding the development of response inhibition.

4. Still another central concern of the present theory is an effort to conceptualize and integrate the varieties of adaptive behavior. In situations of stress, some individuals are characteristically maladaptive. Their maladaptations are various and almost uniformly regressive in

nature. These maladaptations may be grouped into two broad classes—disorganized, fitful, transient, highly variable maladaptive behaviors or rigidified, perseverative, overly focused, unvarying maladaptive behaviors.

Other individuals are characteristically resourceful in responding to environmental or existential stressors. They psychologically rise to the occasion and resourcefully increase their organization of thoughts and behavior in adaptive response to the objectively pressing demands of the moment. However evolved, this characteristic ability to dynamically and progressively "adapt to stress" in specifically unrehearsed yet effective ways as required by existing circumstances, appears to be a decisive dimension in terms of which to order individuals. It should also be noted that, within a person, over short and long periods of time and also as a function of context, there may be changes in the individual's capacity to cope effectively with the flux of experience.

5. There is another property of the personality systems of individuals that warrants consideration, one that is a kind of converse of the progressive ability to "adapt to stress." Just as certain contexts appear to demand a tighter, more directed organization of the personality if the situation is to be mastered, other contexts demand a looser, less directed organization of the individual's personality in the interests of surmounting or easing a problem. This latter capacity for change is what Kris (1952) has called "regression in the service of the ego" (see also Schafer, 1958). Individuals appear to vary widely in their ability (or affectively controlled willingness) to permit these nominally lower, less contained (normatively, more "primitive," "childlike," "irrational") levels of personality organization to operate. Indeed, individuals change over time and over context in their capacity to "regress" in deliberate ways, to willingly release what has been restrained. This capacity for willful, "playful" cognitive reversion is important because many hunches about the essential basis of creativity revolve about some such notion (Martindale, 1990; Russ, 1996). The present formulation, by the terms of its system, attempts to encompass both "progressive" and "regressive" forms of adaptation.

6. Studies of attachment have consistently observed that a toddler of a certain age repeatedly ventures forth by him- or herself to explore the environment and then rushes back to the attachment figure, the mother. This behavioral alternation has been called *secure-base behavior* or *the exploration-attachment balance* or the *attachment behavior system* (Hinde, 1984). However, this cyclic phenomenon may be viewed not as a "balance" but rather as an alternating sequence. Within the young

and still world-constructing child manifesting this behavioral cycling, there are fluctuations in priorities of two quite different motivations: There is a going out to an attracting world so as to experience and encompass it and then a rushing back to mother—the safe base—when there is too much of the world to make comfortable and comforting sense of. How shall this undoubted observation be conceptualized?

7. Although psychology has tended to emphasize *behavior response* processes, to escape the dangers of introspection and to objectify behavior, it should be remembered that a case has also been made for emphasizing as well the necessary preliminary of perceptual reaction processes (Gibson & Gibson, 1955; Tighe & Tighe, 1966). Thus, we have "response generalization" and "response discrimination," a widening or narrowing of behavioral responses, and we have "stimulus generalization" and "stimulus discrimination," a widening or narrowing of perceptual reactions. The intrusion of the computer metaphor as a model of mind has also brought attention and respect to the idea of *input* (percepts) as well as *output* (actions)—one must consider what is being entered into the system as well as what is being derived from the system, and the connections between them. These distinctions, between perceptual processing and behavioral processing, if they are useful for the "cold" field of cognition, may also have implications for the study of "hot" personality.

For a further recognition coming from the clinical literature, there appears to be a difference between individuals manifesting attention deficit without hyperactivity as compared with individuals manifesting hyperactivity that is not plagued by attention deficit (there is, of course, attention deficit conjoined with hyperactivity, a confounded and frequent case also requiring understanding). And in the ordinary sphere of interpersonal functioning, there seem to be individuals who know how they are perceived but are poor perceivers of others in contrast to individuals who are good perceivers of others but do not know how they are construed by others (Block & Bennett, 1955). Instances can be multiplied of why it would appear worthwhile, for general and specific reasons, to keep under consideration the separation and difference between what goes into the individual's psychology and what comes out.

8. One can readily observe, within oneself or in others, that emotions, especially negative ones, can summate their effects. A succession of closely timed frustrations—rejection by a sought-after one, an incessant traffic jam, the return of an unaccepted manuscript, and so forth—can prompt a vehement kick of the unwitting cat one has almost stumbled over. Such accumulation of diversely based but also commen-

surately summating affects poses a problem for conceptualizations of personality functioning that do not recognize the existence of this phenomenon.

9. Individuals appear for the most part to live psychologically in an interpersonal, social world more than in a physical world. They must construct intake, output, and integrational structures for dealing with this interpersonal world. But this social world is complex and perhaps ultimately fractious, behaving in ways only fuzzily comprehensible. Efforts by the individual to test the nature of the interpersonal reality have erratic or dim results. Social feedback is often indirect, delayed (sometimes forever), and equivocal, permitting only the uneasiness of uncertain inference instead of the pleasures of certain deduction afforded usually by the physical world. Because there may be little or no external feedback on the basis of which to build intrapsychic structures for dealing with the social world, the individual inferentially evolves personally functional structures sufficient for the predication of behavior. In doing so, the principles that come into play, construed in the absence of unmistakable, unambiguous feedback, are principles that may be construed as less than rational when judged by external logical and empirical criteria. They include the forms of "irrationality" called *primary process modes of thought* (Freud, 1963; Hilgard, 1962), *primordial thought* (Martindale, 1990), the *cognitive illusions* of Tversky and Kahneman (1974), and *attributional errors in social judgment* (e.g., Nisbett & Ross, 1980), among others.

These irrational biases are generally prepotent or heuristically evolved. They are usually helpful or correct on a quotidian basis, but being only evolutionarily or heuristically based, they can go wrong or be misled. Thus, we tend to attend to the rare to which we have not yet accommodated rather than the daily, which is clichéd and boringly predictable; the immediately vivid attracts attention rather than background base rates; what is superficially or apparently similar is dramatic rather than what is deeply similar or a similarity slow to realize; the immediately recent is given more weight than the long past; what information is easily accessible, even if perhaps untrustworthy, is depended on rather than looking further and laboriously for validity. All of these are "Darwinian algorithms," a phrase of Cosmides and Tooby (1987, p. 296).

Although these formally irrational modes of perception, action, and cognition are due at least in part to limitations of the human mind, these limitations provide the possibility for individuals to be influenced by strong motivations, pervading fears, and prevailing aspirations.

Thus, one can formulate a fully encompassing paranoid view of the world that is never diametrically contradicted; one can live a lifetime believing—unwarrantedly—that one is smarter than everyone else or that one is unloved (or loved). The achievement of personally functional but not-so-rational structures—unresponsive to, unclear, or rationalizing about received behavior; fuzzy in their workings; projective; affectively involving—involves adaptations that may be quite effective if they go undiscorroborated (albeit to an outside observer they may appear not fully "rational"). The study of personality must consider these adaptations that are not deemed truly "intelligent."

10. Attending more deeply to what was earlier mentioned only in a developmental context, it should be noted again that individuals vary widely in the degree to which they delay or do not delay responding to immediate environmental contingencies, to emotional or somatic pressures, or to the possibilities and costs of pleasuring. Within a person over time and contexts, there can be variation with respect to reflection or a relative absence of reflection before emitting behavior. This observation has been well noted by psychologists who over the years have offered various descriptions of and terminologies for this latent construct, labeled to describe one end or the other of the continuum. Thus, in research on temperament and personality, we have such concepts as *externalization* and *internalization* (Achenbach & Edelbrock, 1989), *underregulation* (Baumeister, Heatherton, & Tice, 1994), *fear of novelty* (Bronson, 1968), *emotional reactivity* (Carver & Scheier, 1998), *self-sentiment control* (Cattell, 1957), *novelty-seeking* (Cloninger, 1986), *hesitation* (Doob, 1990), *extraversion* (Eysenck, 1970), *psychoticism* (Eysenck, 1981), *thrill-seeking* (Farley, 1986), *self-control* (Gough, 1987), *impulsivity* (Barratt, 1965; Dickman, 1990; Fowles, 1994; Gray, 1987; Revelle, 1987), *rhathymia* (Guilford & Guilford, 1939), *behavioral inhibition* (Kagan, Snidman, & Arcus, 1993; Rothbart, 1989), *reflection–impulsivity* (Kagan, 1966), *inhibitory control* (Kochanska, Murray, & Coy, 1997), *compliance* (Kopp, 1982; Polivy, 1998), *willpower* (Metcalfe & Mischel, 1999), *delay of gratification* (Mischel, Shoda, & Rodriguez, 1989), *strong–weak control of behavior* (Pulkkinen, 1988), *temporal discounting* (Ainslie & Haslam, 1992; Rachlin & Raineri, 1992), *the ability to inhibit thought and action* (Logan & Cowan, 1984), *emotion control* (Roger & Najarian, 1989), *reactivity* (Rothbart, 1989), *impulse expression* (Sanford, Webster, & Friedman, 1957), *hyperactivity* (E. Taylor, 1998), *constraint* (Tellegen, 1985), *behavioral disinhibition* (Watson & Clark, 1993), *restraint* (Weinberger & Schwartz, 1990), and *sensation-seeking* (Zuckerman, Kuhlman, Joireman, P., & Kraft, 1994), to name but a few.

Their common denominator is that they all relate to the way impulse is monitored, by degree of restraint or expression.

This latent dimension is also integral to clinical descriptions, as presented in the fourth edition of the *Diagnostic and Statistical Manual of Mental Disorders, DSM–IV*; American Psychiatric Association, 1994), of psychiatric personality disorders such as, Attention Deficit Disorder, Cluster B Personality Disorders (Antisocial, Borderline, Histrionic, Narcissistic), and the Substance Use Disorders. These personality disorders all significantly involve unrestrained behavior. What were once known as the manic–depressive psychoses, but are now called Bipolar Disorders, also involve a significant component of impulsivity when mania rules the day. Representing the other end of this dimension are the Cluster C Personality Disorders (Obsessive–compulsive, Avoidant, Dependent), which appear to involve excessive behavioral restraint.

The widespread ramifications of this underlying dimension, variously labeled and variously conceived, attests to its importance in accounts of personality functioning. Often, this dimension taken alone has been connotatively identified as reflecting "impulsivity" or, reversed, "inhibitory-control" (or "self-control") or "willpower." However, such evaluative connotations fail to acknowledge and therefore to recognize that, although it may be undesirable to be extremely impulsive, it may also be undesirable psychologically to be extremely controlled. As insightful William James (1892, p. 436) wrote, there is "the explosive will" and "the obstructed … will."

Thus, although alcoholism, drug abuse, and sexual promiscuity may all illustrate an insufficient self-control, it is also the case that teetotalers of alcohol, absolute abstainers from all culturally available drugs, and individuals normatively very late or never to start their sexual lives appear to be rigid individuals, uneasy with affect, and leading relatively joyless existences (J. Block, Block, & Keyes, 1988; Jessor, Costa, & Donovan, 1983; Jones, 1968, 1971). Self-control to such an extent can hardly be thought of as positively adaptive although it may not be societally viewed as troublesome. Unqualified positive usage of the term, "self-control," fails to recognize that inhibitory control, although often adaptive, in many contexts and with certain individuals may also influence behavior to be rigid, unexpressive, routinized, with flattened affect, and excessive delaying of gratification sensibly enjoyed.

The casual and unthinkingly negative usage of the term "insufficient self-control" fails to recognize that in many contexts and with certain individuals, such "insufficient" self-control may provide the basis for spontaneity, flexibility, expressions of interpersonal warmth, openness to experience, and creative recognitions. As so often invoked in this nonpermissive nominal culture, however, impulsivity per se continues to be decried, and inhibitory control per se continues to be lauded. Although the idea of self-control is generally praised by society (and by many psychologists) for its adaptive effectiveness, there are many contexts wherein spontaneity rather than self-control is appropriate and desirable, where self-control may be maladaptive and spoil the experience and savorings of life and even attenuate reproductive fitness. Thus, although the ability to resist distractions in many contexts or to delay gratification can have obvious adaptive implications, there can also be an excessive degree of control of interferences leading to perseverative, inattentive, narrowly focused, delaying behaviors that are also maladaptive but in quite different ways.

In order to rise above this conceptual obtuseness, we early chose (J. Block, 1950; J. H. Block, 1951) to conceptualize (and label) this fundamentally important, multiply cognized underlying dimension as *ego-control*, ranging from *undercontrol* to *overcontrol*. We believed the related, frequently used, descriptive constructs of impulsivity or inhibitory-control were theoretically vague, societally shaped, and psychologically misleading. By the construct of ego-control we hoped to acknowledge both the positive and the negative behavioral implications of each end of the continuum.

11. As already noted, individuals also vary widely in their effectiveness of adaptation, in their ability to dynamically adapt to their personal worlds and the flux of experience, to equilibrate and re-equilibrate in response to their ever-changing being and the ever-changing world. Within a single life, too, it will be observed that at times a person is much more resourceful and adaptively effective than at other times. Because of the recognition of such inter- and intraindividual differences, a central conceptual preoccupation of the field of personality over the years has been with how to most fruitfully theorize regarding the factors underlying human adaptability.

An early and still invoked approach, pragmatically concerned with societal requirements, has focused on the idea of adjustment rather than the idea of adaptability. The term *adjustment* is a conceptually undemanding (even innocuous) layperson's way of saying whether an individual is getting along or not getting along in the world as it is. Such "adjustment" is not without societal importance, of course. Ultimately, such adjustment must be taken into account when a person's adaptability is considered. But the term adjustment seems also to imply a conformance to conditions and values that, from an intrapsychological rather than societal standpoint, may not mean psychological health. As Thoreau implied in his remark about lives led in quiet desperation, an "adjusted" person may not be a happy person but rather a person who has settled for less. A related recognition is that a person may be adapted but not adaptable. The individual may have sought and found or fortuitously encountered a niche in which to abide and perhaps hide, one that suffices, one that keeps despairs and anxiety within tolerable bounds. This kind of static fitting-in may not be publicly troublesome or obvious to others, but it is not what should be meant theoretically by "adaptability." Being vegetatively adjusted or not in a mental hospital is not quite the way to think conceptually about adaptability and psychological health (White, 1973).

More recently, there appears to have been recognition of the insufficiency of societal preoccupation with adjustment and the atheoretical view of "mental health" in terms of such "objective criteria" as the absence of "symptoms" or "days outside the mental hospital." Various concepts have been brought forward as theoretically useful, more psychological abstractions to characterize human adaptability. Most recently, explanations have been phrased cloaked in emotional terms: "emotional regulation," "emotional intelligence," or "emotional stability." However, as Depue, Collins, and Luciana (1996) remarked, "adaptive behavioral systems, in the broadest sense, are really emotional systems that motivate and, in a general way, guide behavior in response to critical stimuli" (p. 48). To the extent that psychologists currently involved in emotions research are introducing new understandings, the centering on emotions is of course worthwhile and advancing. But it should also be noted this work may be only the study, using different terms, of previous recognitions regarding motivation and personality.

To provide a sense of current conceptual offerings, consider the following: *the Central Executive* (Baddeley, 1986), *meta-cognitive components* of intelligence (Brown, 1978; Sternberg, 1985), *emotion regulation* (Campos, Campos, & Barrett, 1989; Shields & Cicchetti, 1997), *social intelligence* (Cantor & Kihlstrom, 1987; Keating, 1978), *self-regulation* (Carver & Scheier, 1998; Kopp, 1982), *constructive thinking* (Epstein & Meier, 1989), *regulatory control* (Fabes & Eisenberg, 1997), *left-brain interpreter* (Gazzaniga, 1989), *executive functions* (Barkley, 1997), *action control* (Kuhl & Kraska, 1989), *decision and adaptive systems* (Kosslyn & Koenig, 1992), *response modulation* (C. M. Patterson & Newman, 1993), *attentional and effortful control* (Posner & Rothbart, 1992), *emotional intelligence* (Salovey & Mayer, 1990), among others. In earlier times, other terms involving different concepts or metaphors—such as *ego-strength*, *coping*, *competence*, *self-efficacy*, and *hardiness*—were invoked that were conceptually functionally equivalent.

These various contemporary concepts have been of diverse conjectural origin, have used different terminologies, and have often been scientifically ineffable. They have even been occasionally inconsistent. For example, Kagan (1966) at one time lauded *reflectivity* as opposed to *impulsivity*. More recently, he has suggested *behavioral inhibition*, which involves reflection, is adaptively inadequate, whereas *behavioral uninhibition*, another term for impulsivity, implies a more suitable connection with the world (Kagan et al., 1993).

But all these notions have been proposed to encompass the quite remarkable phenomenon of human adaptability in more theoretical ways that might be advancing of our understanding. I note that, with increasing frequency, the broad labels self-regulation or emotional regulation seem to have come into use in psychology to characterize such adaptation (cf., e.g., Carver & Scheier, 1998; Eisenberg & Fabes, 1992; Kopp, 1982).

However, when the popular terms self-regulation or emotional regulation, are used to describe personality functions, they often prove to have an uncertain meaning. It is often unclear whether such regulation refers to dynamic and resourceful adaptability per se or whether the term means behavioral control per se and perhaps—even likely—overcontrol; or whether it refers to some confound of adaptation with impulse control per se. The difficulty with the latter interpretation is that dynamic adaptability should in certain, not infrequent contexts call for a reduction of control. There are occasions (e.g., brainstorming, sexual circumstances, vacations) when behavioral control per se is psychologically maladaptive. One should not go to a Mexico beach attired in a business suit and with a schedule in mind.

There is recognition in developmental and personality psychology of the crucial importance of both regulation and restraint. But there has been little thinking and research regarding a fundamental commingling and confounding of regulation and constraint. It is far better—even necessary for theoretical purposes—to keep these constructs distinguished. The idea of regulation does not necessarily mean a move toward restraint, per se. The commingling between the idea of uncontrolled versus controlled behavior on the one hand and the idea of maladaptive versus adaptive regulation of behavior on the other has been a fatal conceptual flaw. There are important, inevitable connections between these two ideas, but there are crucial differences as well. The failure to recognize and respect these distinctions may lead to crucial errors in psychological thinking and in the planning and interpretation of empiricism.

In the present conceptual view, an adaptable individual will regulate behaviors so as to be controlled or to reduce control as a function of the evocative quality or contextual cues afforded by the existing situation. He or she will be able to work planfully on a distant goal and also be able to relax and be pleasuring when the circumstance permits. To express this conceptualization of the latent dimension underlying such dynamic and resourceful adaptability, and to convey the particular sense of involved agentic structures, we early chose the label of *ego-resiliency*. This may have been the first conceptual usage, a half century ago, of the terms resiliency or ego-resiliency in personality and developmental psychology.

As formally and specifically defined, the full construct of ego-resiliency requires the ability to effectively reduce control as well as to effectively increase control, to expand attention as well as to narrow attention. The construct is further described in chapter 2 and later in chapters 6 and 7.

12. An enduring problem in personality psychology is that equivalent or highly related recognitions or findings have not been recognized as such. Decades ago, such occurrences were called instances of the "jangle fallacy" (Kelley, 1927). It is sadly surprising how often, in our joint, extraordinarily broad, but also compartmentalized scientific field of psychology, bodies of relevant past or contemporaneous research have not been encountered by serious investigators. There are various reasons for this compartmentalization, mostly having to do with differences among schools of thought or training and their consequently different terminologies. Freud (1961a, p. 114) also noted "the narcissism of minor differences" that leads to unique but functionally interchangeable terms.

In personality psychology, the various terms alluding to the sufficiency or insufficiency of behavioral restraint all seem to have rather similar functional implications. Similarly, the various terms alluding to complex perceptual and behavioral governance all seem to have very similar functional implications. To the extent that a strong common core is indeed present in these sets of differently named constructs and operationalizations, many separate lines of inquiry may be brought into the same conceptual tent. It would be worthwhile for the field to conceptually and empirically interrelate these similarly intended constructs in order to ascertain in what ways they are equivalent and in what ways they warrant being distinguished. To the extent that these seemingly similar constructs are indeed the same, convergence is attained; if seemingly similar measures are considered to be insufficiently equivalent, conceptual argument and refining empiricism should seek to specifically identify the differences claimed. To some extent, the present work is an effort in this direction.

In working toward achieving a more calibrated, perhaps even consensual language, it is important to remember to be historically grounded as well as au courant. The field of personality is too frequently ahistoric. Certainly, past recognitions should be recalled but of course not necessarily deferred to. What is most recent should be evaluated for what is new and what is significant. However, what is new is not necessarily significant, and what is significant is not necessarily new. Too often, contemporary lyrics have been created for an old tune.

Some other matters that the theory will propose to speak to or derive are the reactions that emerge after prolonged isolation or sensory deprivation (Zubek, 1974); the effects that follow upon imbibing such drugs as alcohol, the psychotomimetic drugs, amphetamines, and tranquilizers; the difference between surprises that are funny and surprises that frighten; the generation of apathy under conditions of prolonged terror; and a catalogue of kinds of psychotherapy and forms of psychopathology.

I begin this theoretical development attempting to speak usefully regarding the earlier mentioned and related phenomena only after having stated in chapter 3 certain orienting attitudes and premises as well as the aspiration that has guided this effort at system-building. The reader will be in a better position to evaluate the arbitrariness to be encountered at various subsequent steps in the specification of the system if it is understood how the decisions are suggested and sometimes forced by the outlines of the approach being followed. But before this third orienting chapter, chapter 2 discourses on various presystematic matters that also influence this effort.

Some Logical, Psycho-Logical, and Definitional Matters

In this chapter, before commencing the theory proper, it is useful to consider more closely a variety of current developmental issues with implications for theoretical matters soon to arise and for the field more generally.

TWO KINDS OF PSYCHOLOGICAL VARIABLES

With constructs that stay close to obvious observation or experience, I suggest that it is difficult and perhaps impossible to formulate dimensions or variables that have conceptual properties. This statement requires elaboration along several different lines.

A variable has conceptual properties for a theory of personality, in my terms, if separately or in conjunction with other variables it can generate a web of nontautological consequences, consequences that are not circularly entailed by the way the variable has been defined. Variables that might be mentioned as having conceptual properties include *susceptibility to interference, intolerance of ambiguity, anxiety level, personal tempo, extroversion, empathic sensitivity, ability to maintain integrated performance when under stress,* and the like. Historically, conceptual variables have been both esthetic in property and theoretically satisfying.

Consider now such variables used in personality research as *adjustment, neuroticism, social effectiveness, conduct disorder, hardiness, agreeable-*

ness, positive character integration, survivorship, mastery motivation, academic conscientiousness, and even many interpretations of the psychoanalytic conception of *ego-strength*. All of these variables—herein termed *societal dimensions of personality*—take their meaning from a particular societal referent; they are "culture-bound," and can be understood only within a specific (if not always acknowledged) societal context. They are naming or descriptive variables, not having deeper explanatory implications.

Once labeled, naming variables are usually employed as independent variables, although inspection of their operationalization identifies them as dependent variables, influenced by the particular societal environment. They are treated as causes although they are derived as consequences. Societal dimensions of personality always, latently or blatantly, carry a connotation of descriptive evaluation, incorporating a culturally defined concept of what behavior is to be preferred and what is to be discouraged.

Societal dimensions of personality are widely used because of their undoubted convenience and effectiveness for certain practical descriptive purposes. It is helpful—even fundamental—for many kinds of planning or for summary societal purposes to be able to characterize an individual's adequacy or adjustment within the given societal milieu.

As theoretical variables, however, societal dimensions have proven disappointing. They offer multiplicity but do not promise coherence. Societal variables have been able to generate only the vague and unexceptional hypothesis that the "integrated" person will perform "better" or at a more consistent level than will the "unintegrated" individual. Because of the kind of experimental situations psychologists tend to select and the way behavior tends to be indexed, confirmation of this essentially trivial hypothesis has been frequent and may be multiplied almost at will. Witness the remarkable array of procedures wherein psychologically disturbed individuals perform less well and with greater variability than "normals" (Hunt & Cofer, 1946). And yet, after all of these findings are duly noted, societal dimensions appear to have led us in a circle rather than further.

The difficulty with such dimensions of personality is that their very origin in a specific societal matrix prevents them from having conceptual properties, properties that would make them commensurate with other nonsocietal variables and thus permit the system properties of a theory to be generated. For example, it is readily possible to theoretically find situations where the societally integrated individual performs *less* well than societally maladapted persons. Kounin (1972) has shown that feebleminded persons do better in certain tasks than normal persons. Mednick (1958) demonstrated that schizophrenics will perform more effectively than normals in a situation that requires a strong tendency to generalize from initially learned stimuli. The Iowa investigators (e.g., K. Spence & Taylor, 1964; J. A. Taylor, 1951) and others (see M. W. Eysenck, 1982) have noted that psychasthenic (i.e., psychologically vulnerable) participants learn more rapidly (i.e., "better") than nonpsychasthenic participants in a simple learning situation. Overcontrollers are more, not less, "reality-oriented" than appropriate-controllers; undercontrollers are less, not more, ethnocentric than appropriate-controllers (J. Block & Block, 1951). Relatively narrow categories at age 3 appear to suggest positive cognitive development, but at age 11 relatively broad categories appear to suggest positive cognitive development (Block & Gjerde, 1986a). All of these findings seem contrary in terms of evaluative societal variables but are readily understandable conceptually.

These several illustrative findings all happen to be predicted ones; their essential significance, however, is that their coherent explanation invokes and must invoke variables that are not societally evaluative. Such experimental observations pose perverse problems for societal constructs although presenting no difficulties within a nonsocietal conceptual framework.

The conceptual inadequacy of societal dimensions must be understood as a consequence of the way societal dimensions are defined and not simply as a current empirical conclusion from the historically disappointing contribution of societal dimensions to understanding. This point is perhaps objectified if some reasons why societal dimensions are theoretically unfortunate are briefly noted.

First, societal dimensions are not invariant in meaning over time or across cultures. Comparing representatives of different cultures or different epochs on dimensions such as "neuroticism" or "social effectiveness" has slack meaning because the definitions involved are not constant or, where constant, are no longer cleanly applied given the context. To be socially effective in 21st century America has a different meaning than to be socially effective in 17th century Ghana. In contrast, constructs such as "anxiety," "introspectiveness," "capacity for response modulation," and "tendency toward externalizing or internalizing response" can be conceived and operationalized so as to have a culture-free meaning. The Kwakiutl, Hopi, Alorese, barrio resident, Watts dweller, West Virginian hillbilly, and Protestant New Englander can all be evaluated with respect to "extroversion" or other conceptual dimensions, and indeed such evaluation is quite instructive with regard to better understanding of personality in culture. But comparing representatives of different cultures or different epochs on dimensions such as "social effectiveness" simply has little meaning because the definitions involved are not constant. Indeed, the notion of "cultural relativism" developed as a neutralizing antidote to the uncritical application of societal dimensions in the comparison of cultures. More recently, however, it has been recognized that pan-cultural study validly may be pursued with "culture-free" conceptual variables.

Second, an individual's placement on a societal dimension tends to be equivocal in meaning at or beyond some point along the implied latent continuum. For example, on an "adjustment" scale, a high or a low score may be variously achieved because there are alternative ways to be adjusted and, especially, alternative ways to be maladjusted. More sensitive discriminations are required than calling a playwright and a mechanic equally "adjusted" or a conversion hysteric and a depressive equally "maladjusted." Not more than a gross prediction may be expected from societal dimensions.

Moreover, such gross predictions are made without conceptual understanding of how the predicted relation is mediated. Sometimes, one end of a societal dimension may be well specified but the other end is not, for example, knowing that one is not supercilious does not tell whether one is submissive or egalitarian. The empirical consequence of relating such a dimension to a fully defined dimension is a scatterplot, often observed, displaying a monotonically increasing heteroscedasticity, the so-called "twisted pear" (Fisher, 1959).

To a large extent, the success in the past—only moderate—of societal dimensions as predictors may be ascribed to the lumping together of characterologically diverse personalities similar only in limited ways. There has been subsequent failure to recognize the several developmentally different routes to the societally defined category.

Third, societal dimensions confound and obscure the distinctions and relations between the person and the environment in which that person exists. A dimension of personality that simultaneously (implicitly but effectively) characterizes the environment in which the person inextricably finds him- or herself confounds two fundamental sources of behavioral variance. This recognition often escapes some transactionalists. However, any analysis of a process becomes an analysis of sequence, the term "process" simply referring to an unanalyzed sequence. And analysis of a sequence requires consideration of the influences involved and their transactional effects over time.

Because the goal of personality psychology is understanding sequences of development (over short and long terms), it seems inescapable that distinguishing the person and contextual factors involved should be preferred so that transactional effects may be discerned. Only then will the contextual and procedural relations influencing personality in situ be recognized. No loss is entailed by distinguishing the individual's personality structure from his or her autochthonous environment; personality and environment may always be subsequently conjoined to enable prediction of behavior. However, prediction in the opposite direction, from the behavioral consequence to the preceding constituent variables is not univocally possible. Knowing an individual is "adjusted" offers no information as to the individual's personality structure or the situational condition in which the individual happens to function.

For example, the construct of the *difficult temperament child* (Thomas, Chess, & Korn, 1982) confounds characteristics of the child with the characteristics of the parent (i.e., the "situation") labeling this child as "difficult." By conceptually separating the person from the surround, we are enabled to recognize ways of empirically assessing or even manipulating these different influences on behavior independently. With this possibility comes the possibility of discerning and understanding personality–environment transactions. Why is a person neurotic in one context but not in another? Why is a child constrained in strange situations but spontaneous in familiar environs? Why do certain situations seem to "pull" uniformly adaptive behavior (e.g., driving on the left-hand side of the road when in England), whereas other circumstances are associated with heterogeneous and highly idiosyncratic reactions (e.g., what one chooses to do on a lovely Saturday morning).

As long as societal dimensions of personality are employed, it is difficult to make sense of these confounded, amorphous, multivocal influences on behavior. Understanding and anticipations cannot rise above the highly general but also highly innocuous level permitted by the way the societal dimension initially has been defined. So here is a reason for a try with only conceptual notions.

It should be noted that although the conceptual approach to understanding personality is largely intrapersonal rather than interpersonal, evolved intrapersonal structures almost inevitably have large consequences for the interpersonal behaviors emitted. For example, individuals with high energy levels and a tendency to spontaneity may be expected to be more dominant in new interpersonal contexts than individuals with a reverse pattern of intrapersonal qualities. Certainly, interpersonal experience may have large developmental consequences for the shaping of the intrapersonal structures that evolve (Loevinger, 1976, p. 375; Vygotsky, 1960). However, in the contemporaneous moment, the intrapersonal structures of the individual fundamentally influence subsequent interpersonal transactions and how an individual happens to be perceived societally.

REGARDING "RISK" AND "PROTECTIVE" FACTORS

The preceding discussion leads naturally to consideration of the traditional focus in psychiatry and psychology on "risk" and "protective" factors in psychopathology. This emphasis has been implicitly concerned with societal criteria of adjustment rather than conceptual criteria of adaptiveness. Therefore, research on risk and protective factors is largely societally and empirically driven, not conceptually motivated. It is, sometimes usefully, concerned with epidemiological prediction, a prediction however that is generally made without conceptual understanding. Unfortunately, such atheoretical prediction may be on rather shaky ground, especially subject to an infirm foundation as cultures or contexts change or there is great heterogeneity in a given culture.

Epidemiologically identified risk or protective factors seem infrequently to have been closely thought about conceptually with regard to the psychological processes involved in amplifying or damping adverse outcomes. Rather, the risk and protective factors reported usually have remained at a distal, epidemiological level. But what may seem only a statistical finding when viewed with an epidemiological telescope may be further understandable when viewed through a psychological magnifying glass.

Thus, it has been suggested by an unreflective epidemiologist as evidence of how complex and contrary a world we live in that the presence of much autonomic nervous system activity in individuals is a risk factor for a diagnosis of "neurosis" but a protective factor for the diagnosis of "conduct disorder." The deeper psychological meaning in individuals of autonomic nervous system activity or inactivity has not been considered. However, it is well known that much autonomic activity in humans reflects the presence of introspection, the activation of inner life, and experienced emotion (e.g., J. Block, 1957; Porges, 1991). And it is well known that, psychodynamically, too much introspection by individuals is conducive to what societally has been called neurosis, whereas a lack of introspection in individuals is conducive to what societally is called conduct disorder.

As another instance of uncontemplated findings, there has been much quite separate research on the adolescent risk factors predictive of alcohol abuse, drug abuse, and early sexuality. These risk factors for various societally frowned-upon outcomes all turn out to be the same or rather similar (J. Block et al., 1988; Jessor & Jessor, 1977). However, little thought is expended by disparate risk investigators regarding what the common denominator in all these adverse outcomes might be conceptually.

Relatedly, and as noted in the preceding chapter, the personality qualities of individuals who are alcohol teetotalers, drug abstainers, and normatively much delayed in sexuality all turn out to be much the same (Block, 1971; Jessor et al., 1983; Jones, 1968; Shedler & Block, 1990). What is the common denominator in all these diverse outcomes, conceptually?

These findings suggest an increased alertness to the possibility of conceptual explanation could well be helpful in furthering coherent understanding of risk or protective factors and the various forms and complexities psychodynamics can take.

WHAT SHALL WE MEAN BY RESILIENCE?

In concert with emphasis on risk and protective factors, the term "resilience" has come into popular usage, especially recently, and is frequently invoked as a term of broad applicability, a term for all seasons and reasons. The "resilient" person is intrinsically protected, the "unresilient" person is intrinsically at risk.

PsycINFO, the psychologist's electronic literature searcher, reports resiliency as a key word of 103 studies in 1998, 32 studies in 1993, 8 studies in 1988, 4 studies in 1983, but 0 studies in 1978. In the preceding 25 years, it received only occasional mentions, never more than once per annum. Clearly, the notion of resilience is now in vogue.

However, like many words in psychology, resilience has come to mean different things for different people at different times. The sliding, slippery, diverse ways in which the term resilience is currently employed by psychologists is troubling. There is no need to be obsessional about definitions. Certain constructs such as "anxiety" or "curiosity" are entitled to be ultimately undefinable primitives and the term resilience, may well be one of these. However, at the constructual level there should be a sufficient sense of consensuality among the individuals using the term to be mutually persuasive that all are talking about the same phenomenon. Often, one cannot be sure this is the case.

It may be useful to convey a bit of the provenance of the term in developmental psychology, to consider just how the single label resilience came into its currently popular usage in psychology and psychiatry.

Psychiatrist E. James Anthony (1974) evaluated children who appeared to be surprisingly healthy psychologically despite having experienced environmental contexts that, according to received psychiatric and psychological views, should have created severe psychopathology—that is, these children defied psychological expectation. Anthony chose to label these children as "invulnerable."

However, the initial label of invulnerability seemed overly dramatic and absolutistic and was rather quickly abandoned as the humble recognition took hold that, of course, no human being is invulnerable. Instead, invulnerable children were relabeled as "stress-resistant." A variety of important studies, sparked often by Norman Garmezy (e.g., 1983) and Michael Rutter (e.g., 1987), focused on stress-resistance or "survivorship," to refer again to children surprisingly unaffected in their psychological development by environmental conditions generally adjudged by mental health professionals to be adverse and stressful.

The terms, "stress-resistant" or "survivorship," apparently seemed somewhat graceless and soon were superceded by the connotatively more positive term, "resilient" (e.g., Werner & Smith, 1982; see also Hauser, Vieyra, Jacobson, & Wertlieb, 1989; Masten, Best, & Garmezy, 1990; Milgram & Palti, 1993; Neiman, 1988; Richmond & Beardslee, 1988; Sroufe, Cooper, & Marshall, 1988). In this psychiatric terminological passage, it was not historically recognized that the attractive term resiliency had been employed much earlier in personality psychology and with a highly specific conceptual meaning (as I discuss later).

In much contemporaneous developmental and clinical psychology parlance, then, a "resilient" individual was conceived as a person who has "survived" psychologically despite the significant presence of acute or chronic life stressors; a resilient person was deemed a survivor.

Problems immediately arise with this clinical definition as it has been empirically used in developmental psychology and psychiatry. Why does a particular individual "survive"?

Survival may not be an intrinsic outcome for the person. Some individuals survive just by the luck of the draw, by chance. A concentration camp survivor may have been permitted survival because of being sent one day one way rather than the other on the basis of an adventitious decision by a prison guard. A ghetto adolescent might have gone along a constructive life path rather than a sad, bad path simply by the chance concatenation of events or a mentor who happens, luckily, to be encountered. To the extent that surviving the Holocaust or escaping the ghetto is not some function of the particular surviving individual, it is incorrect to call the survivor stress-resistant or resilient. It seems likely that, with a frequency that has never been closely examined, individuals who were unquestionably only lucky have been awarded the more desirable label of being resilient.

Further, there is something intellectually unsatisfying in the view of resilience as seemingly successful adaptation to seemingly adverse circumstances. Resilience, so construed, is said to be present when mental health professionals are surprised by a positive or nonnegative outcome given environmental conditions thought to be detrimental; pessimistic expectations are apparently defied.

However, as Luthar and Zigler (1991) have shown, a child may appear resilient in terms of overt social competence but may be covertly experientially vulnerable when studied more closely.

The approach to a definition of resiliency that is based on unevaluated presumptions of adaptation and unevaluated presumptions of adversity certainly creates the pleasant possibility of attractive surprise. However, another scientific approach, differently oriented, might well discern lawfulness in what now seems surprising, might find that what seemingly is successful adaptation to seemingly adverse circumstances is too often not all that it seems. There needs to be more of a push to go deeper, empirically and conceptually, into what is now being called resilience or instances of resilient behavior.

Going beyond these definitional concerns, it is necessary to consider more closely how a genuinely based survivorship or resilience—one that cannot properly be ascribed to fortuities—is thought to come about. Garmezy (1993) has insightfully and incisively called attention to three factors that may insulate the child (or, if reversed, put the child at risk) from the adverse effects of particular environmental stress: (a) the warmth and solidarity of the parental–family surround creating an evolved premise system in the child regarding what the deep security of a situation is now or ultimately will be; (b) the accessibility and the individual's understanding of accessibility in the larger society of support systems for the child and the parent; and (c) intrinsic or evolved personality characteristics of the child.

One can readily accept the importance of these three distinctive factors and acknowledge their positive influences on the manifested resilience of the child in dealing with a psychologically traumatizing context. It is crucial to recognize, however, that the first two of the three factors perceptively noted by Garmezy—family warmth and societal support—need to be explicitly distinguished etiologically from his third factor—intrinsic or previously evolved personality characteristics.

Recall that an "influence" is not the thing being influenced. An influence on height (e.g., protein intake, constitutional endowment) is not height, and an influence on intelligence (e.g., number of books in the home, constitutional endowment) is not intelligence. Likewise, an influence on resilience achieved, whatever may be influential, is not resilience. It seems that in our emphasis on identifying the protective factors and risk factors influencing what is called resilience, we sometimes have lost sight of this distinction between an influence and what is being influenced.

For the moment, presume that resilience, if and however influenced and achieved, in time represents an enduring characterological qualia indicating the individual is generally adaptively versatile in the expectable environment; the individual generally well forfends stress and promotes effective adaptation. Consider, now, the recent argument by Sroufe (1997) and others (e.g., Cowan, Cowan, & Schulz, 1996), viewing resilience as a "developmental process" influenced "organizationally" by its surrounding context. I believe this latter perspective is worth discussing here as a seemingly opposite but also, I suggest, apposite point of view.

Sroufe (1997) has brought forward proper criticism of the "medical model," so often used implicitly to guide mental health research and interpretation. He singles out the frequent psychiatric use of the term *deficit* as implying that there is an endogenous or inherited problem in the child or adult. For example, *DSM–IV* (American Psychiatric Association, 1994) follows the organic disease analogy by considering behavioral and affective disturbance to be a consequence primarily of underlying neurophysiological pathology, whether due to genetic defects or psychological pathogens in the enveloping surround or their conjunction. Sroufe noted that the medical model leads to considering resilience to be "an inherent robustness," an "endogenous trait" that is viewed as "an explanation for the observed phenomenon" (Sroufe, 1997, p. 256).

Sroufe (1997) contrasted this psychiatric, endogenous view with a developmental model in which the individual and the surrounding context are viewed as inseparable.

> Behavioral and emotional disturbance is viewed as a developmental construction, reflecting a succession of adaptations that evolve over time.... Just as ... the emergence of competence involves a progres-

sive, dynamic unfolding in which prior adaptation interacts with current circumstances in an ongoing way, so too does maladaptation or disorder. (Sroufe, 1997, p. 252)

Sroufe's (1997) criticism of the medical or psychiatric model and his cognizant articulation of the developmental model is apt. However, in discussing the concept of resilience, I suggest Sroufe draws or over-draws a distinction between resilience conceived as a "developmental process" and resilience conceived as what he called a "trait." He views resilience as representing a pattern of relationships, a pattern of learned adaptations developed over time; for him, resilience is not a static trait. Sroufe does not closely indicate how he means the word trait but for him the word is clearly a pejorative, implying the existence of a habitual behavioral manifestation of an unchangeable, yet unobserved, neurophysiological factor.

However, as typically employed by personality psychologists rather than developmental psychologists, the term trait neutrally refers to intrinsic characteristics of an individual, however achieved, that influence behavior. Allport (1937, p. 295), for example, defined "trait" as "a generalized and focalized system (peculiar to the individual), with the capacity to render many stimuli functionally equivalent, and to initiate and guide consistent (equivalent) forms of adaptive and expressive behavior."

Contemporaneously, the term trait has often been used by psychologists in multifarious ways, a reason perhaps why the term should not be used. Unarticulated and unexplained, the term is indeed only statically descriptive and is no more than a summary label for a class of past observed behaviors. The term disposition, frequently used as a substitute, is perhaps somewhat better for personality psychology but does not rise above stating a probability of a particular class of behavior subsequently being emitted.

It is more useful to think in terms of personality structures, which mesh with the pushes and pulls afforded by the immediate situation to lawfully forge the behaviors then emitted. That is, personality structures order or codify a set of procedural rules that then, depending on the context, can shape a variety of determinate behaviors. In this conception, resilience is a high-order personality structure, a set of internalized, generalizing, and discriminating relations that encompass the range of circumstances an individual will encounter.

A resilient personality structure, once evolved and established, is relatively stable and will only change (likely, slowly) when the generalizing and discriminating relations on which it is predicated change. Certainly, Sroufe's view is correct that the *evolvement* of resilience occurs in crucial ways via the pattern of interactions the individual earlier encounters and is a part of. Also importantly involved are constitutional factors (genetic, pre-, and perinatal), albeit in yet unknown ways.

But it should be recognized that, as Loevinger (e.g., 1978) has often remarked, what is initially interpersonal becomes what is intrapersonal. What has evolved developmentally from the individual's pattern of interactions with others can be viewed subsequently—in the contemporaneous moment—as a well-established personality structure operating when behavior is called for to effect situation-relevant adaptive behavior. Thus, the growing organism may have developed a lasting "working model of attachment" (Bowlby, 1986); he or she may have stabilized "a representation of interactions that have been generalized" (Stern, 1985).

Although resilience is a developmental process from a long point of view, when viewed subsequently in the later moment of behavioral observation, resilience is a function of now-existent personality structures formed and carried over from earlier developmental times.

If one accepts this reconciling construction, there is no real diametricality between the relationship view (which is developmental) and what Sroufe called the "trait" view (which is usually concerned with contemporaneous function). Understanding developmental process—how patterns of adaptation or resilient personality structures take form or fail to take form—is different from but important for understanding the subsequent operation of evolved and established patterns of adaptation and maladaptation, of resilience and brittleness of personality structure.

Considering achieved resilience as varying among individuals, how shall it be meant? If we are to use the word sensibly, a seriously offered *conceptual* definition is needed that attempts to go beyond loosely referring to resilience as a set of observed phenomena characterized by successful adaptation despite significant challenges or threats to adaptation. The sets of phenomena that observers have noted in a variety of contexts and denoted as manifestations of resilience certainly cannot be denied relevance. To advance understanding, however, what is necessary or at least useful now is to seek a theoretical, more analytical underpinning for these diverse but converging observations.

Historically, as noted earlier, a usage of a personality construct called *ego-resiliency* was evolved in the mid-1950s and may be useful to mention here. Although conceived in the 1950s, it was first reported in J. Block (1963; 1965), apparently the first published conceptual usage of the term resiliency in psychology: "The word, resilient, implies the resourcefulness, adaptability, and engagement with his world that characterizes the individual placed high on this continuum; the word, ego, implies that an enduring, structural aspect of personality is involved" (Block, 1965, p. 111). It is envisaged, in Allport's (1961) phrase, as "a complex system of potential *ranges* [italics added] of behavior that may be evoked (within the limits of possibility for the person) by the various physical, social, and cultural conditions that surround him at any given time" (p. 181). The concept was further discussed in Block and Block (1980) and most recently in Block and Kremen (1996). It is further elaborated in later chapters and may provide a theoretical foundation for the various phenomena that so far have only been listed or described by mental health workers. The concept comes from an effort to integrate Lewinian notions with psychoanalytic writings.

Because our 30-year longitudinal study of personality development has focused on the nature, antecedents, and consequents of ego-resilience from its inception when the participants were assessed at age 3, and in subsequent assessments at ages 4, 5, 7, 11, 14, 18, 23, and 32, the construct may have implications for unifying the findings of the past and in setting priorities for future empirical research (J. Block, 1993; J. H. Block & Block, 1980).

HOW SHOULD THE TERM, "SELF," BE USED?

The term "self" is used by psychologists in broad, enveloping, often uncertain ways. It is often unclear how this protean term is being employed. I wish to be quite clear as to how I will and will not use the term.

A familiar, quite ancient distinction in discussions of conceptions of self is between the "self as an object of one's knowledge" and the self as "active, independent, causal agent" (Harter, 1983, p. 283). The *self as object* is viewed as a subsystem of or falling within the *self as agent*.

The self as object of appraisal—the "Me" of Mead (1934)—refers to those moments when the individual's self-percept (my preferred term) has been activated, when one is introspective, recursively aware. One is not just participating in life but is simultaneously observing and influencing one's participation in life.

For example, one can be dancing marvelously well, be in "flow" (Csikszentmihalyi, 1990), with no subjectively held sense of self. Someone comments on how well one is dancing. Quite abruptly, the dancing becomes halting and clumsy; the dancing participant has also become a dancing self-observer; the self-percept has been activated and come into play. Why? Because the previously inoperative self-percept has been activated and suddenly what has been "unthinking" behavior comes into consciousness, and one "chokes" in the behavioral moment. There is premeditated rather than spontaneous psychomotor behavior—no longer flow—and there is a fundamental restructuring of self-perceptions. The psychology of the individual has changed fundamentally and discontinuously when the self as object of appraisal and source of influence comes into play.

Generally, the self-percept becomes activated when things go badly or function without ease; the individual is under psychological load or stress. There develops some, at least beginning, awareness of self-doubt and anxiety; the activated self-percept consequently comes into play.

It should be noted that the self-percept, as an object of appraisal involving self-awareness, need not be and is often not present when much—perhaps, most—perception occurs, cognition happens, and behavior is forged. Most human beings are not always or even usually activated to introspect.

Prior to the activation of self-awareness and after self-awareness is no longer regnant, it is the self as agent—the "I" of Mead—that is operative. The self as agent refers to the individual's psychic apparatus, to the organismic integrative structures that regulate perceptions and predicate behavior. In this second meaning, there is no necessary implication that self-awareness is present; rather, the organization of perception and behavior proceeds in automatic, context-sensitive, perhaps overlearned, coordinated ways of which the individual may be introspectively unaware.

Certainly, the self-percept when activated crucially influences subsequent behavior in regulatory ways. But behavior is also being regulated even when the self-percept is not operative. Of course, there often may be a spiraling interplay between self-percept functions and the underlying psychic apparatus (on which the self-percept system ultimately depends).

The distinction between self as object of appraisal and self as agent is often lost. Although sometimes expressed at the outset in formal essays, the distinction is often ignored or muddled in subsequent discussion and in colloquial presentations. It becomes simply too awkward or slowing to consistently keep adding the necessary qualifiers to the term "self" so that communication is clear. And so the term "self" is used alone or imprecisely, and therefore in inevitably confusing ways.

I submit that the single term, "self," cannot serve two conceptual functions, as both object of appraisal and as agent of regulation. Doing so has created what has been called the "jingle fallacy" (Thorndike, 1904), wherein two concepts or measures that are really different are given the same name or label.

I prefer the term, "self," be reserved for the meaning of self as object of appraisal, as implying the presence of self-awareness. It seems to me that such a denotation is connotatively closer to what most people mean by the locution, "self," and it is this way that I use it.

If this particularized usage seems reasonable, then the much broader term, "self-regulation," becomes unfortunate if the mental processes involved may not involve self-awareness. There may be regulation of what one sees and what one does, but is it self-regulation in the sense that an awareness or consciousness is involved? Often not. Certainly, there may be on occasion—even frequent occasion—an awareness or consciousness that indeed influences how perception and behavior are regulated. But usually there is regulation of behavior although there is no activation of self-perception. It follows that an alternative, nonconfusing term is needed to characterize the broad underlying regulatory system of integrative structures.

The term, "ego" suggests itself. "We have formed the idea that in each individual there is a coherent organization of mental processes, and we call this his ego" (Freud, 1961b).[1] So, if one is not vehemently anti-Freudian, the needed term becomes "ego-regulation" or "ego-functioning." If one prefers a more antiseptic but equivalent term, "executive regulation" or "executive functioning" will serve the same purpose.

THE COHERENCY OF PERSONALITY

The criticism is sometimes advanced that the kind of behavioral coherence implied by the concept of personality exists only slightly or even is not to be seen empirically. An individual behaving impulsively in one situation may behave in a most contained way in another circumstance, thus apparently denying the usefulness of a generalizing personality concept.

This kind of datum suggesting an incoherence of personality cannot be questioned; it is simple to embarrass the construal of generalized,

---

[1]Loevinger (1976) has offered an alternative but quite equivalent definition: "The striving to master, to integrate, to make sense of experience is not one ego function among many but the essence of the ego."

consistent behavior as underlying any proposed personality dimension. All that is necessary is to select seemingly contrary observations. What can be questioned, however, is the implication immediately drawn from such unimpressive observations. It does not follow from mediocre or clashing findings that a personality dimension then necessarily loses its cogency as a basis for conceptualizing and anticipating the behavior of individuals. We can question this adverse implication if, and only if, a higher form of lawfulness or coherence can be found in the behaviors pointed to as evidence for temperamental or personality inconsistency.

It is not enough to point alternatively to the many kinds of countering evidence for a common thread through a large variety of perceptions or behaviors and over very long periods of time, as can be readily done. This is evidence only for a "dual aspect" point of view—a highly unsatisfactory intellectual circumstance. The apparent discordancies must be resolved within the framework provided by a theory, or at least a theory must have the promise of integrating these otherwise upsetting data.

Years ago (Block, 1968), and prior to Mischel's influential volume, I cataloged four conceptual ways in which some superficially embarrassing behavioral inconsistencies may come about. It is still useful to mention them here.

The first of these inconsistencies is when the behaviors being related exist at different levels of relevance or psychological cogency for the individuals concerned. The association between the behaviors involved becomes a function of chance because of the essential unimportance to the individual of one or both of the variables involved. For example, it is psychologically uneconomical and, as a rule, not necessary to deliberate excessively before deciding whether to walk down the right aisle or the left aisle of a theater. Consequently, an individual may make theater lobby decisions in a rather cavalier, impulsive way. Or the individual may give reign to a slight position preference that, because it is consistent, may suggest a rigidity of his or her behavior. In neither instance is core behavior being studied, and so it is specious to contrast such peripheral behaviors with the way the individual copes with a genuinely significant situation such as friendship formation or aggression imposition. Yet, unwittingly, the comparison between different levels of personological relevance is often made. The behaviors being contrasted and related must all be significant ones for the individual. Failing this, behavior is likely to appear whimsical, and consistency will be a sometime thing.

A second and no less important reason why behavior often appears capricious is that the nature of the stimulus situation in which the individual finds him- or herself is not taken into account by the observer. For example, a generally spontaneous child may in certain circumstances behave in a highly constricted way. This vacillation toward constraint readily becomes understandable when it is realized that these certain circumstances are always unfamiliar ones for the child. We may expect that a formulation of personality functioning that attempts to take environmental factors into account will be able to integrate behaviors that from a context-blind viewpoint appear inconsistent. This expectation still has to be realized, of course, because situationists have not yet provided a formal conceptual basis for psychologically characterizing the demand quality of environments. But achievement of a set of cogent situational dimensions may provide a way of assimilating the observations of seemingly inconsistent, apparently unlawful behaviors.

A third way in which behavior can appear paradoxical occurs when the mediating variables underlying a given action are not conceptually analyzed or considered. Thus, in a basketball game, two players may demonstrate a wide variety of shots at the basket. The one player may have spent solitary years before a hoop, developing precisely his or her practiced repertoire. The second player, in the heat of athletic combat, may in spontaneous, fluid, and impromptu fashion manifest the same variety of basket-making attempts (and with no less accuracy if a good athlete). These phenotypically equivalent behaviors (diverse and effective shot-making) are in the first instance mediated by practice and *inculcation*; in the second by a spontaneity and *fluidity*. In a changed context, where inculcation and fluidity have behaviorally divergent implications, the "equivalence" between these two individuals may be expected to vanish, thereby suggesting an "inconsistency" in behavior. For example, the first athlete, shifting to baseball, can be expected to be a better pitcher, since pitching is a deliberated activity; the second athlete may be expected to be the better hitter in baseball, because good hitting is based on snap, unpremeditated, opportunistic action. The moral here is that the behaviors to be related must be mediated by the same underlying variables if behavioral congruence is fairly to be expected.

A final way in which behavioral inconsistencies can come about is when an individual has reached certain personal limits so that previous consistencies are now breaking down. The notion of bounds or limits is one that has received insufficient attention and application in psychology. Relations tend to be posited unequivocally, without recognizing the bounds within which the relation can be expected to hold and beyond which the relation fails and is replaced by other relations or by system chaos.

Thus there is the phenomenon earlier labeled "bimodal control" (J. Block, 1950), where individuals manifest in highly variable and not yet fully predictable ways, behaviors that are extremely overcontrolled and, conjointly, behaviors that are extremely undercontrolled.

Etiologically, one way this character structure appears to come about is when an individual ordinarily quite controlled in behavior finds the ability to control exceeded or unnecessary in certain directions of expression, with a resultant absence of modulation in these special areas. A second way is when an individual ordinarily undercontrolled in behavior becomes overcontrolled abruptly and categorically. Such extremist behaviors, via either route, are likely to be judged psychopathological. Indeed, one of the explanations of why psychiatrists and clinical psychologists may argue against the existence of an internally consistent ego-apparatus is that they in their practice encounter so often those comparatively few individuals in whom the generally expectable coherence has been disrupted. Later, when I consider various forms of psychopathology, the origins and implications of inconsistent control are treated in some detail and seen as consequent to the formulation being advanced. For the present, I simply note the phenomenon.

Now to begin the presentation of a personality system.

Chapter 3

Theoretical Orientation and Aspiration

ORIENTING ATTITUDES

The theoretical formulation to be presented is derived from, and at times limited by, six general commitments about the way a personality theory should proceed. As will be seen, none of these principles is by any means new, the arguments involved having been pleaded before by various writers. Nor are these six guiding attitudes independent of each other; it simply is convenient to present them separately so that their special emphases are most clearly drawn. The six orienting premises broadly underlying the present theoretical construction are:

1. A formulation of personality should define a system rather than simply be a listing of variables.
2. A formulation of personality should be, in the Lewinian sense, contemporaneously oriented.
3. A formulation of personality should be stated in terms of "metapsychological," evolutionarily reasonable, intrapersonal constructs.
4. A formulation of personality should, in terms commensurate with its other constructs, offer some way of characterizing in psychological terms the stimulus environment, context, or situation in which an individual must function.

5. A formulation of personality should encompass both the propulsive influences of drive-reduction and the experience-increasing attentional influences operating within the individual that conjointly forge behavior.

6. A formulation of personality should be phrased in psychological terms rather than in terms of neural, hormonal, genetic, and other biological mediators of mental functions.

These six preferences (and constraints) require amplification and justification.

The Emphasis on System Properties

It is well to begin a discussion of the virtues of a system emphasis by a definition. For our purposes, a convenient and quite sufficient definition of "system" is available from Floyd Allport (1955). For Allport, a system is "any recognizably delimited aggregate of dynamic elements that are in some way interconnected and interdependent and that continue to operate together according to certain laws and in such a way as to produce some characteristic total effect" (p. 469). More formal is the definition of Ashby (1960), wherein a system is considered as a set of selected variables whose defined properties are capable of yielding transformations that are closed and single valued.

The essence of the conception of "system" in both of these definitions would appear to be the concern with the coupling or interlocking of variables so that changes within the system over time become determinate. In brief, a system is what turns inputs into outputs. "For systems that change through time, explanation takes the form of laws acting on the current state of the system to produce a new state—endlessly" (Simon, 1992, p. 160).

This notion of system may, for some readers, imply nothing more than an alternative definition of the term, "theory." Certainly, the conception of a theory as a body of relations that logically flow from a small number of explicitly defined concepts and posited relations is coordinate with the notion of system. The term system is preferred here for the reason that the word theory is by now often multiply understood and multiply abused.

The term "theory" means very different things to different people. Sometimes "theory" is used to describe a hunch that research in a particular area will prove fruitful or that certain distinctions among variables are worth keeping. Sometimes a relation between a single pair of variables is proposed as a "theory." By and large, the term theory is not used in a stern, explicit, restrictive sense by psychologists, perhaps because of the responsibilities such usage places on the would-be theorizer; it is very difficult to theorize in this last sense of the word.

I like very much a three-word definition encountered many years ago: A theory is an "interpreted deductive system." This definition of theory is a most succinct and demanding one, far more demanding than the version usually used by psychologists. A theory is a system, concerned with interlocking relationships; a theory is deductive, submitting to certain rules for consistency; and a theory is interpreted, its logical elements standing in some posited correspondence to properties in the real world. Thus, a theory requires statement of the laws linking a closed set of variables, on the basis of which specific deductions follow, which can be reasonably or sufficiently mapped into the real world. To my knowledge, very few published presentations relevant to personality approximate these definitional criteria. Some examples in different realms are the model of Norbert Bischof (1975), the theoretical statement of Carl Rogers (1959), the systems of Herbert Simon (1952) and George Homans (1950), and some of the systematics of psychoanalysis as presented by Fenichel (1945). Much can be learned about serious model building by consulting such efforts.

In asserting that a personality theory should define a system, I mean that at the present stage of knowledge and existent insights some such effort at constructing a system can be heuristically useful. It is not enough now simply to enumerate a list of variables that, in the view of the propounder, should prove empirically to be important. Of course, establishing the necessary and sufficient set of variables in terms of which personality can be understood would indeed be a worthy endeavor. But how can we be assured that a given set of variables truly "carves nature at its joints" and is not simply one of many possible descriptive schemes? The sufficiency of a suggested set of variables cannot be tested without some additional theoretical assertions about the relations existing among the proposed variables. Failing this, alternative sets of "important" variables can be and have been proposed without end.

Looking over the various "theories (or "models") of personality" in the literature, one finds an extraordinary number of competing lists of variables or needs or drives or wishes or values, all presented as consummate ways of understanding humankind. The journals continually turn up "new," "improved," "final" dimensions of personality, brought before the psychological public as better ways to phrase our understanding of behavior. How shall we choose from among these offerings when more will soon be available?

The promise some investigators have made for factor analysis in the realm of personality psychology has not been fulfilled either; it has not provided automatic, compelling clarification of what is important to consider. The method has many vagaries; its findings can be wittingly or unwittingly manipulated; it algorithmically creates a set of conceptually unrelated, artificially (and unstably) orthogonalized factor dimensions; the behavioral and conceptual interpretations of the factors decided upon as relevant are open to dispute; and rival taxonomies continue to exist (J. Block, 1995a). Also, the data on which such factor analyses generally have been based derive primarily from responses to self-report or peer-report, often patent, personality inventories. However expedient the acquisition of such data may be, and convenient the subsequent analyses, the intentions of a theory of personality cannot be seriously realized within this restricted empirical vision.

The common aspiration of efforts thus far to achieve a (or "the") sufficient set of personality variables is also its common limitation: The empirical search or conceptual proffer has been to provide the dimensions for characterizing the differences existing *between* individuals. The study of personality, however, is not simply the study of differences between individuals, as it too frequently has been construed. The proper study of personality requires as well a dynamic, integrative model of the individual's functioning in a variety or succession of enveloping situations. Toward that end, there have been few efforts to find or formulate constructs, to identify the parameters in terms of which to represent differences existing *within* an individual over time or context (i.e., the concepts relevant for characterizing intraindividual psychodynamics).

A half century ago, Kurt Lewin (1946) recognized and saw the solution to the apparent *within* and *between* dilemma in psychology:

> A law is expressed in an equation which relates certain variables. Individual differences have to be conceived of as various specific values which these variables have in a particular case. In other words, general laws and individual differences are merely two aspects of one problem: they are mutually dependent on each other and the study of the one cannot proceed without the study of the other. (p. 794)

Contemplating the Lewinian recognition, it is difficult to see how an intraindividual approach to personality can be fitted into an interindividual approach. By the application, for example, of the five-factor approach to the description of between-individuals differences, we would not gain a theory of the individual person in the sense of a dynamic, integrative model of functioning in a variety or succession of contexts. However, the opposite seems logically quite feasible and perhaps even required: interindividual differences can be readily understood in terms of different, rather unchanging or only slowly changing specific values of intrapersonal parameters. I believe we need to look for personality parameters or variables that can do conceptual service in both intra- and interindividual contexts. Logically, then, primacy should be given to specifying the necessary intraindividual variables, whereupon subsequent between-individual differences can be understood simply as different values of the intrasystem parameters. It would be a sweet intellectual accomplishment if the theoretical constructs required for dynamic understanding within individual functioning could also be used for understanding the differences between individuals.

Our first point, then, in support of a system emphasis is that such an orientation, by the consequences it entails or promotes, requires that looser schemes advance to become proper theories. By so doing, coherent conceptual approaches begin to be recognized and separated from those schemes that were only asserted or that represented a conceptual potpourri.

A second reason for urging a system emphasis is perhaps a personal but not unique one. Psychologists no less than lay people are subject to a desire for closure or a sense of understanding. One of the necessary conditions for being interested in the science of personality psychology is a belief that an order exists and can be found underlying the diverse details of experience and behavior. However, if one looks at the empirical results thus far produced in the domain of personality psychology and related psychological disciplines, one cannot be pleased by past accomplishments and excited by immediate prospects. Too often, the objectively charted behavior of individuals has shown seemingly little or trivial coherence. Contradictory reports, failures of cross-validation, and low relations are frequent, and as a result a naively nihilistic position has too often been presented as the most reasonable professional attitude to maintain regarding the relevance of personality psychology for understanding behavior.

There are a number of reasons for this still unhappy state of affairs. Our empiricism is frequently absurdly shallow, our thinking concretistic, our methods or scope of approach simply inappropriate. Research quality varies widely, and it is difficult and often impossible from published accounts for the reader to separate the empirical wheat from the empirical chaff. Yet the faith with which the study of behavior must be approached requires that a coherence exist, even if the evidence for it is not yet sufficiently strong or clearly to be seen. If one tries to discern this coherence, one is still likely to fail; however, if one does not try, failure is assured.

A system emphasis suggests a way, perhaps the only way, of establishing an order among what otherwise is a listing of scattered observations. John L. Holland once casually mentioned: "there is an important sense in which a good theory defines the objects with which it deals." By positing a set of variables and their presumed relations, it becomes possible to see whether trees observed singly can be seen to arrange themselves into a forest of the theoretically required form. A system emphasis helps identify the maverick observations, the findings that are embarrassing to the system. These anomalous findings can then be more closely examined to see whether they are genuine and thus embarrass the effort of theory as thus far stated or whether they are ephemeral or irrelevant or "auxiliary" to the theory.

It is clear at this point that a reading of the psychological literature must be highly selective, that respect cannot be accorded to all findings that emerge from the empirical hopper. The empirical literature is vast, some would say half-vast, with many inconsistencies, many very complicated results. The guide to the required selectivity in appreciating present-day empiricism must be some kind of (preferably explicit) conceptual system. If a coherence is ever to be found in the thickening "litterature" on personality research, it will be noticed only when the "empirical integrator" (Underwood, 1957) is guided by a conceptual scheme.

My own feeling is that one can already make important sense in our results. Sense can be made in part by a proper discounting of some findings that have already been reported and in part by presuming the existence of certain yet unsought relations. In part, too, it must be admitted that a coherent view of the domain of personality psychology can be achieved only by arbitrariness, by speculation, and by a narrowed delineation of the field that still retains sufficient interest.

The reason, then, for a system emphasis is that it provides a way of perceiving or imposing an order on what otherwise is amorphous and intellectually inaccessible. Admittedly, there are dangers to be encountered as the effort is made to fit theory to data and data to theory. Constructs have surplus meaning, which implies an operationalization is an insufficient translation or manifestation or indicator of the construct.

And all operationalizations rely on "sweet reasonableness," an intuitive judgment of its conceptual sufficiency. Since this judgment is an essentially arbitrary decision, it follows that there can be no truly critical test of a theory. Perhaps an overall "batting average" is a kind of answer to the problem of evaluating a theory

One can only hope to be cognizant of and resistant to the temptations of simplistic and imperious thinking, and duly tentative regarding theory and its attendant empiricism. No implication should be drawn from the present model of personality that anything ultimate and complete has been created. If the model should prove at all useful, it will soon be bettered and even outmoded, for as Orwell says in quite another context, "one must prepare to be defeated in the end." Yet the effort at a system—any system—may well have been worth the while.

The Contemporaneity Emphasis

In this preference, I again follow Lewin (1951), who has stated well the case for a contemporaneous approach to behavioral prediction. The interested reader is referred to a thoughtful discussion by Chein (1954) of the arguments against and the counters for the contemporaneity viewpoint.

The task set for this book is to state the properties of the individual's personality system and how it changes and adapts to the various presses impinging on it at a given psychological moment. In this effort, I am not especially concerned with the very important but very separate historical questions of temperamentally given or otherwise inborn behavior-shaping characteristics, of how particular personality systems evolve, of the social learning contexts that predispose children toward one form of personality organization rather than another. This is the vast province of developmental psychology, what Lewin called "genetic psychology." I attempt to comment later regarding some of these developmental matters (see chap. 11).

Lewin (1951) once succinctly formulated the principle of contemporaneity as follows: "Any behavior or any other change in a psychological field depends only upon the psychological field *at that time*" (p. 45). Unfortunately, and especially in the field of personality psychology, this principle has been misunderstood or set aside, for it has been interpreted as implying that developmental and historical factors in an individual's past are unimportant for understanding the flow of the individual's current behavior. The contemporaneous emphasis, were this interpretation correct, would of course be a silly one to maintain; the weight of evidence, formal and informal, is indeed that in the child is to be seen very much of the adult that will be (see, e.g., J. Block, 1971). Behavior is so transparently influenced by our prior intrinsic temperament, learning, and experience as to make arguments here a product of straw construction. The big question, however—and this is where a proper understanding of the contemporaneous emphasis takes on its significance—is what *kind* of function characterizes the relation between prior life and present behavior?

It is not enough simply to correlationally link an early happening to a current action. Scientific understanding requires in addition a close specification of the sequence of events by which what is identifiable early comes to affect behavior later. And this generally is lacking in empirical efforts to establish connections between childhood characteristics, situational press, and subsequent behavior (but see, e.g., G. R. Patterson, DeBaryshe, & Ramsey, 1989; G. R. Patterson & Reid, 1984, for efforts to rather closely track ongoing sequences of person–situation interaction).

The obtained findings of association between early and later behaviors are of course of interest (see, e.g., J. Block et al., 1988; J. Block, Gjerde, & Block, 1991; Kremen & Block, 1998), but usually they only serve to tantalize and to elicit speculation. Moreover, these statistical associations have tended to be relatively slight in magnitude if only because, over time, there are multiple influences also operating on subsequently observed behaviors (Ahadi & Diener, 1989). Correlations between early and late behaviors fail to respect the impact of intervening events and of currently operative situational factors in shaping the behavior of the moment. Both of these sources operate in powerful ways to limit and even prevent the findings of strong, simple relations between early happenings and late happenings.

The contemporaneous approach, on the other hand, would attempt to trace lines of behavior. It aspires to study the sequence of development from moment to moment, respecting always the complex of factors operative at each moment. In this expectably quite tedious, very complicated, empirically forbidding fashion, later eventualities would be understood because the links in the chain of events would all be available. As Lewin (1951) has said, "field theory is interested in historical or developmental problems, but it demands a much sharper analytical treatment of these problems than is customary" (p. 64). It seems to me that the recent interest in what are called "dynamic systems" in psychology (e.g., Thelen & Smith, 1994; Vallacher & Nowak, 1994) may be viewed as concordant with Lewin's concern for contemporaneous understanding of the psychological moment.

It is true that Lewin sometimes appeared to overstate the contemporaneity position. Certain of his writings are perhaps insufficiently qualified, and in his own research he paid little attention to how the residues of past experience take their effect in the present. For the current theoretical formulation, structural variables are used to characterize the person, variables whose parameter values are the product of the individual's developmental history. However, these variables, no matter how their values happen to have been achieved, will be treated as they influence and are themselves influenced by the other variables operating within and upon the individual's personality system at the psychological moment under consideration. If these "structural" variables of personality, in their system interconnections, appear to provide a useful way of encompassing an interesting variety of behaviors, then it will be time enough to seek out and examine the antecedents of different values of these historically evolved structural parameters and to attempt a theoretical developmental understanding.

For present purposes, then, I am concerned with stating the relevant variables operating at a given moment together with their rules of relations. Once the definitions and relations are specified, the behavior that then issues from the personality system becomes required rather than simply likely. Although certain of the structural variables to be defined may be studied in their own right to ascertain the historically antecedent conditions associated with certain parameter values, as mentioned earlier, I reserve consideration of these developmental questions for a later chapter (but see also J. Block, 1971; J. H. Block, 1983; Kremen & Block, 1998).

The Emphasis on "Metapsychological" Constructs

If one is going to construct a model of personality, how shall one grab hold of experience, how shall the variables of the system be selected and defined? There are so many ways to proceed, so many possible levels of analysis as to dazzle and then depress the would-be theorist. Moreover, the richness of alternatives does not suggest that decisions at this juncture can be casually made since the later character and capacities of a theory are vitally affected by these early choices and preferences.

In the nature of things, there can be no definitive statement or advice about the proper way to proceed in putting together a theory. The fruitfulness of a way to proceed can be judged only post hoc, not a priori. Yet, it may be helpful if some strategic considerations in constructing dimensional schema are discussed here. The viewpoint expressed will provide a basis for understanding the particular choices that have been made.

To begin, it seems to me that a personality theory should be constructed to be a "grand (grandiose?) theory" rather than a "miniature system." For a number of reasons, such as its intrinsic difficulty, the focusing on separated dimensions, and the discouraging temper of recent times (see, e.g., Mendelsohn, 1993), efforts at theoretical systematics have been rare. However, the miniature systems so espoused in psychology can issue consequences of only the same order of implication.

By anyone's definition of personality, a proper personality theory must range over a polymorphous (and often perverse) set of behaviors. Behavior in intensely interpersonal contexts (e.g., romantic style, self-esteem, charade expressiveness) must be explained by the aspiring conceptual scheme. An individual's social acuity, value system, behaviors in a group situation, or style of neurosis are further phenomena that traditionally fall within the domain of personality psychology.

But behavior in impersonal, highly instrumented, highly controlled psychological situations (e.g., Witkin's rod-and-frame test, photic driving, attentional deployment) must also be explained by the offered conceptual scheme. For example, an individual's perceptual reactions while observing a point-source of light in a pitch-dark room or while wearing aneisokonic lenses or when subjected to the Stroop interference effect also should be grist for the theoretical mill.

Because of the tremendous diversity of behaviors with which a personality theory must deal—and an absence of "grand" theory—concepts have been tied closely to the specific circumstances that have originated the concept and have proliferated without measure. A new behavioral context has seemed to require a new concept for its explanation, a progression ad infinitum. And yet the ostensive reason for theory is cogent economy of representation.

The simplifying function of a theory can be achieved, I am convinced, only by personality concepts that are abstract, broad, general notions. The variables of a personality theory must be abstracted out of and also be applicable to contexts and data of widely different and even superficially incommensurate content. If efforts are only reportorial rather than seeking to be incisive and generative, they will not achieve the cognitive economy of a proper theory. Someone once remarked that "what they call the content is only impure [that is to say, *muddied*] form." Relatedly, "the mathematician (read, would-be theorist here) must resist the tug of rich, very voluptuous descriptions of reality" (Berlinski, 1995, p. 63). It is acknowledged that "every theoretical explanation is a reduction of the intuition" (Hoeg, 1993, p. 46).

Many psychologists are likely to be troubled by this particular emphasis because it seems distancing from the content of subjective experience and the interpersonal connections that so affect subjective experience. Illustratively, consider John Dewey's (1965) definition of psychology: "the ability to transform a living personality into an objective mechanism for the time being" (p. 302). However, it has not been enough, scientifically, to remain as much as we have at the contentual, subjectively apprehendable level. The anthropologist's emphasis on "thick description" is certainly valuable, even necessary for establishing a personal sense of understanding and for providing a context of discovery. But immersion in content is insufficient because the economy of theory cannot be realized there. Emphases on content are bound to the single situation or data in which the notion of content works. It is by pursuing the good abstraction and by rising above content per se that the possibility lies of perceiving an order in the experienced and motivated behavior of individuals.

This is not to deny the unruly difficulties that must be faced if we seek out or propose the essential forms underlying behaviors of manifestly different content. Ciphering actual behavior into this strange, deeper language and translating back into behavior involves formidable problems of coordinating levels and specifying translational rules. Often these highly removed personality concepts will seem more abstruse than is worthwhile—the compelling immediacy of experience will have been lost, irreversibly. But the hope and promise of a good theory is that, in the Murray Gell-Mann phrase, it will generate "surface complexity arising out of deep simplicity." A remark by David Spiegel (1997) may be pertinent here: "We are often caught in the dilemma that our theories are too elegant to be meaningful or too full of meaning to be elegant" (p. 170).

Clearly, a problem of choice is involved here. In part because of what is no more than my own esthetic preference and in part because of the failure to date and in immediate prospect of conceptual approaches immersed in (and immobilized by) content, my choice is for the more formal, more abstract construct. This level of conceptualization has come to be known as "metapsychological" (Freud, 1952; Gill, 1959).

The Emphasis on Characterizing Environmental Contexts

Psychologists may be placed, almost without ambiguity, into one of two camps—they are either "organism-centered" or "environment-centered" (MacLeod, 1947). Students of personality traditionally, fixedly, have been organism-centered—they have focused on the differential personal qualities that underlie differential behaviors. Cognitive and social psychologists have tended to be environment-centered—they have concerned themselves primarily, often exclusively, with the properties of stimuli or tasks or situations and their mentation effects on the behavioral outputs of a hypothetical "average" individual. A corollary distinction is made by Cronbach (1957), who talks of "the two disciplines of scientific psychology"—correlational psychology, which is primarily concerned with variation among or within individuals, and experimental psychology, which studies the consequences of conditions imposed upon individuals.

Historically, these two preferred orientations have often been intensely polarized—it is the rare soul who can move freely (or comfortably vacillate?) from one emphasis to the other. There has been an appreciable tradition for representatives of one camp to point to the follies of the other while basking in the (partial) truths they themselves have achieved. Gladiators for the organism-centered view will proudly publish still another demonstration that the presumption of an average or normative individual is patently wrong and leads only to predictively trivial relations. Additionally, it is argued that the normative presumption prevents attention to obviously important and lawful interindividual differences in intraindividual variables (e.g., gender differences).

Champions of the environment-centered view may ignore or slight embarrassing findings of interindividual differences except to label them as "nuisance variance." Instead, there are further demonstrations proving yet again that individuals are responsive often in impressively uniform ways to certain stimulus manipulations, a finding that is lost on many proponents of the exquisite individuality of response.

And so the arguments have gone, serving to divide rather than inform their opposites, or to confuse and depress both camps. For clearly, as any elementary psychology student would say, there should be no issue here. As Allport (1961) said many years ago, "the situational theorist is right when he claims that psychological theory looks too much inside the skin. But it is likewise true that the situationist looks too much outside the skin" (p. 178). And "if there is no personality apart from the situation, it is equally true that there is no situation apart from personality" (p. 181).

The passions that have been invested would be better spent in meshing the two emphases rather than in scholastic argument. A conception of personality must respect environmental considerations; a proper understanding of situational effects must recognize the differential significance seemingly identical situations may have for different individuals. Some large conceptual and practical problems are involved in bringing the situation into play as a modifier of affectively relevant behavior but these difficulties are inescapable and should be faced.

The simple recognition that a personality theory must also consider the environment does not lead simply to a way of incorporating contextual factors. Unfortunately, the environment-centered approach has never come to terms in a useful way with its own central problem: What is a "stimulus" or a "situation"? Psychophysical representatives of the environment-centered approach have not satisfyingly resolved the conundrum (see, e.g., Gibson, 1960). Social psychologists—users of situations—have also offered little help in conceptualizing the environment. Although there has been much emphasis on the importance of the inferred situation by pointing to personality findings that often were empirically weak (Mischel, 1968), social psychologists have not positively proffered comprehensive or systematic formal characterizations of situations.

The dilemma is this. A stimulus is a stimulus for an individual because it has meaning. But a stimulus must be defined independently of the particular individual if we are to use the concept of stimulus or situation as an independent variable affecting behavior. Otherwise, we are entangled in circularity and solipsism (and deconstructionism). Can the meaning of a stimulus situation be said to exist and have a meaning separate from the particular individual experiencing that situation?

Environment-centered psychologists, in their desire to achieve unqualified objectivity for the science, have sometimes reacted to the problem by disregarding the meaningfulness property of stimuli. For them, the properties of stimuli may be physical (size, color, form, frequency, parsing, and so on; (see Davis, 1953), properties seemingly cleanly specifiable without regard for the perceiving organism and hence conforming to the ideal of independence. But elementary epistemology brings forth quickly and clearly the recognition that "physicalism" can only be an implicit, vague, and unsystematic attempt to substitute the experimenter's restrictive and often naive perceptions of the stimulus environment for those of the participant. Some moderate successes have been recorded with this approach, but numerous embarrassments have also been recorded and can be multiplied at will. The successes depend on an unrecognized (or unadmitted) confounding of the physical variables with variables that involve meaning. The failures are generated by separating or opposing physically specified stimulus properties with stimulus properties having psychological implication for the organism.

In general, it may be said that discontinuities in one's experience are especially attended-to and learned, for it is such events that are likely to have the greatest adaptational consequence for the perceiving individual. Stimuli that are easily encoded, or that are made frequently available for encoding, or that are presented in contexts where it is imperative for the organism to form some connections, are all readily learned because of their adaptive relevance or meaning or salience for the individual. But an important recognition is missed if these findings are understood solely in such "objective" terms as "frequency" or "reinforcement schedules" or "classical conditioning."

In the psychological literature, awareness of the need to distinguish between the objective, nonpersonal environment and the environment as apprehended by the perceiving organism appears to have come primarily from the gestaltists (e.g., Koffka, 1935; Kohler, 1940; Lewin, 1951; Wertheimer, 1945). In various demonstrations or illustrations, they were able to show that the physical stimulus situation (the "geographical environment") could not predict behavior, whereas the stimulus situation as subjectively understood (the "behavioral environment") could quite readily. These demonstrations served as one important basis for attack upon the stimulus–response psychology of the time.

Later, the point was generalized to more social situations. It was recognized that the immediately determining factor in an individual's behavior was the social context *as perceived by the individual*, not the social context as defined in some absolute or abstract sense (cf., e.g., Lazarus, 1991; Lewin, 1951; Rogers, 1959; Rotter, 1955; Snygg, 1949).

This criticism of the physical definition of the stimulus was thrown, however, from a glass house. Countercomplaint has validly been made against the interpretation of stimuli in terms of their "functional significance" for the individual because psychology will then be able to know the meaning of a context only through the subsequent behavior of the individual. The opportunity of predicting behavior will have been abdicated because we will know the significance of a stimulus-environment for an individual's behavior only after the fact of that individual's action. More important, I would suggest, is the utter capitulation a subjective definition of the stimulus context would offer to the philosophical position of idealism, an orientation I consider to be incompatible with a scientific view of the world.

In one sense, of course, this stand on the uniqueness of an individual's experience cannot be denied, and it is therefore trivially true. It should be recognized, however, that this position, by itself, may not be maintained within the confines set by the scientific method. If the subjective environments of individuals are fully unique so as to deny the possibility of a useful classificatory scheme, and if the nature of a personal perception cannot be extrapolated on some theoretical basis rather than realized circularly after the fact of that perception, then we cannot make use of this phenomenal stuff for science. The canons of science cannot apply where infinite, unclassifiable variegation exists or where only post hoc definitions can apply. In short, some means of bringing each and every environmental experience into a normatively functionally relevant conceptual scheme is required. Diverse phenomenologies must be brought into a sufficiently common, yet psychologically useful, frame or metric.

It is necessary then, but is it possible to avoid the insensitivity and irrelevance of physical definitions of stimuli without foundering (or reveling?) in an unrestrained, scientifically unusable idiosyncrasy and phenomenology?

One way of escaping this dilemma—the way favored here—takes its cue from an inconsistency in usage (and perhaps of thinking) in Lewin's discussions of the "psychological environment." Sometimes Lewin used the term environment to refer to the objective, external physical–social reality. I call this environment the *objective psychological environment*, the contextual situation that ought to be seen by the individual. The objective psychological environment is that totality of situational factors presented to the participating person. It includes representations of physical ("geographic"), societal, and cultural realities; it contains all the features present in a situation that affect or presumably would or should affect an idealized "normative" individual.

At other times, as Leeper (1943, p. 207) remarked, Lewin would mean the term "environment" to contain "only those things which exist psychologically for a given person at a given moment." I call this filtered perceptual environment the *subjective psychological environment*, the stimulus context as it gets through to and is experienced by the apprehending individual. Murray (1938) made a similar distinction, between "alpha press" (the objective psychological environment) and "beta press" (the subjective psychological environment).

We should explicitly acknowledge and make conceptual use and empirical study of these two kinds of environment or situational press. With this distinction, we may understand the difference between objective and subjective psychological environments as due to personality differences or personality changes in regard to modes of perceiving. In "processing" the objective psychological environment so as to create the individual's subjective psychological environment, various differential emphases, sensitizations, and distortions may occur as a function of the total personality system operating at the moment. This complex of intervening factors can thus, in principle, account for a less-than-perfect relation that may exist between the two kinds of psychological environments, objective and subjective.

It should be noted that this conception of the objective psychological environment does not presume its identity with the geographical (i.e., physically-defined) environment, nor is a one-to-one relation between the two implied. Also included in the objective psychological environment are cognitively presented aspects and social aspects of the situation. The objective psychological environment is certainly influenced by the characteristics of the physical stimuli present, but the relations of the physical environment and the objective psychological environment cannot be unthinkingly assumed; they must be evaluated empirically. This point has been made by a number of writers (e.g., Jessor, 1956). A priori pronouncement by experimenters of what is to be considered the stimulus situation by the participant is still frequent, however; experimenters too often do not anticipate or subsequently recognize the actually operative psychological "press" on the person of the situational circumstance under study.

All is not lost, however, if the investigator devises an experimental situation that brings all participants to the same objective psychological circumstance, that creates the same pushes and pulls for all. A superb instance is to be found in the studies of Asch (1956). The basis for suggesting that the famous Asch procedure elicits reactions to conformity pressures is that, intuitively and obviously (and in manipulation checks as well on the introspections of participants), competent observers consensually judge the experimental setting and sequence of events as one that should develop in each participant a sense of being deviant from group norms. What each participant subsequently does then is, of course, dependent on the individual's personality structure. The crucial matter is that each participant is brought to the same experienced choice point. For each participant, the objective psychological environment is effectively the same. The differential behaviors that ensue are therefore a function of the different personalities experiencing the situation.

We do not usually bother to confirm the conceptual and operative validity of the experimental situation devised to provide the psychological setting desired. It may seem unnecessarily cumbersome to verify procedures, especially when psychologists tend so often to deal with the intuitively obvious. However, where a greater degree of subtlety or complexity is being approached experimentally, it is necessary to be more explicit and more certain about the normative psychological presses provided by a stimulus context.

Acceptance of the necessity of distinguishing two kinds of psychological environments—the objective and the subjective—is a vacuous recognition if the problem of specifying conceptually the objective psychological environment cannot be usefully solved. However, as Oehman, Hamm, and Hugdahl (2000) remarked, "evolution has primed organisms to be responsive to stimuli that more or less directly are related to the overall task of promoting one's genes …. Such stimuli include those related to survival [and bettering] tasks [and] are embedded within emotional systems" (p. 546). Extending this recognition, Cacioppo, Gardner, and Berntson (1999) remarked that "stimuli and events in the world are diverse, complex, and multidimensional—in short, seemingly incomparable. Yet each perceptual system has evolved to be tuned to specific features, resulting in the expression of these stimuli on a *common* (italics added) metric" (p. 840) of psychological salience. That is, each stimulus situation, although potentially existing in infinite complexity, is processed conceptually at a metapsychological level, by an evolution-based abstraction into broad categories or dimensions of general functional relevance for all individuals living in an expectable physical–social environment. Stated somewhat differently, it is the affordances or demand qualities or psychological salience of a situation that constitute the objective psychological environment of all commonly cultured individuals. Individual differences or changes in attention allocation and articulation create the subjective psychological environment and can bring the objective psychological environment into or out of subjective focus.

The important phrase in the preceding definition is "psychological salience"—a notion that need not begin a regress of unwieldy, unreachable terms. The meaning of psychological salience, it is argued here, may be quite specifically stated and made usefully operational.

A thoughtful discussion of the problems associated with specifying the objective psychological environment has been contributed by Jessor (1956). Further relevant efforts are by Block and Block (1981), Murray (1938), Chein (1954), Arsenian and Arsenian (1948), and Fuller (1950). These several, not-recent analyses of the problem are recommended to the interested reader for their consideration of ways by which the objective psychological environment may be specified.

The problem of operationalizing the objective psychological environment is a sticky one, not apparently touched seriously by contemporary conceptualizing psychologists.

Summarizing the discussion to this point, I have pointed to the necessity within a personality theory of conceptualizing the situation existing for a particular individual if we are to understand the subsequent flow of behavior. I have briefly considered the essential problem of "defining the stimulus" and have argued for the acceptance of two kinds of stimulus environments in a proper system of personality. The objective psychological environment—broadly and deeply evolution- and experience-shaped—is not more than roughly fashioned by the physical objects present and has been proposed as specifiable independently of the particular participant's subsequent responses. The participant's actual behavior is to be understood as a relatively immediate function of—among other things—the subjective psychological environment. In turn, the subjective psychological environment is a resultant or modification, to a greater or lesser extent, of the more distal, consensually salient objective psychological environment. This modification is forged by the individual's intervening perceptual modes or schemata. Inter- and intraindividual differences in these perceptual schemata can provide conceptual and research entry for understanding alternative behaviors and changes in character over time.

The Emphasis on Integrating Drives With Attentional Influences

In the field of psychology during the 1950s, there was an intensification of dissatisfaction with the then-ensconced views of why it is people do what they do. The basis of this discontent was empirical—unassimilable discrepancies were being repeatedly observed between what should happen, according to the dominant theoretical views of drives, and what did happen. Although the concept of drive was paramount at the time, observed behaviors in the field of animal psychology (the predominant locus of research on behavior at the time) did not seem to conform well enough or extensively enough to theoretical anticipations. Moreover, within the field of psychoanalysis, which also strongly emphasized drives and drive-reduction, there were many observations that were theoretically or seemingly anomalous.

Gradually, discontent accumulated regarding the sufficiency of the drive conception that had prevailed for so long. This burgeoning of dismay was summarized brilliantly at the time by White (1959) in a scholarly essay still well worth reading by contemporary psychologists.

White made the critical case *against* drive-reduction as a sufficient paradigm for conceptualizing behavior by portraying the many kinds of behavior neglected or too tortuously explained by drive orthodoxy. Beyond pointing out these conceptual and empirical embarrassments, however, White went on to constructively argue for deeper recognition of an intrinsic motivation in individuals that earlier had been only dimly perceived. Specifically, he called attention to the universal developmental achievement by children of what he labeled "competence" and proposed that the achievement of competence was driven, universally, by what he termed the pleasures of "effectance motivation."

By competence, White (1959) had reference to the "adaptive mechanisms ... or ego processes ... which have to do with effective interaction with the environment" (p. 317). Such mechanisms, such processes involve slow development from infancy on of learned skills such as

> sucking, grasping, ... visual exploration ... crawling and walking, acts of focal attention and perception, memory, language and thinking, anticipation, the exploring of novel places and objects, effecting stimulus changes ... , manipulating and exploiting surroundings, and achieving higher levels of motor and mental coordination." (White, 1959, p. 317)

Such evolved and articulated skills provide, as a common effect, an increase in the individual's understanding, facility, and therefore effectiveness in operating on the environments encountered. And such competencies are poorly understandable in terms of drives if only because competencies must have been achieved *before* they can begin to serve to reduce drives.

What then brings about competencies? White (1959) proposed an inborn motivational tendency to achieve effectance, "an intrinsic need to deal (effectively) with the environment" (p. 318). Although White did not especially employ evolutionary phrasings in his rationale, he did remark upon the "biological significance" of the effectance motive. In the present zeitgeist, the seeking of competence can be construed as a powerful and gratifying way by which individuals may improve their ultimate reproductive fitness.

The operation of effectance motivation can be expected to create a broad variety of behaviors: directed, selective, persistent action; curiosity; manipulation of the environment; behaviors betokening of efforts at mastery per se; and so on. As White (1959) characterized the developmental process underlying the achievement of competence, behavior ... is constantly circling from stimulus to perception to action to effect to stimulus to perception, and so on around; ... these processes are all in continuous action and continuous change. Dealing with the environment means carrying on a continuous transaction which gradually changes one's relation to the environment. Because there is no consummatory climax, satisfaction has to be seen as lying in a considerable series of transactions, in a trend of behavior rather than a goal that is achieved. It is difficult to make the word "satisfaction" have this connotation, and we shall do well to replace it by "feeling of efficacy" when attempting to indicate the subjective and affective side of effectance. (pp. 321–322)

White's essay coincided with (and abetted) the dropping away of psychological interest, conceptually and empirically, in drives. The evidence for the insufficiency of drive-reduction seemed compelling since, despite great theoretical contortions by drive-reductionists to encompass the marshaled contrary observations, there remained confronting problems. The continued convenience of working exclusively in a drive-reduction framework had become simply outweighed by the fantastic complications of the relations that therefore had to be posited and heaped upon each other. In the search for conceptual economy—that implicit reason for theorizing—the question had become where we wish to place our parsimony. Should we have relatively few concept-based variables and, consequently, extraordinarily complex relations among them or a larger number of concept-based variables, all of which are relatively simply related?

With the waning of the emphasis on drive-reduction, there began reciprocal waxing of respect for the idea of exploratory, competence-enhancing, proactive behavior in the field of personality psychology (e.g., Berlyne, 1965; McReynolds, 1956; White, 1959). The concept of drive by the 1960s was largely put out to pasture. Where earlier there had been emphasis on the preemptive, affectively tinged, immediately motivating, short-term influence of drive-reduction on behavior, the new motivational emphasis—insofar as it was pursued—was on recurrently emerging, long-term affective tendencies underlying adient, experience-increasing, competence-enhancing behaviors.

However, concern regarding the relations between and relative importance of motivations for drive-reduction and motivations toward increasing experience and competence has largely languished for the past 30 or so years. With the excited and exciting emergence in psychology of "the cognitive revolution," psychology turned away from issues regarding motivation toward issues of cognitive functioning per se, of how information is organized and processed in the brain and how cognitive behaviors are influenced by various external experimental manipulations.

Remarkably fruitful though this psychological movement has been, it has proceeded with little consideration of the significant motivations and affect that underlie naturalistic behavior. This insufficiency has been remarked on recently by a number of investigators (e.g., Damasio, 1994; LeDoux, 1996). As Izard (1993) has noted, and as cited earlier,

> the emotion system preceded the cognitive system in evolution and outpaces it in ontogeny. It is highly adaptive for animals to be able to feel before they think, as in the case where pain elicits withdrawal or pain-induced anger motivates defensive actions. (p. 73)

The emphasis on cognition per se has been, perhaps, a stage in the dialectic by which a science progresses. Old truths regarding affective considerations are abandoned—but too vehemently—for new, affectless, cognitive ones. As Meehl (1978) remarked, psychology does not solve its problems. Rather, it just drops them and goes on to another, quite different problem. Hopefully, time—that great arbitrator—will bring about the balance and integration that is required.

White's early conceptualizations of the motivational tendency to obtain percepts was an attractive effort to employ his broadly based observations in a positive manner as a cornerstone of a theory instead of solely as a basis for criticism of earlier formulations of the concept of drives. I follow him (and others; e.g., Woodworth, 1958) in acknowledging the significance of this evolution-wired influence on experience-increasing, percept-processing, order-seeking behavior. However, White (1959) did not throw away the construct of drive (p. 317), although he did not conceptually deal with it. Atkinson (1964) also recognized the existence of two alternative conceptual approaches to motivation when he noted that behavior could be formulated as a function of drives × habit, whereas perception required a formulation in terms of expectancy × value. I wish to reconcile the crucial emphasis on effectance with what may still be called the drive- or impulse- or urge-reduction influences I continue to recognize as psychologically important.

What remains needed for personality psychology is a conceptual framework that does justice to the important but partial truths justifying competing views, one that can intermix in coherent ways what proponents of the importance of drives and drive-reduction have to say and what acclaimants of the importance of experience-increasing motivations insist on. The present formulation is an attempt to construct such a model, one that respects both the propulsive influences of drive reduction and the experience-increasing influences operating within the individual that conjointly forge behavior.

This attempt fails, of course, because of daunting difficulties and the prematurity of any such effort. The present endeavor, however, may offer some useful, advancing recognitions and be instructive for future and better theorizing.

The Emphasis on Conceptualizing Personality Psychologically Rather Than Biologically

The biological fields have infiltrated the field of psychology in exciting and implicative ways. Psychologists cannot afford to ignore the new findings stemming from functional imaging, anatomic and physiological studies, findings regarding DNA markers, and so on; they must attain and maintain sufficient such knowledge relevant to inform their own psychological theorizing. There is an intellectual obligation to not ignore the directive and controlling conceptual implications at the psychological level of the findings of various kinds of biological knowledge, whenever they can be drawn. We are well beyond the old notion that the brain simply functions like a telephone switchboard or a serial computer.

However, it is also important to recognize the ways in which neuroscience, so important and attractive in its own right, is often internally equivocal[1] and may have little relevant to say as yet to the science of psychology per se. Thus, it has been recognized since the days of Phineas Gage that the prefrontal cortex mediates impulsive behaviors (see the volume by Macmillan, 2000). More recently, we know that the complicated amygdala complex is involved when emotions are experienced. But the subsequent neuroscience articulation

---

[1]The neuroscientist Richard Ivry (in the Berkeley Magazine of the University of California, Fall 1998, p. 13) has remarked regarding the limitations on imaging devices and procedures: "They are very useful in telling you what areas of the brain are active, but they are not all that good for telling you why those areas are active or what they are actually doing." More generally, consider the "binding problem" besetting neuroscience. We know there exists an executive system, a superordinate area or system of the brain that "binds" together and integrates the functional modules underlying organized perception, cognition, action—in short, behavior. But the binding problem has not been solved at the first, lower level of integrating within modules. It remains to be seen how the binding problem will be solved at the higher, "executive" or "ego" level.

of these mediated relations has been uninformative or inconsistent, and therefore not conceptually constraining in theorizing regarding the psychological dynamics and conditions underlying impulsive and insufficiently impulsive behavior, between various conditions of felt emotion, between the adaptive and maladaptive solutions attempted. The last dozen pages of the chapter by Pickering and Gray (1999) on the neuroscience of personality frankly demonstrate the limited findings, empirical incoherence, and speculative neurologizing still riddling the field.

The remark of Cacioppo et al. (1999) is telling: "The extant of neurophysiological data cannot resolve the nature and structure of affect" (p. 844). Freud is said to have once said, "I have no inclination to keep the domain of the psychological floating as it were in the air, without any organic foundation .... Let the biologists go as far as they can and let us go as far as we can. Some day the two will meet." I agree with him and look forward to a mutually helpful meeting. But so far, biological psychology—by itself important and fascinating—has not met well the specific conceptual needs of personality psychology (Turkheimer, 1998). Just as particle physics does not explain plate tectonics, neuroscience does not explain personality and its development.

It needs to be remembered too that physiological or neural "predictors" tend to be no more than correlates or markers or associations of psychological states. They may, in principle, be causes, effects (as witnessed by placebo evidence of how the mind can affect the body and brain), or concomitants of these states. At the present time—whatever the future may bring—studies of localized brain activity or autonomic functioning or hormonal changes or different brain hemispheric proclivities, themselves of intrinsic interest, may serve personality psychology well primarily and perhaps only as indicators or markers that something psychologically relevant is happening within an individual. And what is happening psychologically may be understood only if the psychological context within which these neurohormonal changes occur is known via reported mentation, reasonably inferred cognitions, and contextualized physical behaviors. Thus, neurophysiological changes may serve well to objectively indicate the presence of certain concurrent affectively experienced but unreported states. By themselves, skin conductance, heart rate changes, localized brain activity, cortisol levels, and so on are of uncertain psychological implication. When given context, however, they can be uniquely informative. But then such measures serve only as "operationalizing indicators" or "markers"—they do not "explain."

To extend this argument somewhat in a more philosophical direction, consider that the neuroscientific emphasis often seems to imply or presume the possibility of a reductionistic view of psychology, that neuroscientific knowledge in principle can supplant the intellectual need for efforts at psychological understanding.

Jessor's (1958) definition of reductive explanation remains a fair one for the immediate purposes: The idea of reductive explanation posits that "the terms or concepts and the relations or laws of one discipline may fully and without loss of meaning be translated into or deduced from those of a lower (and more 'basic') discipline" (p. 171).

However, the logical and practical problems besetting the ambition of reductionism should be recognized. As Gell-Man has aptly noted, although one can reduce to a lower level, it does not follow that one can go the other way, toward a higher level of complexity. Lively arguments for the emergent qualities of systems based on but not predictive from lower level components challenge the supposed simplicity and all-embracingness of a reductionistic view (see Bock, 1998). Two apt analogies are worth quoting here: "Trying to understand perception by studying only neurons is like trying to understand bird flight by studying only feathers: It just cannot be done" (Marr, 1982, p. 25). "Knowing the structure of water is H_2O gives no clue as to why water goes down a drain in a vortex," an analogy informally offered by Brian Goodwin.

Such counterarguments resisting or even denying reductionism, it should be recognized, do not displace the need for close analysis in any way available of the phenomena under consideration. But they do suggest the reductionist explanation should not be too hastily invoked.

In the present formulation, I stay at the psychologically emergent level of analysis and therefore theorizing. The brain inexorably mediates the many aspects of perception, behavior, and experience, but these many aspects may profitably be conceptualized and studied with little regard for the specifics or "hardware" of nervous system function. The present approach is therefore not especially concerned with the way psychological functioning is realized or mediated neurologically; "the mind is not the brain" (Hyland, 1985). In what follows, little will be said of the higher nervous system, the middle ear, or lower organisms.

Finally, I must comment on the unfortunate tendency among some neuroscientists to neurologize, to talk rather loosely in nominalistic, but not explanatory, terms. Thus, "the left-brain interpreter," vaguely characterized, is proposed to explain integrated behaviors (Gazzaniga, 1989). Other neuropsychologists invoke the label of "executive functions and dysfunctions" to explain various actions and mental disorders

(Barkley, 1997; Lezak, 1983; Stuss & Benson, 1984). Certainly, there is
an organization or sometimes a disorganization of behavior but its basis
is as yet not comprehensible by neuroscience (or by personality psychology). The usage of such portentous, homuncular labels seems to
represent scientism rather than serious science.

PLAN OF PRESENTATION OF THE PRESENT FORMULATION

A previous, private version of this monograph was sequenced so that all
the constructs chosen were first defined in all their particulars. The interrelations of these constructs were then posited and, finally, the systematic consequences of these definitions and posited relations were
considered. This way of proceeding seemed to place too heavy a memory burden on preliminary readers because the definitional details of
the various constructs and relations were numerous, and their logic or
ultimate function could not be immediately apprehended when initially presented. When the pieces of the puzzle were later assembled,
there was uncertainty still and much back referencing to the earlier definitions in a way that was unsatisfactory.

In the present organization, I have reversed this plan and chosen
what might be called an "unfolding" method of presentation. System
properties are described and justified and then the constructs required
to explain the properties of the system are introduced, in the succession
and detail judged appropriate, so that the logical structure and conceptual purpose of the further complications is made apparent. It is hoped
that this way of proceeding will not be too tantalizing for the reader and
I will not have simply exchanged organizational faults. In any event, the
reader is asked to accept, graciously, the delaying tactics often employed as the main line of theory development is pursued.

Another deliberate choice in regard to the plan of presentation is
that no thoroughgoing documentation of the evidence in support of
the formulation is attempted. Although many references are mentioned at junctures where it is useful to introduce support for an assertion, a scholarly, searching review of all the relevant literature has not
been an aspiration of the present work. In my judgment, an effort at
more elaborate documentation would have disrupted the flow of the
theoretical argument. The intent of this work is a restricted one: to introduce in somewhat skeletal form a systematic conception of personality functioning. I must leave for others the task of evaluating
comprehensively the pertinence and support of experiment and observation of the present formulation.

Chapter 4

A First Characterization
of the Personality System

This chapter begins a formulation of the ongoing, moment-to-moment personality system. The essential, primordial motivation of anxiety is considered, how it arises, and how it may be brought within bounds.

A CAPSULE STATEMENT OF THE ARGUMENT

(a) For evolutionarily adaptive reasons, there is a phenomenon called "anxiety": a sensed indicator to the individual that survival, physically and/or psychologically, is in the immediate apprehended moment under severe threat.

(b) A primary consequence of this urgently pressing system threat is that it abruptly invokes the primitive built-in system tendency of attempting to reduce anxiety to below a certain, sufficiently low level. Viewed psychologically, the individual is organized and impelled naturally and without prolonged articulation or serious analysis of the threat to seek anxiety-reduction, to lessen sensed threat. "The conditions that give rise to natural fear are statistically related to conditions that are actually dangerous but are far from identical with them" (Bowlby, 1970, p. 85). Because sensed threat is heuristically related to objective threat, the system orientation toward anxiety-reduction usually serves to escape the individual from the objective threat. By so doing, the immediate, proximate, "short-term viability" (the continuing

57

survival) of the individual is enhanced. However, it should be noted that in achieving psychological short-term viability, "non-rational aspects can be imbedded ... as the limiting conditions that 'bound' the area of rational adjustment" (Simon, 1954, p. 394). In "non-rational aspects," issues of emotion and psychological survival are paramount.

(c) A primary tendency evolutionarily ingrained in humans is a tendency to seek, articulate, analyze, organize, and simplify the internal representations of perceptual inputs, an orientation that is labeled herein as *perceptualizing*. Individuals naturally "perceptualize" because, in the long term, so doing is evolutionarily adaptive. Ceteris paribus, it enhances, ultimately, "long term viability" (the continuing survival of the individual's genes—i.e., reproductive fitness).

(d) The orientation to reduce anxiety is posited to be preemptive. When anxiety develops past a (generally) set point for the individual, the system tendency to reduce anxiety predominates over the tendency to perceptualize. That is, the perceptualizing orientation of the individual is deeply influenced and even subverted and displaced when anxiety levels reach regnancy and trigger system efforts at anxiety-reduction. An evolutionarily adaptive reason for subordination of the perceptualizing tendency to the anxiety-reduction tendency is that, effectively, short-term viability sensibly must precede long-term viability.

(e) When anxiety is reduced sufficiently and is no longer regnant, the perceptualizing tendency asserts or reasserts regnancy, and the individual is again oriented toward articulating the experienced world. Now, to elaborate.

PERCEPTUALIZATION AS A "NATURAL" STATE OF THE INDIVIDUAL

I start with the proposition that the personality system, when not otherwise controlled, assumes a state or orientation whereby the individual takes in new, novel, complex, variable information to organize, and therefore widens experience. That is, the individual may be thought of as biologically "tuned" to attend to and even seek fresh experience, to—in McReynolds' (1956) terms—"obtain new percepts" for personally held organization (p. 294). This is the natural, evolution-shaped, neurologically ingrained, orienting posture of the personality system wherein it operates as an "open system" (Bertalanffy, 1950), as a receptive and adaptive part of the larger ecosystem in which it finds itself. After McReynolds, I term this organismic tendency as *perceptualization*. Piaget (1967, p. 103) viewed this tendency to organize experience as being sui generis, as biologically given. Cacioppo and Gardner (1999) more approximately called this tendency a "positivity offset" (p. 205). There are individual differences in the organizational efficiency or rate of perceptualizing, with efficiency and rate being positively related to what may be called elementary information-processing functioning.

I need to explain the meaning of certain of these notions, and will attempt to do so shortly. But for now as this unfolding method of presentation is pursued, I depend on the widely held, albeit somewhat vague, meanings of these words among psychologists.

By positing an ever-welling tendency in individuals to differentiate novel features in the surrounding environment and to search for their organization, I am of course attempting to respect the indisputable phenomena of curiosity and the implications arising from observations of the stimulus seeking of infants, children, and adults. Historically, various writers (e. g., Angyal, 1941) have spoken out for some such assumption if only to permit humans to escape the discomforts and negativity of a totally animalistic, drive-driven self-image. But this emphasis, as already noted, proved convincing as well to more empirically oriented psychologists engaged in close scrutiny of the drive-reduction hypothesis and its empirical insufficiencies (e. g., Dember & Earl, 1957; Hinde, 1966; McReynolds, 1956; White, 1959).

Also, the recognition that evolution has shaped "modal action patterns" (G. W. Barlow, 1977) toward adaptation to the "average expectable environment"[1] brought with it the corollary recognition that an orientation toward attending to and organizing novelty improved cognitive understandings of the environment in which one abides. Such cognitive understandings can have crucial implications for adaptation within the surrounding ecosystem, thus fostering long-term viability and the ultimate evolutionary achievement of reproductive fitness.

The first proposition, then, simply says that the individual naturally and spontaneously is attuned to look for and process new experience in the outer environment, to attend to unaccustomed or previously unapprehended impingements from outside the skin, and to make sense (and use) of them. The developmental function, and consequence, of this percept processing is the establishment of assimilative cognitive structures, schema for economically organizing the inflow of perceptual experience. This tendency to be vigilant for and encompassing of

---

[1]Interestingly, the phrase "average expectable environment" has arisen in two seemingly quite distant intellectual fields, the ego psychology of psychoanalysis (Hartmann, 1958, p. 51) and ethology (e.g., G. W. Barlow, 1977).

new information is posited as perpetually, latently present, asserting itself or reasserting itself in behavior whenever the personality system, as a whole, is not dominated by other sources of motivation.

We may expect inter- and intraindividual differences or changes in this tendency. This tendency may be characterized more broadly as life zest or energized curiosity or perhaps what the Chinese call "chi." It may be viewed also as a precursor of or as underlying what has been called "positive affect" (Watson & Tellegen, 1985).

The usual or "natural" behavioral manifestation of (or evidence for) this proposition is curiosity or undriven exploratory behavior. Given that short-term viability is not threatened when the particular environmental context is registering on the particular individual as familiar and predictable, it is not presenting new perceptual or behavioral possibilities for assimilation. In such circumstances, the individual—if not otherwise controlled—is intrinsically oriented to seek more and uncommon percepts or a faster rate of percept impingement than the particular situation affords. In that interval when percept impingement, either in unusualness or in rate, lags behind a personally preferred tempo of incoming stimulation, the individual may be said to be "bored."

Individual differences or changes in the uncommonness of or rate at which percept impingement is preferred are of great significance. This individual difference variable may be termed *percept organizational–processing capacity*. Thus, an individual with a relatively high percept organizational–processing capacity, however evolved, will tend to be bored by a given situation well before an individual with a relatively low percept organizational–processing capacity. The spontaneous seeking of excitement or of thrills which is sometimes observed may perhaps be understood as due to a comparatively strong tendency to go out to one's world, a thirst or "zest for life," an "openness to experience."

Individuals characteristically or temporarily with a low percept organizational–processing capacity will tend to be overwhelmed—remaining or becoming disorganized or becoming rigidified—by situations relished by others with greater percept organizational–processing capacities. Such individuals will therefore seek to avoid percept organizational circumstances that would be preferred by a comparatively zestful person or by the same person at a time of higher percept organizational capacity. To a comparatively passive soul, only an adventurer takes a walk after lunch. Compared with the great many of us, the thrill-seeker—certain thrill-seekers—may simply be taking a walk.

To summarize this first assumption and its direct implications: When precedence is not taken by other factors, the individual is oriented toward increasing articulation of the environmental context. The continuing and comfortably progressing articulation of experience is recognized as providing one kind of pleasure, a sense of what White called *effectance*. The absence of sufficient variety or pace in the percepts psychologically impinging upon the individual develops a form of boredom—a latent impulse that is not yet goal-directed. The impingement of percepts at a rate or of a kind that does not permit continuing and comfortable processing overloads the individual's personality system. The consequence of this overload is that anxiety signals arise, and the individual may find the circumstance to be seriously unpleasant.

Because of temperamental characteristics and developmental history, individuals vary in their established insistence or appetite or "set point" for novel experience; some tend more to prefer and some tend more to avoid new and varied contexts. It should also be noted that, within an individual, there can be fluctuations over time and context in percept-processing capacity due to stress, fatigue, surgent drives, and other factors.

By this first assumption, we are enabled to encompass, if only by the easy trick of postulation, a variety of behaviors that earlier were viewed as puzzling or paradoxical for more instinct-ridden, drive-driven approaches. The matter now to be discussed is the connection and integration of this first proposition and what it entails with propositions that attempt to respect other kinds of recognitions about personality functioning. Before these connections can be offered, a definition of anxiety is required together with consideration of its place within a theory of personality.

ANXIETY AS THE SENSED INDICATOR OF SYSTEM INSTABILITY

There are universal phenomenological experiences and consensual observations of certain phenomena in humans that have come to be understood as instances of what commonly has been labeled "anxiety." Formally, anxiety may be conceived of as a deviation from a tenable-state condition of the personality system wherein the greater the deviation, the greater the anxiety. By "tenable-state of the system" I mean a conjunction of system variable values such that the temporal continuity of the system is not threatened—that is, the system is not close to those boundary conditions beyond which it cannot exist as a system. In contrast to the relatively "open" characteristic of the personality system when it is receptively and dynamically oriented to the external world, when anxiety achieves rule the personality system functions as a relatively "closed" system emphasizing internal rearrangements directed to moving away from boundary conditions.

To connect this conceptual assertion with earlier offered formulations, anxiety in the present context is being equated with deviations from psychological homeostasis (cf., Stagner, 1951); in psychoanalytic terms, with an "insufficiency of mastery, a state of being flooded by excitation" (Fenichel, 1945, p. 43), a "disintegration" or "overwhelming of the ego." Mandler (1980) suggested that anxiety results from a disorganization of previously flowing behavior and thought, frustrations of actions, discrepancies between expectation and reality, unanticipated conflict—all occurrences not under the control of the individual. Other theorists (D. H. Barlow, 1988; Beck & Emery, 1985; Chorpita, 1998) similarly conceptualize anxiety in terms of insufficient control or influence by the individual on a situation perceived as catastrophically threatening. There is anxiety whenever the individual does not know what to do, given impending and impinging environmental or intrapsychic events, and a sense of threat and helplessness is—at some level—experienced.

It is important to note that the nature of the state of the personality system in which such deviation or flooding or insufficiency of organized control has occurred is *not* specified. The present definition thus permits anxiety—a consequent variable—to arise from various states or combinations of the personality system's contemporary parameter values. Anxiety, as conceptualized here, represents a special kind of relation among system variables denoting that system boundary conditions have been or are being approached. Given the "satisficing" or strain-reduction organization (or "goal") of the system, the system—qua system—seeks to move away from the boundary conditions beyond which irreversible system instability would occur.

Strictly, anxiety is a primitive term, an open concept in the present formulation and as such is not completely definable (cf., e.g., P. E. Meehl, 1990). Amusingly but not incorrectly, the philosopher of science, Lakotos, has remarked to P. E. Meehl (1990) that some "open" concepts are more open than others.

At the subjective level, of course, our notion of anxiety is intended to have the surplus meaning usually accorded the concept of anxiety by psychologists. It is the basic mammalian emotion, inborn and reflexive for life-preserving evolutionary reasons; it developmentally precedes and contemporaneously dominates all other emotions. In its primary, intensely phenomenological form, the anxiety with which I am here concerned may be described as a primordial, ungovernably experienced panic (or terror or acute dread or horror, or an ultimate sense of hopeless helplessness) that, if sustained, could not be psychologically tolerated. In lesser intensity, anxiety phenomenologically may be manifested by a sense of uneasiness. Objectively, the experience of anxiety may be accompanied by a variety of autonomic (primarily sympathetic but also parasympathetic) nervous system reactions: hyperventilation, instant heartbeat changes, precordial pressure, dryness of mouth, palpitations, pupillary dilation, sweating, tremor, vomiting, abdominal pain, and other motor or verbal reactions such as startle, immobilization, transient and diverse behaviors such as unpremeditated aggression, distorted impressions, substitute stereotyped behaviors, behavioral disorganization, and so on. Massive, primary anxiety, if protracted, is postulated to be ultimately unendurable physiologically and therefore to terminate life.

In the beginning of life, there are prepotent causes of anxiety, evolution-based, that capture our nervous systems and instantaneously cause panic. Thus, one is compelled to be aware, anxiously, of a rapidly oncoming object in one's peripheral vision. The infant is uneasy, panicky, when on the edge of a "visual cliff." The sudden absence of a caretaking figure activates a built-in primary anxiety in an infant. In all of these and other instances, there is pre-emptive, affectively based perception, occurring without reflective cognition, reflexively directed toward immediate survival.

To experience a personal sense of what is meant here by the prepotency of primary anxiety, the reader should recollect in tranquility the sudden, flooding, surging panic momentarily and inevitably experienced on the realization a deadly car collision was about to befall one. Consider also how it would be, psychologically, to experience such terror prolongedly, indefinitely. Fortunately, beyond infancy and for most reasonably arranged lives, such primary anxiety is infrequent and fleeting and is not therefore chronically overwhelming. However, it is presumed by this formulation to be lurking as an omnipresent possibility—evolution-based—of which individuals are only dimly or occasionally aware. And when prepotent perceptions are activated, all human beings submit to life-continuing imperatives.

In its less extreme forms, a deviation toward personality system instability may be experienced as an uneasiness or unpleasant restlessness, a feeling of diminished control of the enveloping circumstance, an indication that the world or a portion of it does not make sense or have meaning, a sense of foreboding. In its less extreme form, anxiety is not as compelling or as dramatic as the panic constituting primary anxiety. These smaller instances, however, are considered to be conceptually continuous with the larger ones; both are to be thought of as instances of anxiety, of threat to the organism, of auguries of system instability. Perhaps the use of a more neutral term than "anxiety" would be desirable to characterize these less extreme states signaling an affective disequilibrium. However, no more general label readily suggests itself as connotatively superior (but consider "anticipations of dread," "apprehension," "trepidation"), and this usage need pose no difficulties for a forewarned reader.

The reader should also note that there is no implication in what has been said that anxiety is necessarily a phenomenon of which the individual is always aware. In attempting to characterize the primitive meaning of the anxiety concept as employed here, illustrations out of human experience have been used. The notion of anxiety, however, is one that has been developed out of observation as well as introspection. There are many instances of behavior that can be economically understood only by inferring the operation of some such underlying construct. Although the individuals involved, because of their patterns of mentation and affective expression (e.g., repression or other defenses, alexithymia, cultural or verbalizing style), may be unable to report their state of feelings, they may manifest symptoms clearly indicative of an underlying anxiety.

We may further distinguish anxiety that is proportional and rational, with a specifiable source, from anxiety that is disproportionate, irrational, and without a specifiable source. Experientially, whether realistically or unrealistically based, they are the same—anxiety is anxiety. For verbal convenience, we may label the first of these, realistically-based anxiety, as *fear*. But whether called fear or anxiety, we are referring to an elemental, instinctive, natural source of disturbed emotion indicative of an unsatisfactory state of the personality system and directed toward dire future anticipations.

ANXIETY-REDUCTION AS A PREEMPTIVE BASIS FOR BEHAVIOR

It follows, from the previous definition of a personality system and of anxiety as a deviation from a tenable state of that system, that attempts to reinstate some kind of tenable system state are anxiety-reducing. Anxiety-reduction is, by natural definition, sought by the individual and therefore can be viewed as motivating.

I assume that anxiety, when it occurs, displaces from motivational regnancy the tendency to take in and organize new information. Cacioppo and Gardner (1999) in their review article alluded to this tendency in terms of what they called "negativity bias" (p. 205). The consequence of this shift in priorities is that subsequent changes in the functional characteristics of the personality system and its moment-to-moment behavioral adjustments then derive primarily from their influence on anxiety-reduction rather than an outgoing approach to the world.

By virtue of the linkages among the set of variables constituting the system, reduction in anxiety level is associated with changes in the values of system variables. Invoking evolutionarily prepared adaptive response tendencies, the individual unthinkingly ducks the oncoming object; the infant hesitates and turns away from the visual cliff; the forlorn infant insistently seeks and usually finds a solicitous caretaker—all reflexive ways of undoing or ameliorating the causes of anxiety.

To the extent that changes reinstate the previous tenable state, anxiety is, by definition, reduced. However, I emphasize that, superimposed on prepotent recognitions and preadaptive responses, is the glorious cognitive capacity of the human being. This capacity, motivated by affect, permits the achievement of anxiety-reduction via a variety of alterations of system parameter values. The personality system, in seeking a sufficient tenable state, a modus operandi, may settle upon a tenable parameter arrangement never before realized. In the implementation of personality continuity, various feedback mechanisms are, within limits, available. To a large extent, the formulation to be presented herein consists of attempting to spell out some of these and the rules by which they are invoked and sequenced.

The return from system vicariousness or the achievement of a new, within-bounds tenable-state may be understood as a "reinforcing" of the behaviors or system adjustments that have just occurred. If the creation of a tenably improved personality system is contiguous with an action, that action is reinforced although the aim of the action is in a logical (but not psychological) sense quite irrelevant. That is, the personality system contains a "memory" of the outcome of experience such that subsequent, similarly grounded anxieties tend to be reacted to by system adjustments that have proven psychologically effective in the past. Subsequent response probabilities are altered—raised or lowered. Since our present concerns are with a specification of how a personality system functions over relatively short time spans, I do not consider here in any detail the structural changes in the personality system by means of which reinforcement leaves its adaptational residues (but see chap. 11). The nature of certain of the variables in the present formulation, however, suggests the locus of this kind of learning and even indicates certain of the properties of such anxiety-motivated, anxiety-resolving learning (Epstein, 1998). Of this, more later.

Without suggesting that the variety of conditions felt as pleasurable can be encompassed in anxiety-reduction terms, it is nevertheless subjectively clear that anxiety-reduction, when it occurs, provides a sense of relief and security, a feeling of closure and satisfaction that may serve as a not completely negative approximation of a kind of pleasure. In the infant, there can be quieting or relieving by various environmental or organismic events, such as sucking, rocking, or holding. The adult may require other ways of certifying and pleasuring the relief of anxiety. Whereas anxiety is largely mediated by sympathetic activity, anxiety-reduction is largely enhanced by parasympathetic activity.

THE TWO BASIC CAUSES OF ANXIETY

I now postulate that all instances of anxiety can be ordered to one or the other or some combination of two conditions of the personality system. These conditions are as follows:

1. The states where the *percepts* of the system are not being psychologically processed with sufficient organization or rapidity relative to the rate and autochthonous structure with which percepts unavoidably are being presented to the individual. There are instances, evolutionarily prepared, of stimulus configurations that are intrinsically not processible by the organism with a usual learning history; that is, typically, they will arouse anxiety.

2. The states where the psychological processing of motivational directives, generally known or labeled as *drives* (see the next chapter) is occurring with insufficient organization or rapidity relative to the rate of occurrence and the intrinsic structure of the drives. There are instances of drive configurations that are not processible by the organism with a usual learning history; that is, typically, they will arouse anxiety.

Combining the effects of these two classes of anxiety-increasing circumstances, then, the condition of maximum anxiety can be seen as resulting from a high level of accumulated, unorganized, unprocessed drive in the presence of a high level of accumulated, unorganized, and unprocessed percepts. In the extreme, the experience of this ultimate state may be called *panic*.

Minimum anxiety may come about in two ways, both of which are consonant with the above formulation. There can be minimum anxiety when there is the adient meshing of rapid, readily organizable, and intense drive processing conjoined with rapid, readily organizable, and affordant percept processing. The experience of this ultimate form of minimum anxiety may be what has been called "flow" (Csikszentmihalyi, 1990), a special and intense kind of pleasure. Or there may be minimum anxiety predicated on the meshing of low levels of drive experienced within the context of long-familiar and therefore easily organizable percepts, a form of quiet, habitual pleasure.

How are the terms "drive" and "percept," to be understood in the present context? Each of these terms, especially the former, has seen such multiple usages in psychology as to require close definition if they are to be used again. We must consider these concepts immediately, in at least a preliminary or approximate way before going on to the main line of theoretical development.

Chapter **5**

A Beginning Discussion of Drive, Percept, and Anxiety

In order for the reader to have a better sense of how the theoretical constructs drive and percept are meant and impinge on the personality system, the notions of drive and percept are separately illustrated, justified, and then placed in the context of anxiety and anxiety-reduction.

A FIRST DISCUSSION OF DRIVE

By the term *drive*, I refer to a psychological directive, often called an "impulse," inferred to exist within the organism, which activates, energizes, and shapes the individual's behavior. Over time or contexts, drive is in a state of flux, varying with regard to magnitude, the nature of its activation, and direction of expression. When present, drive is "regnant" (i.e., dominant; Murray, 1938) and must be dealt with within the personality system in some way or other and during that particular interval or moment of psychological time—it has an effect although its effect may not be immediately behaviorally or consciously apparent. If a drive is unacknowledged subjectively or a behavioral decision is made to not specifically respond, there and then, to the existing drive, that drive becomes a "psychological load," remaining as a latent, diffuse effect continuing within the personality system and in various ways influencing the system. The accumulation of such unresolved, unprocessed drives constricts or limits the boundary conditions within which the

68

personality system must function. Drive may or may not have some form of subjective representation, depending on its directional properties and other characteristics of the personality system at the psychological moment.

Drive, like anxiety, is a primitive term, a construct not completely definable in formal language. Consequently, it is necessary to build up a sense of what is meant here by the notion of drive through illustrations out of behavior and experience, where drive or the necessity of the concept of drive is intuitively apparent or logically compelling.

In part, the concept of drive is introspectively based. To an observer—at least this observer—it seems clear that not all behavior is determined by the details or "pulls" or affordances of the particular stimulus situation in which the individual has been immersed. Rather, much of what we do appears to be shaped by or be expressive of internal psychological pressures and "pushes." We are motivated organisms in the sense that some kind of lawfulness pervades our behavior, in ways not comprehensible by an exclusive focus on the external stimuli that happen to be present at the moment of action. We are not simply and only at the mercy of our surrounds.

How then is the initiation and urgency of these lawful behaviors to be conceptually understood? One answer that is still viable is that some kind of internal psychological initiator, triggered from latency by maturational processes and certain experienced environmental contexts, is involved. Ethologists (e. g., Tinbergen, 1951) talk of such occurrences as involving an "innate releasing mechanism." An individual hormonally achieving sexuality or long sexually quiescent may be aroused by the entrance of a sexually provocative, implicitly available person. With the recognition of behaviors that arise independent or partially independent of environmental stimuli, a concept of drive would seem to be required.

Among animal psychologists and ethologists in earlier years, the concept of drive was rationalized by pointing to the activity catalyzed by food or water or sexual deprivation (i.e., arising from so-called primary or unconditioned stimulus contexts). Bowlby (1986) viewed a constellation of object-seeking, attachment behaviors of infants as a drive in its own right. The behavioral changes that unquestionably have been observed are due to internal factors that have intrinsic, biologically based survival value and therefore implications ultimately for reproductive fitness.

For personologists, certain directed sequences of complex behavior have been viewed as arising from so-called secondary drives or abstractions from conditioned environmental contexts. Examples, among many others, of psychologically evolved motivations include Murray's *needs* (1938), *n* achievement (McClelland, Atkinson, Clark, & Lowell, 1976), the *need for intimacy* (McAdams, 1989), and Maslow's need hierarchy (1962). Consideration of these and other internally based motivations suggests that they have what may be called "psychological survival value" for the individual.

In the current psychological literature, it is apparent that the concept of drive has received serious inattention. The rise of the cognitive revolution has largely displaced thinking and empiricism regarding the problems previously considered under the rubric of drive and motivation more generally. True, some aspects of the drive concept are being obliquely studied by biologically oriented psychologists, but they invoke conjectured neural models of inhibition and activation without conceptual mention of what, psychologically, is being neurally inhibited or neurally activated. The present essay reasserts the conceptual usefulness of a notion of psychological drive.

The view being espoused here is that a drive, once actuated, may then exist essentially independently of its initial actuating circumstances and will remain to influence subsequent experience and behavior if not processed during its immediate psychological moment. Certainly, the circumstances of arousal of the drive, via modal action patterns operating within expectable environments or via learning, may also provide the circumstances relevant for its processing, release, and cessation. In this case, the claimed separation of drive from its activation may not clearly appear or seem confounded. However, and importantly, drive often may not be reducible by behavior available within the arousing situation. Thus, an experiment involving participant humiliation may be terminated abruptly, leaving the participant still bursting with aroused hostilities but with no environmental opportunity for their release. A sexy person may simply tease and leave, with the other individual now vigilantly oriented toward unavailable sexual activity. In the "unnatural" situation now existing for the individual, the psychological motivations that have been developed by such external environmental stimuli *must still be coped with* if only ultimately by the subsequent attenuation of memory. The existence of this kind of impelling residual, and its belated or indirect effects even though the precipitating circumstances no longer are immediately present, provides another basis for the construct of drive.

I emphasize again that drive, although to be posited herein as contributory to anxiety, is *not* anxiety in the present formulation. Drive, when it increases faster than it is being reduced via processing, will create anxiety by our definition of the relation between the two concepts. But drive level can be high without causing anxiety if its processing proceeds apace and therefore reduction is also high; indeed, as already has been mentioned, such circumstances can be excitingly pleasurable— the individual has achieved "flow."

Experientially, drive per se is not anxiety-inducing unless and until it can find no or insufficient expression or release and hence accumulates. For example, voluntary holding of one's breath activates a drive, a need to breathe. The consequent anoxia-caused drive creates no anxiety in the volunteer breath-holder until replacement of the required, and anticipated, oxygen is cut off. At that point, panic—massive anxiety—wells up. Reducing the drive by reintroducing a supply of oxygen will lower anxiety. However, if the perceptualizing individual anticipates further oxygen severance within the situation—thus raising anxiety level—then anxiety level may be psychologically high although the anoxia-based drive is being continuously processed.

These illustrations call attention to a circumstance where drive is high, but not anxiety, and also to a circumstance where drive is low, but anxiety now is high. Although in general drive will tend to covary with anxiety, the relation is not one-to-one. For this reason again, a conceptual separation between anxiety and drive is required.

We also observe that, historically, for stimulus-response psychologists such as K. Spence and Taylor (1964), anxiety was simply one kind of drive. However, in the present theory, drive is conceptually separable from the concept of anxiety. So much, for the moment, on the nature of drive and its relation to anxiety.

A FIRST DISCUSSION OF PERCEPT

The notion of *percept* is equally difficult to think about clearly and to convey. As I wish to employ the term, a percept is a subjectively registered, schematic representation of the stimulus situation or environmental context in which the individual exists at that particular psychological moment. By emphasizing the feature of subjective registration, the definition distinguishes between what is "out there" and what happens to get through to an individual. It is with what has effectively registered on the individual that the personality system must deal. I note, in passing, that the definition speaks of registration, not of awareness of what has registered. Although this distinction is not especially used here, I mention it to prevent misunderstanding.

This definition also calls attention to the schematic or abstracting property of a percept. A percept never registers in all its dazzling complexity the infinite set of facets in terms of which a stimulus situation conceivably can be understood. The percept instead is a simplifying abstraction created or imposed by the perceiving individual. The individual operates on the endlessly knowable environment, seizing on provided affordances (e.g., the importance of edges, verticality, color contrasts, and other evolution-shaped, neurologically honed reality indicators) and other adaptationally relevant, learned attention grabbers to evolve and establish what is usually an astonishingly small (and frequently rather consensual) set of relevancies for apprehending the world.

Often and perhaps usually, an incoming percept proves to be interpretable by means of the previously established schema the perceiver brings to the situation. When this happens, we say that the current percept has been *assimilated*. But sometimes the percept—what registers on the individual of the outside world at that moment—is not encompassable by the settled schematizing structures available to the perceiver. The structuring dimensions being brought to bear upon the percepts may simply not apply or apply well enough. When this eventuality arises, we say the percept has not been assimilated and that, more generally, percepts are not being processed at a sufficient organizational rate with the consequence that anxiety may arise. As will be noted later, when assimilation fails, accommodation efforts must be brought into play to generate a newly sufficient assimilatory structure that can keep anxiety level within bounds. The individual follows the adaptive maxim, "assimilate if you can, accommodate if you must" (J. Block, 1982).

Assimilation, then, refers to the ongoing compatibility of an individual's current percepts of the world with the highly selective schema previously evolved for integrating or organizing the individual's percepts. Percepts are continually impinging upon the individual, a new one registering whenever the psychological situation changes, and often when the personality system is subject to change. With rapid changes in the "objective" outside world, changeable received percepts may impinge upon the personality system rapidly, with the result that the organizational capacity on which assimilation depends becomes a highly relevant consideration. By the present definition of how anxiety comes about, if the individual's rate of percept processing or organizing is insufficient given the rate at which percepts requiring assimilation are impinging—if established schemas for percept assimilation are simply wanting given the nature of the pressing percepts—anxiety is increased. If percepts are comfortably processed as they register upon the individual, then anxiety level is unaffected from this direction. The process of assimilating percepts, after McReynolds but with an importantly different meaning, is called *perceptualization*.

As with anxiety and drive, the notion of percept is a primitive term whose meaning can only be suggested, instanced, or circumferentially specified. We cannot be formal or truly explicit about what a percept is.

I intend the term to provide a way in which "external forces" or conditions outside the individual can affect anxiety. In particular, I am presuming that a received percept may operate directly, in its own right, and not through activating an inner, dormant drive that is then coped with. By way of illustrating my conceptual intention here, consider the phenomenon of "photic driving."

An individual sits, with eyes closed, before a stroboscopic light perceptibly flashing at a rate within range of the alpha rhythm. Very readily, a synchrony develops between the flashing strobe and the rhythm of the brain. As the rate of flashing is gradually increased, the pace of the brain quickens also—until its upper bound on rhythm variation is reached and it falls behind the still accelerating light. It is at this point, when the photic stimulus can push the brain no further and the relation between light frequencies and brain rhythm breaks down, that the individual begins to experience a vague and unanalyzable, ineffable sensation of intense, content-free panic or anxiety.[1] How can this be understood?

In the present model, this phenomenon would be explained as due to a biological inability on the part of the personality system to assimilate percepts at the rate finally imposed from outside the individual. At a stage where the input to the organism is pressed beyond what the system can integrate, anxiety results. Now, it does not seem sensible—at least to the writer who has lived through this experience—to invoke a drive interpretation of this phenomenon. The phenomenology of the experience is such that one feels simply overwhelmed by the onslaught of incessant, intensifying stimuli. The stimulus situation seems to be having its effect directly, powerfully, immediately, and it has no specific psychological content or reference. Consequently, the separate status of some kind of concept such as percept would seem to be required.

---

[1]According to newspaper reports, a group of Japanese children watching a strobe light on TV experienced the phenomenon of photically-induced stress *en masse*.

Another kind of datum that supports the recognition of something like the percept notion comes from research on the so-called "psychotomimetic" or "hallucinogenic" drugs (e. g., mescaline and lysergic acid diethylamide, or LSD). To the extent that the consensus of testimony by individuals experiencing these drugs may be respected, their fundamental effects have to do with perceptual changes. Perceptual inputs, not behavioral outputs, are primarily affected. Individuals, when affected by mescaline or LSD are no more rampant than usual. They tend to be quiet and well modulated in their behavior. Indeed, the casual observer may note little or no significant behavioral change in the person under the influence of the drug. But experientially, and as suggested by certain specifically sought-for behaviors, the range and quality of perceptions is profoundly affected. "The doors of perception" (a line from William Blake, the poet and artist; see Huxley, 1954) have been "cleansed." The world is seen by the individual as never before, in something closer to its infinitude.

For some individuals or in psychologically unsupportive, strange environmental contexts, the hallucinogen lets in too much from the outside that ordinarily goes unattended. Consequently, the characteristic perceptualizing modes of the individual are overloaded, unassimilating, with resultant anxiety. In a benign, structured, supportive context or with individuals who have personality systems with an adaptational reserve to deal with the strains imposed by the suddenly astonishingly new world, the unusualness of the perceptual experience can be enjoyed and even relished.

Analogous to these differences between individuals in their reactions to psychotomimetics is the sequence of reactions often to be seen occurring within individuals. In a person new to such drugs, appreciable anxiety can be observed as the drug effect takes hold—the individual recognizes that perceptions are being fundamentally, increasingly, and uncontrollably altered and does not know how far this strangeness and absence of perceptual control will go. Assimilation is thwarted and anxiety is therefore frequently observed. But the drug effect ultimately flattens out and, although it is still appreciable, the person recognizes that the effect is decreasing rather than deepening, that continued metabolism will in time provide return pretty much to the way he or she was. During the recovery phase, the individual tends to savor the hallucinogenic experience more than when the experience is being entered.

I shall need to say more about percepts and bring in more supportive illustrations. For the present, however, these observations of photic driving and the effects of the psychotomimetics provide a further inferential basis for a notion of percept impingement and percept assimilation that is separate both from the concepts of drive and drive reduction and the concepts of anxiety buildup and reduction. The rate of percept impingement may be high, with little anxiety resulting, as where an individual appreciates or accommodates to the phenomenal experience provided by mescaline. The rate of percept impingement may be low, yet appreciable anxiety may be present overall by virtue of the presence of high drive levels. Often, the organizational rate of percept impingement will tend to covary with anxiety. However, because the correlation is far from unity, it is necessary for a theory to distinguish among these several concepts. While perceptually influenced by mescaline or LSD, individuals do not generally appear to be concerned with or susceptible to the various internal urges that usually rise up or can be activated. Appetites do not increase for food or sex or whatever. The psychedelic experience, paradoxically enough, is respected more for its revamping of perceptions than for its internal hedonistic qualities.

Having conveyed at least approximately the sense in which drive and percept are to be understood herein, I now cite some evidence in support of the present twofold classification of anxiety-arousing conditions. Later, more articulated chapters discussing the components of drive and percept will elaborate on certain points first made here.

INSUFFICIENT REDUCTION OF DRIVE AS A CAUSE OF ANXIETY AROUSAL

This condition is the classical one, considered extensively in psychoanalytic theory and experimentally by animal psychologists concerned with motivating learning.

In Freud's (1936) little volume devoted to "the problem of anxiety," he sees primary anxiety or the experience of panic (distinguished from secondary anxiety, which is a signal of danger to the organism) as an "economic disturbance brought about by increase in stimuli demanding some disposition made of them," as "an increase of tension arising from non-gratification of ... needs" (p. 76). For Fenichel (1945), long the definitive voice of orthodox psychoanalysis, anxiety is equated with "painfully high tension," with "amounts of tension beyond [the organism's] capacity to master" (p. 42). Other psychoanalytic writers, when explicit about the psychological economics by which anxiety comes about, do not diverge significantly from the conceptual positions just quoted, and accordingly one may draw upon the body of psychoanalytic theory not as proof, but as consistent with the assumption.

As noted earlier, research at the animal level where anxiety has been conceptualized as a drive can be viewed as supportive of the presently posited relation. Although there has been much dispute in the journals regarding the appropriateness of the drive concept, my point is simply that evidence is widespread that organisms, when manipulated so that their ordinary motivations (drives) are not realized by the achievement of goals (i.e., drive-reduction), subsequently manifest an agitation of behavior from which it seems reasonable to infer a latent variable such as anxiety. Essentially, the evidence to be mustered here is the nature of the behavioral effects of prolonged deprivations or drive containment.

Although previous clinical theory and findings from empirical research are supportive, it is at the level of subjective experience that the argument for the proposed relation must prove telling. Is it reasonable to assert that drive unresolved precipitates that feeling known as anxiety?

Drive, as I have defined it, is an internal behavioral directive that ordinarily helps activate actual behavior. It must be dealt with by the personality system when it is present. It is there and by posit, if not dealt with immediately in some way or another, it will be incremented or intensified and persist into succeeding psychological moments. If drive increases, and by the nature of the circumstances no means of coping with the unreduced drive is permitted, the welling up of drive will cause anxiety to be experienced.

With respect to drives for which physiological origin can be readily seen, the relation appears to easily hold. As already noted, the sudden unavailability of oxygen will certainly cause panic; thirst will drive men mad; prolonged hunger breeds something reasonably entitled to the anxiety label, at least until certain psychological and physiological mechanisms come into play to dampen its intensity and create an apathy.

At the more complex level of psychological drives, such as the motivation for love or money, it seems intuitively apparent that individuals intensely driven in such directions experience anxiety when the goals they seek are unavailable. Especially supportive of the relation I wish to establish here is the observation of the appearance of anxiety when the individual's conventional means of seeking drive-reduction are, one-by-one, made unavailable. One can get by with very little love from the outside world so long as an intimate or the family provides this kind of affective nourishment. If one finds a receptive, affirming world, it is easier to be at odds with one's partner or family. But let all the supplies of affectional sustenance be cut off (or appear to be cut off) from the individual motivated for affiliation—a derivative of early attachment—and a desolating and panicky sense of "aloneness," not simply a sadness, appears to develop. It is this kind of observation, multiplied by the kinds of retrospections the reader personally may bring to bear upon the question, that I suggest as justification for the relation proposed.

INSUFFICIENT PROCESSING OF PERCEPTS AS A CAUSE OF ANXIETY AROUSAL

This condition for anxiety is perhaps equally compelling subjectively. Research related to this assertion, however, is much sketchier than the research that can be brought to bear upon the drive-accumulation hypothesis. There are, however, several lines of evidence bearing on the contention. The reader may well wish to refer also to the prior paper by McReynolds (1956) where he brings together, for his own purposes and in somewhat different terms, diverse evidence for precisely this relation.

Perhaps the most widely available evidence for the present proposition comes from observation of reactions to "strangeness." We have all experienced momentary or sustained panic or perturbation when a familiar, predictable situation is suddenly and radically changed. The "startle response," abrupt skin conductance changes in reaction to a new stimulus, the chimpanzee's fright when a familiar attendant wears the familiar coat of another attendant, the child's concern when an often retold story is trivially changed—these are all illustrations of the posited relation. Or consider what happens when an infant is confronted with a "still" (i.e., nonreactive) face of a parent who had previously been facially reactive. The strangeness appears to provide threatening percepts which, if only momentarily, cannot be assimilated by the schemata then available to the infant.

More formal evidence may be seen in experiments that have varied the dimension of environmental entropy—that is, the randomness or orderliness of the environment, the independently defined ambiguity or structure of the field presented to the individual. Presumably, a more chaotic or cue-less or contrary environment will develop percepts that are less likely to be integratable by existent structures for percept processing. The literature on the effects of this environmental dimension has not been brought together. However, representative studies include (a) those on concept attainment where instances of concepts are arranged systematically or at random (Bruner, Goodnow, & Austin, 1956); (b) recognition thresholds where illumination, exposure time, or stimulus distinctness are varied so as to make the task easy (because it is clear) or difficult (because it is ambiguous); (c) the development of frames of reference, where an individual is asked to establish a reference frame in an unstructured as compared with a partially structured situation (Sherif, 1936); (d) postural orientation toward the vertical where individuals are asked to judge the true vertical when deprived of certain usually present cues to verticality (Witkin, Lewis, Hertzman, & Machover, 1954); (e) reactions to rumor where the ambiguity of the situation is varied (Allport & Postman, 1947); (f) judgments made in opposition to group pressure (Asch, 1956); (g) perceptions of size when deprived of typical visual cues (Ames, 1951; Dion & Dion, 1976).

In all of this research, it is clear from the reports of participants and as a straightforward inference from participant behavior that a destructured or unstructured registration creates a psychological context that is not assimilable by previously established means. A strain is imposed and is experienced as psychologically stressful, perhaps verging onto anxiety, in contrast to registrations permitting ready understanding and utilization by the individual.

Whereas the preceding argument of support employs normative evidence for the anxiety-inducing effect of situational entropy, research on the meaning of individual differences in reaction to ambiguity is also relevant. Here may be cited, for example; (a) differential studies of *intolerance of ambiguity* and the need to categorize (Frenkel-Brunswik, 1949); (b) differential studies of tendencies to establish a frame of reference (J. Block & Block, 1951); (c) differential studies of tendencies to "level" or to "sharpen" incongruities in perceptions (Gardner, Holzman, & Klein, 1959; Klein, 1953); (d) differential studies of the effects of the latency and magnitude of perceptual reactions on wearing aneisokonic lenses (Becker, 1954; Martin, 1954); (e) differential studies of interpretations of an authority's vaguely defined expectations (J. Block & Block, 1952) and group pressures (Crutchfield, 1955).

The central finding of these and other experiments on individual differences in perceptual modes is that identical stimulus contexts give rise to behaviors differentially reflecting the presence of strain or anxiety and the attempt to eliminate this subjective discomfort. A most reasonable explanation of these differing levels of anxiety is that the identical stimulus contexts are somehow being understood differently. In the present terminology, these identical situations are being assimilated differentially. An environment relatively assimilable by one individual proves to be relatively unassimilable by another person, this difference in ability to assimilate thus accounting for the difference in anxiety level that is manifested. These research findings provide another leg of support for the proposed relation that inadequate assimilation of percepts arouses anxiety.

THE TWO BASIC MODES OF ANXIETY-REDUCTION

It follows, as a trivial corollary of the assumption of the two ways by which anxiety is aroused, that the reversal of these conditions will prove anxiety reducing. Anxiety can be lessened by lowering the level of drive or by more efficiently processing or assimilating percepts.

The anxiety-reducing function of drive-reduction is well supported by a variety of researches, especially those of the Iowa group (K. Spence & Taylor, 1964; K. W. Spence & Farber, 1953) and those concerned with avoidance learning (Brush, Brush, & Solomon, 1955; Kamin, 1954). Although most of these researchers make anxiety but a drive, we may still avail ourselves of their experimental evidence that a relation exists between anxiety-reduction and drive-reduction. The question of the hierarchical placement of anxiety and of drive is a separate one, for which other arguments must be introduced.

Further evidence for a relation between drive-reduction and anxiety-reduction comes from noting the effect of catharsis, the release of pent-up impulses, and from various psychoanalytic observations of behavior during psychotherapy.

The anxiety-reduction function of percept assimilation is not so well evidenced by formal studies. From my own standpoint, I take the proposed relation as a premise, based on experience and observation, and as adapted from the premise system of other theorists. I am most obviously indebted here to the formulation advanced by McReynolds some years ago (although he did not consider the internal urges of the individual), the emphasis of Harlow (1953), and the psychoanalysts (see, e.g., Fenichel, 1945). The gestaltists too (Koffka, 1935; Kohler, 1940; Lewin, 1951; Wertheimer, 1945) and their successors (e. g. Hochberg & Gleitman, 1949; Postman & Bruner, 1948) may be brought in to further support the hypothesis of the anxiety-reducing function of percept assimilation. They contend that the function of perception is equilibration or compromise as manifested by pragnanz tendencies. All perceptions seem to move toward simplification, in some way or another, in order to resolve disequilibrium. But what is the nature of the disequilibrium the organism "seeks" to resolve? I suggest the disequilibrium involves what has been labeled "anxiety," in both its system-influencing and experiential aspects.

Although no systematic body of research on the relation seems to exist, a variety of observations and experiments can be fitted to the assimilation hypothesis. Thus, children appear to find a certain comfort in repetitive play—a phenomenon that may be known as "belated mastery." The usual tendency for skin conductance reactivity to lessen as the participant accommodates to the initially strange experimental situation may be thought of as support for the proposed relation. The "leveling" effects reported by Klein and his collaborators (Klein, 1953) and by the Dartmouth group (Ames, 1951), where objectively changed stimuli are still viewed in familiar ways may be interpreted into the present frame of reference (Dion & Dion, 1976). Sherif's (1936) experiment on the sequential establishment of personal norms in the autokinetic situation is also suggestive, especially in the light of subsequent studies on the personality correlates of differential behavior in the situation (J. Block & Block, 1951; Millon, 1957). Research by Broadbent (1971; 1977), Easterbrook (1959), Wachtel (1968), and Bacon (1974) indicates that individuals, when made anxious, tend to narrow their focus to the dominant cues in the surrounding environment, excluding irrelevant cues and thus making what remains more readily assimilable. Often, this restriction of perceptual range may be effective, but sometimes it is maladaptive, depending on the situation. Other experiments could be cited but perhaps these are enough for the while.

RECAPITULATION OF WHERE WE ARE NOW

The personality system so far described is a simple one, but it may be well to review its capacities and mode of operation, if only to set the stage for the next complications to be developed.

In the present characterization, the individual will, in the natural or expectable or "normal" course of events, be open to experience and will act to take in and organizationally process new percepts. The individual will be curious, broadly attentive, and actively engaged with the world.

This intrinsic (life-force, protoplasmic) tendency to seek new, organizable inputs, however, can be preempted at any time by a phenomenon known as anxiety. When anxious, the individual is no longer enabled to maintain this relaxed, uncommitted yet encompassing orientation to the situation and must instead rearrange functioning so as to cope with the anxiety that has arisen.

There are two basic ways in which this anxiety develops. The first of these is when inner drives or behavioral directives or impulses break through and achieve regnancy but have no or insufficient outlet—the condition where drive level is extreme but drive-reduction techniques are insufficient or unavailable to the individual in the particular situational context. The second basic way in which anxiety can be developed is where the individual's world appears to be hopelessly and overwhelmingly chaotic—the condition where percept impingement is high and unstructured but processing and assimilation of these to-be-organized percepts into comfortable-enough schemas lags behind.

Maximal and massive anxiety, by the definitions thus far, would develop when the two routes to anxiety reinforce each other—when extreme levels of unreduced or disorganized drive are concomitant with a subjectively incomprehensible world.

At levels of anxiety less than the maximum, the formulation permits equivalent levels of anxiety to be differently composed. Thus, an intermediate and perhaps tenable degree of anxiety may be based on the conjunction of unreduced drive with readily assimilated percepts, or it may be a resultant of a comparatively low drive in the presence of an unstructurable environment. The possibility of alternative patterns of tenable anxiety carries with it the important implication that prediction of the subsequent behavior of anxiety-ridden individuals must assess first the underlying basis or form of the motivating anxiety.

There are two ways by which anxiety may be reduced—by organized reduction of drive or by assimilation of percepts, by finding an effective means of releasing the activated behaviors or by finding a schema in which, as apprehended, the disturbingly disorderly environment may be integrated or awarded gestalt qualities. Given maximal and psychologically untenable anxiety, both means must be invoked to diminish the individual's panic. At intermediate levels of anxiety, the one or the other mode of anxiety-reduction or a conjunction of the two may be employed.

A most important property of the formulation even at this early point of the theoretical development should be noted. An intermediate (i.e., less than maximal) anxiety stemming essentially from one of the sources of anxiety may be reduced *directly*, by reversing its source or *indirectly*, by employing the other basic means of anxiety-reduction. Thus, when drive-reduction is not proceeding apace, with resultant anxiety, the personality system has available to it, as one means of coping, the option of structuring the perceived environment even more than would ordinarily be required. That is, in order to reduce an anxiety that may have been initiated by inadequate expression of impulses, the individual may adopt the stratagem of insistently and radically assimilating percepts to ready-made, well-used, narrowed or oversimplified schemata. By so doing, drives previously blocked from reduction or redirection because of the unavailability of perceived instrumental opportunities in the environment may in the now oversimplified view of the world find the means to their end. The observation of a drive origin of "intolerance of ambiguity" (Frenkel-Brunswik, 1949) may perhaps be understood in these terms.

Conversely, in order to reduce an anxiety aroused by a suddenly incomprehensible or strange environment, the individual has the option not only of structuring and making sense of the perceived situation but, alternatively, of preventing increases in and even containing or lowering the level of unreduced drive. If, somehow, the individual can prevent the onset of drives that would then have to be dealt with, the anxiety potential is diminished. Caution and constraint and control may be used to cope with the anxiety provoked by "strangeness." I later attempt to spell out the details of how such an interchange can come about. For the moment, it need only be noted that these possibilities presently exist within the system being postulated and that they have the promise of permitting the derivation of a variety of patterns of adaptive mechanisms individuals can invoke in the effort, somehow, to reduce anxiety.

Thus, anxiety is viewed as a function of the relation existing among several variables. It may be managed within the personality system directly by reversing the effects of the particular anxiety inducers, or it may be attenuated indirectly by changes in variables other than the ones initially involved.

Now to consider the notion of drive in more detail.

Chapter 6

Drives, Tension, and Control

THE NECESSITY OF STRUCTURAL VARIABLES

To go further now, it is necessary to complicate matters by introducing some additional concepts. We must spiral back upon the notions of drive and percept because in the first approximation to these concepts some formidable complexities in their definition were glided over. The conceptual problem now to be confronted is the problem of *structure*.

In talking of drive and percept, nothing has been said so far about structural variables of personality, as these might affect and help influence registered drive and registered percept. A *structural variable* is meant here as a relatively enduring, slowly evolved, more-or-less articulated property of personality systems that serves to give direction or constraint or specificity to the relatively transient energies of and impingements on the individual.

The term structure as used here is similar to the notion of psychological structures characterized by Schafer (1958). In his definition, (a) structures have a slow rate of change; (b) there is a relative autonomy of structures from their origins; (c) there is a high degree of automatization or triggering of structures as a manifestation of their achieved autonomy; (d) there is an acquiring of structures through learning from and identifying with family and the larger community; (e) structures are steadily and preferentially available, not created anew on each occasion of stimulation.

Earlier, in defining drives as *directed*, the prior existence of a structure has in effect been implied. Also earlier, in distinguishing between the objective psychological situation of the individual and the shaped percept that has subjectively registered, schemata have been mentioned by means of which a percept is assimilated—these schemata are also structures. It is by introducing a concept of structure (F. H. Allport, 1955) that the possibility is created of encompassing interindividual differences in functioning and intraindividual changes over time in the effort to elude anxiety.

Introducing some structural variables into a theory of behavior of course threatens an undifferentiated, normative approach. It would be much simpler if a psychological theory could be maintained without the bother of recognizing the "nuisance variance" created by pervasive, reliable, and decisive interindividual differences. The propriety of such a normative stand, once staunchly maintained, for a long time now has been recognized as untenable. It is no longer reasonable for psychologists to aspire for more than trivial normative laws without also evaluating the crucible role of individual differences in the realms of personality, motivation, and cognition (Underwood, 1975). The ancient statistical maxim becomes pertinent here: A mean loses meaning as the reliable variability about the mean increases.

In order to perceive an order in our empirical diversity, a conceptualization is required that includes structural variables, whether these are phrased in psychoanalytic ego terms, in terms of different habit-family hierarchies, or in terms of more contemporary, more fashionable theoretical metaphors (e.g., if–then relations or production rules). The useful question now is with regard to the most incisive way to proceed. My own suggestions on this score are imbedded in this and the next chapter, in more extended discussions of drive and of percept, and their basis.

THE COMPOSITION OF DRIVE

In the earlier characterization of drive, drive was defined as "a directed psychological force ... that serves to activate or energize the individual in his or her behavior." I would propose now that "drive" be viewed in a more complicated way, as a joint function of two prior variables, *tension* and the *control apparatus*. By decomposing the concept of drive in this fashion, it seems to me that some rich possibilities of modeling behavior emerge and we escape some of the contradictions and regresses that have in the past bedeviled the notion of a psychic motive force.

The Concept of Tension

Tension is meant here as an undirected, nonspecific psychological impulsion inferred to exist within the individual that provides the necessary if not sufficient condition for behavior or change in the personality system. Over time or contexts, tension varies in magnitude, and various tension inducers are defined as summating their effects on tension level. Consequently, once induced, the nature of the tension-initiating condition is not necessarily identifiable from the fact of tension per se. That is, the connection, if any, between certain stimulus contexts and discrete tension level changes is primarily a learned one, although there may be fixed or modal action patterns, hard-wired in the individual by evolution, that shape behavior to fit the "average expectable environment." The individual does not, without learning, know the association between, for example, certain periodic tensions and food deprivation, between certain occasional tensions and the common factor in the accompanying stimulus context. By itself, tension is posited as having no necessary subjective (i.e., experiential) representation, although of course it may have many behavioral manifestations and may by its subsequent implications lead to an awareness of itself and its associated context.

Our notion of tension has, in itself, no vectorial properties; it achieves direction only by virtue of being modulated or channelized by another system construct, the *control apparatus*, whereupon as *directed tension* it becomes known as drive. Duffy (1951) has made an equivalent distinction between what she calls "energy mobilization" (our tension) and the direction or guidance of the behavior that has been energized.

Drive always presupposes tension, but as will be seen, tension may exist without representation in a drive. It is in this sense that tension is a necessary but not sufficient condition for the immediate activation of the individual.

I can best elaborate the usefulness and possibilities afforded by the distinction between tension and drive after introducing the concept of the control apparatus. Certain properties and consequences solely of the definition of tension, however, may profitably be mentioned here.

Tension is conceived as a construct existing at a psychological, not a physiological, level. There are various manipulations of physiology that will develop tension, but the relation of physiological manipulation to psychological tension is neither invariant nor necessarily primary in its effects. Other nonphysiological causes of tension exist, and indeed in the usual circumstances of individuals in our abundant society, it is these latter tension inducers that are paramount.

The concept of tension is proposed as integrating into the same or commensurate "psychological units," tension-inducing circumstances of all kinds. Thus, it is implied that the simultaneous existence of, for example, food deprivation and affiliation deprivation would induce a higher level of tension than is caused by either deprivation separately.

Since various tension inducers are psychologically converted into commensurate units of tension and, further, tension is nondirectional, its original causes are not necessarily traceable to particular tension-inducing circumstances. Therefore, *any* method of tension reduction may be effective in reducing the overall tension level. This definition of tension thus makes provision for the cumulative effect of multiple frustrations and deprivations. It also is enabled to encompass the widespread occurrence of substitutive and displacement behaviors (e.g., secondary reinforcement phenomena), where an individual energized by one activator finds surcease in a very different way.

It is true, of course, and not inconsistent with the substitution capability provided by the concept of tension, that different means of tension release will be differently effective. Depending on the context of behavior, the nature of the tension inducer, and the learned or inherited connections between instigating circumstances and environmental alternatives, certain directed behaviors will come to stand higher than others in the adaptive response hierarchy of the individual. The ordering of these behaviors, however, may not be a strong one, particularly where psychologically based tensions are involved.

Thus, hunger—an ultimate biological need—may be alleviated by drinking water—up to a certain point. But the individual still needs food to survive, and biological evolution has been such as to inevitably confront the individual again with tensions not indefinitely reducible by drinking. It needs to be remembered, though, that many tension inducers are "psychological" in nature. The tension they induce can be dealt with psychologically once and for all and sufficiently, but without feedback from the real world or one's physiology that would suggest to the individual that the employed tension-reducing behavior is, after all, only a substitute or a mental creation.

Thus, the invocation of an orientation for achievement and success, when the underlying tension initially stemmed from an affectional deprivation, is not doomed to failure; the substituted behavior may well and indefinitely serve the function of initially more directly relevant behaviors. Although substituted usually because of the unavailability at the time to the individual of more intrinsically related behaviors, there may be a psychological sufficiency of substituted behaviors that enforce or elicit no necessary feedback. When the more directly relevant behavior later becomes an option for the individual, there may not be a motivation for change back to the initially directly relevant behavior, an illustration of what has been called "functional autonomy" (G. W. Allport, 1937).

It should be noted that tension arising but unexpressed, and perhaps cumulated, continues within the personality system as a "psychological load." The fate or consequence of contained tension may be various: It may involve displacement of the tension onto an object or situation quite different from those the tension(s) initially would have called for; it may involve expressing the contained tension via substitution of an object or situation similar to the one the tension initially called for; or it may involve explosive fragmentation as a nonadaptive, immediately relieving but long-term troublesome behavior. The straw that broke the camel's back and, more generally, the phenomenon of small additional inputs having large consequences can be understood in terms of using up available options (resources), or using up the available elasticity (resiliency) so that shattering or crossing the threshold occurs. Later and further stress starts from a different, already used-up system position.

The Concept of the Control Apparatus

Control apparatus is meant here as a relatively enduring, partly genetically intrinsic, but mostly experientially evolved subsystem or structure, existing within the larger personality system, which functions to contain and direct tension. It is posited that tension becomes drive, and is thus in a position to influence behavior, only by virtue of being modulated and modified by the control apparatus. The control apparatus is not a contentual or phenotypical construct; it is a metapsychological and genotypical one. It is not motivational in nature; it is structural in its operation and thus influences the fate of motivations. Although the control apparatus is partly intrinsically given and in part life evolved, it functions contemporaneously in the adult.

The significance and distinctiveness of *drive* in contrast to *tension* can thus be seen to be solely a function of the tension-binding, tension-modulating control apparatus. Where tension may be considered the "potential energy" of the personality system, drive may be likened to energy in its "kinetic" or effective form. Drive is regnant and must be dealt with in the personality system in some way or other and during the particular interval of psychological time in which it arises. Tension, on the other hand, may continue, unallayed, within the personality. Drive, as the transmuted, directed form of tension, is the impelling, activating agency for change in the personality system, change that is usually brought about via behavior or mentation (but which in certain circumstances may involve structural changes).

Tension per se is not regnant; it is not necessarily being directly coped with by the organism. It may simply exist and be contained without being converted into a drive of the moment. The consequence of contained or unrelieved tension is the encumbering or "loading" of the total personality system in a general way, especially by using up the adaptational margin available to the system.

By introducing the notion of a control apparatus, the intent is to create a construct that can begin to deal with the great conceptual problem posed by what has been called *ego* or *executive functioning*. Historically, the terms *ego* or *executive* have been *employed* to signify a recognition that somehow, some way, an incredibly complex arrangement evolves in the personality. This arrangement functions to select or order sequences of behavior so as to optimize or "satisfice" or reconcile certain desires of the individual within the constraints set by the operative environmental situation. In more recent years, the terms, "executive" or "executive functioning" have become popular, but I suggest that the currently unpopular term "ego" and the currently popular term "executive" are no more than synonyms for the same latent but all-important construct.

As descriptive terms ego and executive have been necessary theoretically to invoke. However, the specific properties of a regulatory system that meshes complex inputs and complex outputs so as to keep the personality functioning are only vaguely known. However, an all-purpose, opportunely invoked, reified notion of ego or executive is specious unless its properties and rules of operation are explicitly defined and delimited. Accordingly, the criticism has been leveled that, effectively, the ego (or executive) has been construed as a homunculus, a little man sitting up high in his pineal office directing the fortunes of his empire.

This criticism is, in my opinion, largely justifiable. Many have succumbed to the woolly convenience afforded by a loosely-held and conveniently-invoked notion of ego or executive. The salvage of the concept of ego or executive, if salvageable at all, must come through explicit definition and restriction of the scope of the concept. The person's defensive and adaptational processes, the twisting and turnings of the personality that the label of "ego" initially was invoked to subserve, continue to exist in indisputable importance, but still with little systematic understanding of their lawfulnesses. By explaining too many behaviors, the terms "ego," and its synonym, "executive," have perhaps explained very little.

I do not suggest that the problem of ego or executive function here is truly solved. I do suggest that relevant, even necessary, aspects of the indefinite issues surrounding ego and executive functioning may be conceptually abstracted and that such abstractions may organize many kinds of recognitions that are now only inchoately related.

In order for a concept like the control apparatus to begin to take on an ego or executive function, its several dimensional characteristics must be specified. For the present purposes, I advance three parameters in terms of which a control apparatus is to be characterized. These are its *degree of articulation* (or, in Lewin's terms, *level of differentiation*); its *modal level of tension control*, or threshold for the passage of tension (in Lewin's terms, *permeability*); and its *degree of resiliency*, or capacity for temporary change from and return to the modal level of tension control (in Lewin's terms, *elasticity*). These three parameters, initially due to Lewin (1951), have been adapted here to a personality context.

By the *level of articulation* (or *differentiation*) of a control apparatus, I refer to the complexity or primitiveness of the behavioral alternatives available to the individual. From an articulated control apparatus, a large number of behavioral or cognitive possibilities may issue—given, of course, the appropriate other conditions. By contrast, a relatively unarticulated control apparatus can offer but few potential actions or recognitions as guides for behavior. Something like the degree of fineness of grain or differentiation of the behavioral (including procedural rules) repertoire is to be understood as involved in this articulation property of the control apparatus. The well-established notion of "crystallized intelligence" (Cattell, 1941; Horn, 1997; Horn & Cattell, 1966) seems akin to the notion of articulation. Articulation is the grundlage for what is often called intelligence, but more correctly it functions as a necessary but not sufficient condition of intelligence in the grand sense.

Some tentative ways of translating this notion into operations may be helpful here, to convey what is meant. Operationally, articulation of the control apparatus might reasonably be manifested by a vocabulary test or measure of amount of information, or by some evaluation of the extensity and articulation of the skills and techniques that a person has evolved. Observationally, an individual with a relatively differentiated control apparatus would be recognized as skilled, informed, accomplished, trained, educated, expert, practiced, proficient, a jack-of-all-trades, widely conversant, and so on. A person with a relatively undifferentiated control apparatus would be characterized as ignorant, unprepared, unfinished, unaware of action possibilities, without learning, and so on.

A decisive property of the notion of articulation of the control apparatus is its dependence on the ease of rote learning during development and through experience. Articulation of the control apparatus primarily occurs over time, with rather little occurring in the contemporaneous moment.

The effective articulation level achieved influences behavior contemporaneously. However, it should be noted that the diversity of behavior deriving from behavioral spontaneity or behavioral changeableness per se does not imply behavioral articulation. Impromptu behavioral flexibility or spontaneous, creative behavior due to personally original and new action combinations is differently based. Behavioral articulation instead always implies the mostly prior cultivation or progressive evolvement of action skills, of action knowledge, of a sheer variety of learned behavioral possibilities.

Although the measurement problem is not without its complications, it is intuitively clear, I would suggest, that individuals may be ordered at least approximately with regard to a broadly conceived notion of learned behavioral versatility. Such potential versatility in action provides an important, if latent and itself insufficient, basis for enabling behavior; it provides the information necessary but is insufficient to get things done.

I note that the psychological literature is replete with discussion and measures of intelligent behaviors but these are almost invariably confounds and may stand only in a partial or sometime relation with the articulation of the control apparatus.

By *degree of tension control* or *tension permeability*[1] of the control apparatus, I mean the modal threshold for response to tension which characterizes the individual's set of behaviors. It is assumed that, regardless of their specific content or nature, the behavioral alternatives available for an individual issue into action only when a characteristic "restraining tendency" on tension or a threshold for reactivity is exceeded. A conductive (permeable) control apparatus is one with a low modal threshold for response and permits tension to become drive relatively immediately, readily, directly, and even chaotically. An unconductive (impermeable) control apparatus is one with a high modal threshold for response and permits tension to become drive slowly, with delay,

---

[1]The terms control and permeability with respect to the control apparatus are used interchangeably throughout.

and it may even prevent tension from realizing itself as drive, whereupon the suppressed tension is held over until the next psychological interval that is to be managed by the personality system.

Individuals characterized by a relatively conductive (permeable) control apparatus have been called *undercontrollers* (J. Block, 1950; J. H. Block, 1951). Individuals with a relatively unconductive (impermeable) control apparatus have been called *overcontrollers*.

In order to operationalize the conductivity or permeability of the control apparatus, it is necessary to presume the environmental context is not massively directive and compelling and registers equivalently on all its experiencers. Further, it is presumed that the individual's level of tension or motivational impetus in the situation is constant or equal across all individuals. Whereupon, operationally, the permeability–impermeability aspect of the control apparatus may be reflected by measures of the inability or ability to delay gratification, of impulsivity versus excessive constraint, of the tendency to express or inhibit aggression and other impulses, of unrealistically high versus unrealistically low levels of aspiration, of interpersonal spontaneity and warmth versus interpersonal stiffness and seeming coldness, of wide and unsustained interests versus narrow and perseverative interests, of behavioral uninhibition versus behavioral inhibition, of broad response generalization versus narrow response generalization, and so on.

Observationally, the undercontroller is a person who tends toward immediate gratification or insufficient modulation of desires even when such gratification is inconsistent with the reality of the situation or the person's own ultimate goals. The undercontroller is overly expansive and spontaneous, immediate and direct in expression of motivations, disorderly, with enthusiasms neither held in check nor long sustained, and overly inclusive in considering the factors affecting choices. Decisions are made (and unmade) rapidly; emotional fluctuations, both positive and negative, are readily visible. Social customs and mores are, if not disdained, at least disregarded. The undercontroller's behaviors are highly variable and often diffuse, not especially bothered by ambiguities. Because grooves for behavior are not deeply ingrained, the undercontroller's actions can frequently cut across conventional categories of response in ways that are novel (this originality may be creative or bizarre). Life is lived on an ad hoc, impromptu basis.

The overcontroller is excessively constrained, delaying gratifications even when pleasure is a sensible or no-cost course of action not threatening of long-range intents. Interpersonal relations are distant and restrained, with minimal expression—direct or indirect—of the internal emotional situation. The overcontroller is highly organized and planful, categorical in thinking, overly single-minded in formulating decisions, tending to adhere rigidly to previous understandings. The overcontroller is perseverative, can continue to work on uninteresting tasks for a long period of time, is overconforming and rule-abiding, has difficulty in making decisions, and has interests both narrow and relatively unchanging.

In the conceptualization here, extreme placement at either end of the ego-control continuum implies a relative consistency of behavior that, given a varying world, can be expected to be adaptively dysfunctional. Far better, adaptively, to be in the relatively central portion of the hypothesized continuum.

The permeability property of the control apparatus has been well researched by now under the heading of studies of ego-control (e.g., J. Block, 1950, 1965, 1971, 1982, 1993; J. Block & Block, 1951, 1952, 1981; J. Block et al., 1988, 1991; J. Block & Gjerde, 1986a; J. Block & Kremen, 1996; J. H. Block, 1951; J. H. Block & Block, 1980). For example, Lewinian-type satiation–cosatiation measures and response generalization procedures wherein related responses occur to the unchanging stimulus appear to be indicators of control permeability. Further, a spate of other investigators using different samples and different methods have reported finding undercontrolled and overcontrolled individuals in their analyses. (For some recent empiricism, see Asendorpf, Borkenau, Ostendorf, & van Aken, 2001; Caspi & Silva, 1995; Hart, Hofman, Edelstein, & Keller, 1997; R. W. Robins, John, Caspi, Moffitt, & Stouthamer-Loeber, 1996; van Aken, van Lieshout, Scholte, & Haselager, in press). It is clear now that individuals can be reliably placed with respect to undercontrol and overcontrol and that one's placement on this continuum has a broad significance for a variety of phenotypically diverse behaviors. As noted in the first chapter, many other investigators have proposed and empirically investigated a variety of concepts highly or vaguely related to the construct of ego-control, albeit of course with "jangly" different names.

By the *degree of resilience* (or *elasticity*[2]) of a control apparatus is meant here the range of permeability variation available to it within the per-

---

[2]This term is one used by Lewin (1951) to describe within his system a property of boundaries. Because some of our model stemmed originally from a Lewinian orientation, and because the term conveys some sense of the presently imputed aspect of the control apparatus, the usage is continued. The terms resilience or elasticity of the control apparatus are used interchangeably.

sonality system as it pursues its system bent. Although as previously posited, the control apparatus possesses a characteristic level of permeability, it also has the potentiality of varying about this characteristic mode. When the personality system is stressed, the permeability of the control apparatus may increase or decrease as one means of maintaining or reasserting a tenable personality system within its necessary bounds. That is, a generally low threshold for response may be heightened so that the undercontroller temporarily (and adaptively) takes on the characteristics of an overcontroller, or a typically high threshold may be lowered, permitting the usually overcontrolled person to now (adaptively) function in more undercontrolled ways.

The elasticity notion thus specifies the extent to which a shift in the permeability of the control apparatus—up or down—may be employed in this system maneuver for system maintenance. If elasticity is low, then the limits of variation on the shifting of impulse control are narrow and quickly reached. Shifts of the control apparatus then cannot provide an adaptive reserve since the system bounds are constraining. Other system adaptational modes consequently must be brought into play to cope with the strains of the moment. If elasticity of the control apparatus is great, then the limits of variation are wide; the shifting of permeability control—up and down—can be a deep and prolonged resource for system adaptation. Stated alternatively, the elasticity or resilience of the control apparatus entails a greater number of mechanisms available to the individual in the search for adaptation.

Of course, all human beings will reach a level beyond which further increase in resiliency becomes impossible. As resiliency is increasingly invoked, the sequence of changes observed in behavior may explain what has come to be known as the Yerkes–Dodson law (1908). The Yerkes–Dodson principle asserts there is an inverted-U function (often) characterizing the relation between degree of arousal and performance.

When there is little incoming stimulation or arousal of the organism, there is little motivation, and the relevance of behavior understandably suffers. More motivation engages and activates the adaptive resilience available to the individual, and effective behavior improves. When there is excessive or prolonged motivational arousal of the individual, and the capacity for resilience has been exceeded or exhausted, the quality or effectiveness of behavior again understandably suffers. It is when the individual is more than a little but not too much motivated—when resilience is invoked and operative in its effects—that the individual's behavioral performance is optimal.

The relations between various states of the personality system and consequent permeability shifts of the control apparatus will be posited later. For the present, some of the surplus meanings and operational implications of the notion are discussed.

In terms of everyday behavior, how is elasticity of the control apparatus to be understood? As a hypothetical example, consider two college sophomores equally undercontrolled and of equivalent articulation (or education) and both enrolled in a stiff psychology course that meets at 8 a.m. By virtue of an inability to submit their personal desires to the unbending requirements of an implacable schedule, let us further presume that both students chronically oversleep the lectures, study sporadically, and reach the week before the all-determining final examination equally unprepared. Now, the pressure is really on them because both students must meet and meet well the reality criterion of achieving decent grades and all that grades subsequently can mean. Having frittered away much of the semester, the only way lost ground can be recouped by them is by intensive, systematic cramming in the small time remaining of all that should have been learned more protractedly (and leisurely). Such concentrated studying requires for its success—and it can be remarkably successful—a high degree of self-constraint, of organization, of delay of gratification—in short, of (adaptive) overcontrol. Let us suppose that one undercontrolling student is enabled to adopt temporarily the required overcontrolling characteristics, whereas the second student, equally under the academic gun, continues his diffuse, chaotic ways. The first would be said to have an elastic or resilient control apparatus (even if subsequent to the examination, he reverts again to his characteristic undercontrolling mode of living), the second an inelastic or unresilient control apparatus.

As a second hypothetical illustration of the property of elasticity, consider two highly organized, equally competent, reality-attuned, conservative individuals, perhaps engineers of some kind (presuming that different professions draw on or restructure the characteristics of certain individuals). Let us suppose that they are confronted with an unusual technical problem for which established methods of solution are inappropriate. Creative, ingenious problem solutions require, by definition, departure from ingrained cognitive routes and instead a confluence of unlikely elements in the problem situation in a way that proves to provide a new but also valid solution. Creativity of this kind has in it a significant element of spontaneity and of chance, of only vaguely directed thought processes as the search for possibilities is sustained. The alternatives brought forth subsequently must each be checked for their reasonableness, of course, and here a critical function must be carefully and systematically applied. But logic has no place until the possibilities that must be scanned have been derived. And for their derivation a fluidity is essential, a fluidity that requires an undercontrolling ego apparatus. In the present example, presume that the first engineer is able temporarily to set aside his completely rational and reality-oriented attitude and thus becomes adaptively undercontrolled for the purpose at hand. The emission of original response possibilities that under more constrictive conditions would remain unseen and unannounced by him is thus encouraged—he has "regressed in the service of the ego." The second engineer remains bound to his critical faculties and thus continues, necessarily, in perseverative attack on the unyielding problem. The first individual would be said to have an elastic or resilient control apparatus (even if subsequent to the brainstorming session, he reverts to his characteristic overcontrolling mode), the second an inelastic or unresilient control apparatus.

Elasticity within the behavioral control system, then, is to be understood as a parameter characterizing the individual's capacity to change his typical reaction tendencies when the presses upon him make it efficient or adaptive to be able to do so. And the change may be toward either increased permeability or increased impermeability. With resilience, an individual can be dynamically resourceful, in either direction, to the stresses and strains impinging. By *resilience* I suggest what is by others often called "self-regulation" or "emotion regulation."

Observationally, resilient individuals are dynamically resourceful when confronted by the strain set by new and yet unmastered situations; they manifest more umweg solutions when confronted by a barrier; they can both "regress in the service of the ego" and "progress in the service of the ego," they assimilate when it is contextually convenient or efficient to do so but will also accommodate when so required by hindering circumstance; they flexibly invoke their repertoire of problem-solving strategies; they are deliberative and not ruminative; they quickly adapt and even enjoy new and unusual situations; they have zest for life.

Observationally, unresilient or brittle individuals have little adaptive flexibility; they are disquieted by the dynamic requirements of a new or changed situation; they have a tendency to perseverate or to become behaviorally diffuse when countering changed or strange situations or when under stress; they become anxious when facing competing demands; they have difficulty in recouping from traumatic experiences. Inelasticity implies a kind of frangibility or vulnerability to the personality system. Without a resilience of character structure, the individual can be easy prey to stresses and strains. The inelastic person conceivably can be quite adapted when in predictable and stable niches but is not adaptable when in new and changing circumstances.

It seems to me that this notion of resilience–unresilience in conjunction with the property of permeability–impermeability (too much or too little expression of internally driven presses on one) offers the possibility of encompassing conceptually the meaning of prior societal variables such as "adjustment–maladjustment," "neuroticism," "ego-strength," and so on, earlier mentioned as variables proving theoretically awkward in the past. The advantages to be gained from an interpretation of these societal dimensions in the present terms are several: The ubiquitously observed maladjustment (sometimes called "neuroticism") variable receives an abstract but essence-retaining definition, one that is not tied to a particular evaluative society or culture as referent. Moreover, this reinterpretation, because it is stated as part of an explicitly interrelated system of personality, achieves conceptual properties that the more casual usages simply cannot provide.

Operationally, the manifestations of resilience (or elasticity) seem readily apparent or available. Many of the self-report inventory measures of adjustment, ego-strength, or neuroticism may prove to be usable after close psychometric analysis to purify the devices of now inappropriate or confounding components. Or, a battery of techniques requiring various kinds of integrated performance under different forms of situational stress may be prepared to sample the individual's capacities in this regard (J. H. Block & Block, 1980). Wallace's (1966) suggestion that a distinction be made between response predisposition and response capability offers another way of getting at elasticity.

It is important to note that resilient individuals need not be warm, compassionate, "nice" people; they need only be instrumentally effective in the adverse circumstances in which they find themselves (e.g., William Clinton, par excellence). Indeed, empathic introspection, if overdone by the individual, can prevent or inhibit the decisiveness required for resiliently surmounting a difficult situation.

In any event, there is again good ground for considering the difficulties in this area to be matters of serious practice rather than of conceptual principle.

Percept, Environment, and Perceptualizing

In chapter 5, percept was defined as a subjectively registered, processing-based, schematic representation stemming from what I have called the objective stimulus situation surrounding the individual. I will try now to provide a better sense of what I mean.

The emphasis of this definition was on the abstracting property of an individual's percept, in recognition of the imperfect relation existing between a boundless reality, a two-dimensional recording by the eye of what really is a three- or four-dimensional world, a limited attentional span, and an organized accumulation of remembered experience. The *assimilability of percepts*—how compatible a percept was or could be made to be with the individual's preexisting or quickly evolved schemata for understanding the world—was defined as crucial in understanding much of the nature and flux of behavior. This conception of percept assimilability, however, although not to be disowned, is an insufficient one. It as yet does not face up to the problem of stimulus context representation independent of the perceiving individual, and it offers no way of conceptualizing the processes by which the assimilation of percepts is mediated. Accordingly, it is to a further analysis of the situation and percept assimilability that we now must turn.

Specifically, I now propose that the assimilability of percepts be viewed as a joint derivative of two logically prior variables: (a) the *autochthonous assimilability of the environment*, dependent on the intrinsic,

natively perceived, evolution-shaped environment and/or the culturally provided substrate before the generic individual and (b) *the
perceptualizing apparatus* of the particular individual.

By invoking these complications, it seems to me possible to maintain
certain distinctions about the stimulus environment that it is psychologically crucial to preserve. Moreover, we are enabled to achieve a conceptualization of environments in terms that are coherent with the
other constructs in the formulation. This is an exceedingly important,
if arbitrary, accomplishment because the system possibilities of a personality theory cannot exist unless some commensurate way of conceptually organizing the environment is achieved.

In order to provide a background for the conceptual choices made,
let us first consider the vaguely understood notion of the stimulus environment or situation. We ask, not the timeworn Platonic question,
"What is a stimulus?" but rather a more pragmatic one, "What are the
roles of a stimulus?" With this latter question, the concept of environment may be seen as confounding a number of facets that theoretically
are quite separate. One of these facets provides a way of abstracting a
formally useful aspect of the environment from the otherwise unreachable environmental manifold.

THE INFLUENCES OF STIMULI

A stimulus or situation or environment or behavioral setting—and
these terms are used broadly and equivalently to refer to sequences and
contexts rather than arbitrarily specified, timeless points within the
larger field—has three possibly concomitant but certainly different
roles for the individual.[1]

First, a stimulus situation may instigate the organism by setting internal urges or needs in motion. Or reversely, it may terminate urges and
needs by satisfying the individual. In my own preferred terms, the stimulus may activate the tension system and ultimately drive, or it may operate to reduce the tension level and hence reduce drive. This is the
energizing (or de-energizing) agency of the stimulus.

Second, a stimulus situation may effect a change in the properties of
the psychic structure of the individual. That is, the previously described
control apparatus and the yet-to-be described perceptualizing apparatus are modified in an adaptation to the psychological, relatively universally apprehended, characteristics of the stimulus context. The
outcome for the individual of various stimulus situations conjoined with

---

[1]See also the related articles by Chein (1954) and Gibson (1960).

the behavior memorially recorded in these situations is reflected in an imperfect way in the ego structure of the individual. This kind of effect of and feedback from the environment is the reinforcing or valence or learning-shaping agency of the situation. The valencing of the situation may be negative or positive for the individual.

Third, a stimulus situation guides the organism, determining by virtue of its affordances and the alternatives it allows or disallows the nature of the response subsequently emitted. This is the directing or structuring agency of the stimulus context, its *autochthonous assimilability* (AA).

The energizing role of the stimulus has already been alluded to in the discussion of tension, its origins, and termini. Certain features of the stimulus environment may, by prepotent reactions, prepared reactions, or learnings, elicit internal tensions with which the individual then must cope. The elicitation by situation may be slight or it may be dominant. But the tension elicited is an internal problem, removed from its external prompt.

The reinforcement or valence role of the environment, by its positive attraction or the attraction of avoiding negative reinforcement, importantly influences memory and consequently influences subsequent reactions of the individual. This valence role is crucial to consider and one of the insufficiencies of the present effort is its failure to do so.

For now, this discussion is limited to the third role of stimuli—their intrinsic AA. The directing function of environments provides a means of entry for dimensionalizing in abstract, content-free terms the environmental context brought before an individual and in terms consonant with our other concepts. Specifically, I now propose that all environments may be characterized, independently of any unique qualities of the particular perceiving individual, in terms of their essential degree of unstructuredness or resistance to structuring; reversed, one can conceive of the affordances of situations, their intrinsic AA.

THE CONCEPT OF AUTOCHTHONOUS ASSIMILABILITY

The now strange but historically old word, autochthonous (pronounced "aw-tock-tonous"), in regard to perception refers to what is universally selected as perceptually and contextually influential by all human beings. This universality comes about because the course of evolution has shaped our neural system—we all experience a common physical world, and therefore individually form what is a common ontology.

The objective psychological environment is the totality of situational factors that, in a sense, should be seen by the participating person. It in-

cludes representations of physical ("geographic") realities such as perceptual cues and normative gestalt susceptibilities. But also, for the
present purposes, I choose to extend the notion of the objective psychological environment to include social realities as well; it contains all the
features present in a situation that affect or presumably would affect the
perceptions of an idealized normative individual, someone permeated
by the common (sub)culture. Thus, both physical and social influences
are defined as contributing to the autochthonous input. This broaden-
ing of the sense in which I conceptually use the term autochthonous
should be understood by the reader.

Within the objective psychological environment, the dimension of
AA may be abstracted or formulated. By AA, I mean an objective psychological press variable, inferred to exist outside the individual, that
provides a necessary influence on, although often not the entire condition for, the direction of subsequent behavior or change in the individual's personality system. From context to context, the degree of AA may
vary in magnitude as a function of the intrinsic affordances or gestalt
quality of the external situation independent of the particular individual experiencing that situation.

The various evolutionarily or societally provided AA inducers normatively operating within a particular context are defined as algebra-
ically summating or cumulating their impinging effects on the
individual, whoever he or she may be. They include culturally ordained
as well as "geographic" factors. I mention some typical AA inducers or
detractors later in this section.

Once present, the nature or source of the AA-inducing or AA-de-
tracting condition is not necessarily identifiable from the degree of external structuredness per se. The connection, if any, between the
contentual aspects of a particular stimulus context and the resulting
generally held AA level is (usually) a learned and not intrinsic one. By itself, the objective environmental structure or unstructure (its degree of
AA) is posited as having no necessary subjective—that is, experiential—representation. However, its general or normatively expectable
level may manifest itself through behavioral indicators observed in
many consensual individuals. It may also, by its subsequent processing
within a variety of personality systems, lead to an awareness by an uncommitted, perceptive investigator of its external, typically held level.

It should be noted that the perseveration of unassimilable percep-
tualizations, perhaps cumulative, continues to exist within the subjective psychological environment of the individual and functions as a
"psychological load." The fate or consequence of subjectively unas-

similable percepts may be various: It may involve the perceptualization of ambiguity or uncertainty into another generally assimilable context (a displacement analogue), or because of a prior history of unassimilable circumstances, the immediate environmental situation may be viewed catastrophically as overwhelming.

The very term level of AA implies a potential external shaping influence on the individual. Level of AA exists outside and independent of the particular person but has a supportive or neutral or disturbing impingement upon the individual's psychological harmony. Degree of AA achieves subjective percept assimilability only by virtue of being modulated or channelized by another construct—the *perceptualizing apparatus*. The perceptualizing apparatus, by invoking an already established schema or a hastily constructed one, converts the level of AA into an individual's level of *percept assimilability* (PA) with more or less subjectively apprehended structure. Percepts, whether assimilated by the individual or not, always imply the prior existence of an outside-the-individual environment. But, as will be seen, high or low levels of autochthonous assimilability may exist without representation of their degree of external assimilability in an individual's percept assimilability. With this distinction, it can be seen how AA is a necessary but not yet sufficient condition for situational shaping of the individual's PA.

Before extending the range of this definition more systematically, I attempt to communicate some of the intended surplus meaning of the concept of AA or its converse, environmental unstructure. Speaking generally and rising above the contentual specifics of the particular situation, it may be said that normative environments vary in respect to their "demand quality" or "affordances." Demand quality or affordances indicate the extent and way in which the behavior of the generalized or normative human being living in the specified (sub)culture is modified or affected by the situation. Normative environments reflect the autochthonous features of the physical environment as these are mirrored by the evolved human nervous system, the features singled out by the individual's society as relevant, and the aspects emphasized by the individual's subculture. Excluded are the individual's specific and unique modes of perception.

There is a strong hierarchization of the factors influencing the normative environment such that, in general, geographic aspects take primacy over social aspects that in turn dominate subcultural features in shaping AA. These last two factors allow the existence of what is called social psychology. As I discuss later, idiosyncratic personality influences

on perception subsequently come into play and may be surprisingly ineffective and unimportant or remarkably commanding in shaping the
finally operating PA.

Some objective environments allow behavior to be forged relatively
automatically or habitually; others perplex the organism, any organism.
Ready, facile behavior is precluded by the nature (i.e., ambiguity, uncertainty, complexity) of the environmental circumstances "out there."

This property of the external environment—its level of AA—is independent, in a fundamental way, of the particular individual experiencing that environmental situation. By virtue of certain evolved
neural linkages, special spatial or sequential arrangements of physical
stimuli are more uniformly directing or providing of affordances to
the individual—any individual—than others. Thus, as noted earlier,
randomly arranged stimuli are less assimilable than orderly stimulus
arrangements.

By virtue of similar educative processes, all individuals within a common culture are subject from infancy to certain social stimulus patterns
that achieve a normative significance or common press for behavior.
Thus, the observation of people already in line in front of one is informative that waiting one's turn is to be expected. In individuals who have
evolved in the same social matrix, these externally inculcated expectations may be largely decisive in determining how the individual views
the situation. It seems fair to presume that the neurally or societally
prescribed interpretation of particular social situations is available, at
least in principle, from any individual (or a group of similarly-raised individuals) set down in the context.[2]

The notion of AA, then, is introduced to represent the presence or
absence of environmental gestalt qualities, broadly conceived, in the
objective psychological environment. That is, the external or normative psychological environment—what the individual should see—is to
be characterized in terms of the extent to which the general principle of
structure may be said to apply, its AA. Certain contexts, independent of
a particular individual, may be characterized as relatively orderly, redundant, simple, regular, familiar, predictable; they show overdeter-
mination, closure, good continuation; they are informational in the
sense of negative entropy. All of these are relatively structured or assim-

---

[2]Radical means may be required (e.g., drugs, hypnosis, or psychotherapy) in order to recover from certain individuals a specification of the normative impact of a
stimulus context. Because this route to the specification of the environment is a difficult one, the meaning and directingness of an environment is more readily sought
by other means (e.g., consensual definition).

ilable environments as they impinge upon the individual. Other situations, independent of a particular individual, may be described as relatively random, chaotic, vague, complex, unstable, strange, uncertain; they are underdetermining, open-ended, entropic in their organization; they permit no confident extrapolation or interpolation. All of these are relatively unstructured or unassimilable environments as they impinge upon the individual.

AA or its converse, environmental unstructure, is a primitive concept used to dimensionalize the organizability property of situations. However, it must be remembered that, as the notion is used here, the gestalt qualities in terms of which the degree of assimilability or resistance to assimilability is to be evaluated are a function of social as well as "geographic" aspects. It may be convenient to use physical means such as special spatial arrangements to vary degree of AA, but social means may be used alternatively and perhaps are more usual. In either event, the inducers of AA or unassimilability are distinguishable and exist prior to their merging to form the impinging level of AA or unassimilability itself. AA inducers are psychologically meshable and cumulatively additive to form degree of AA. Thus, the same level of AA may be achieved based on high geographic assimilability conjoined with low social assimilability or low geographic assimilability conjoined with high social assimilability.

The concept of AA is a metapsychological abstraction lifted from the specifics or content of the existing external environment, and its level can, by normative means, be made consensual and psychologically formulated. By the convention used here, the level or degree of external environmental assimilability is to be considered high when the objective psychological environment is relatively simply organized, physically and/or socially. It is considered as low when the objective psychological environment is chaotic in its organization, physically and/or socially.

The concept of AA may be made operational in a number of reasonable ways; it is not inaccessible to an empirical approach. As a paradigm of manipulation of this dimension, consider the widely used procedure of exposing stimuli for varying time intervals by means of a tachistoscope. The presumption of many such experiments has been that with extremely brief tachistoscopic exposures, the environmental input to the organism is informationally insufficient and is therefore relatively uncompelling or undirecting. This condition reflects a state of external environmental unassimilability. Prolonged exposures should aid unequivocal organization of what is out there in the environment and thus should aid in achieving external environmental assimilability.

The partial reinforcement procedure provides another way of manipulating the dimension of environmental assimilability. In a typical partial reinforcement situation, the experimenter uses a random pattern to govern reinforcements of the participant. The participant, with an implicit or explicit set to understand the logic of the experimenter's behavior, tries out various hypotheses by choosing to respond in certain conjecture-testing ways. However, the unfair experimenter, because of reliance on a random (i.e., patternless) device to determine whether or not the participant is to be reinforced, inevitably dooms the aspirations of the participant. Because the partial reinforcement procedure provides less possibility of extrapolating the future of the individual's situation than does 100% reinforcement, where no inconsistencies occur, the partial reinforcement technique may be construed as creating environmental unassimilability. In a 100% reinforcement procedure, environmental assimilability may be said to exist.

Another experimental instance of manipulation of environmental structuredness may be found in the earlier mentioned research by Bruner, Goodnow, and Austin (1956) on concept attainment. In a typical experiment, cards are arrayed on a table before the participant. On each card is a figure, identifiable by a number of clearly discernible attributes (e.g., shape, color, size, nature of bordering). The task of the participant is to identify the nature of a concept, given a particular card as a positive instance of that concept. The concept may require any one or combination of the several attributes or any logically consistent disjunction of attributes. The significance of this procedure for the present discussion is that the cards laid out on the table before the participant are arranged usually in an orderly fashion (e.g., all red figures together, all black figures together; within the red figures, further arrangement into small and large figures; within the small red figures, still further partitioning into those that are triangles and those that are circles). But sometimes, as an experimental manipulation, the cards are placed on the table in an absolutely random way. In the first instance, AA is comparatively high; in the second circumstance, AA is relatively low.

As a final general remark on manipulating AA, note the relevance of creating a rapidly changing and previously unexperienced environmental situation for the individual. Such contexts develop a low level of AA because for all individuals the environmental supports for behavior have lost much of their applicability or pertinence.

In many situations, it may not be feasible to manipulate the environment, but it should still be possible, and useful, to identify the level of

AA present in the situation under analysis. In such circumstances, operationalizing the level of AA present is a straightforward, if tedious, undertaking. A delineated set of environments (including the ones of special concern) is submitted to a group of judges who have (ideally) personally experienced these contexts. The judges, in their subsequent individual and independent judging behavior, must be representative of the kind of individuals later to experience these selected environmental contexts. The stimulus environments being evaluated may be relatively static in nature, as when a set of geometric figures is evaluated for complexity (Attneave & Arnoult, 1956). Or the environments being judged may be more complicated ones, involving temporal sequences or richly intertwined contextual details as when social situations are judged for their degree of scriptedness or extent of well-established procedural rules (J. Block & Block, 1981). The selected set of environmental instances is then scaled by the set of judges with respect to the dimension of assimilability versus resistance to assimilation. This dimension is a highly abstract one, certainly, but judges seem to understand it and empirically agree appreciably with each other in the way they apply this dimension. The most expedient of the many scaling techniques developed by psychologists will serve the scaling purpose here because they all seem to intercorrelate so highly.

The aggregated result of this cumbersome and prolonged judging procedure, if reliable, is a grading of the set of environments that is independent of the ordering or judgment of these environments by any particular judge, or the particular individual under study. The comparison of particular participant performance with normatively scaled evaluations of the situation can now permit, by virtue of the congruence or discrepancy of the individual's perceptions with normatively scaled evaluations, important inferences in regard to the properties of the individual's personality system at the particular moment being studied.

In summary, autochthonous assimilability/unassimilability is conceived here as a construct existing at an abstract psychological level, not a concretely denotative level. It may result from a variety of antecedent and concomitant conditions, but once induced the nature of the initiating and contributing factors need not be identifiable from the fact of assimilability per se. There are various manipulations or arrangements or sequences of geographic stimuli that will develop more or less assimilability. But the relations of these manipulations to autochthonous assimilability/unassimilability are neither invariant nor necessarily primary in their effect. Social as well as physical aspects of the environment contribute toward degree of AA. In the lives of most people, it is the social elements that are likely most decisive of the degree of AA encountered.

Especially to be noted is the position taken that various AA inducers may summate their effects on the objective AA level. By this property, the cumulative effect of various structuring features of a stimulus context is encompassed. Conversely, any method of reducing environmental structuring is effective in lowering the overall objective assimilability level. Thus, environmental assimilability created by a structuring manipulation of social variables (e.g., as in the Asch conformity situation) may be geographically changed (e.g., by placing the lines to be compared in greater proximity to each other). Environmental unstructure developed "physically" by loading a pattern-seeking individual with randomly arranged stimuli may be raised "socially" by a suggestion from another person in the situation as to a cognitively economical way of understanding or patterning the physical stimuli. The functional equivalence of alternative means of raising or reducing AA is a very powerful property to embed in the abstract concept.

THE CONCEPT OF PERCEPT ASSIMILABILITY

With the decision to dimensionalize external environments in terms of their degree of AA or unstructure, it follows as a natural extension of this position that individually registered percepts may be characterized by an equivalent or parallel dimension as well. Accordingly, by *percept assimilability (PA)* I mean here a directed psychological press inferred to exist within the individual as a function of level of external AA and certain properties of the perceptualizing apparatus. It is PA that provides a necessary but not entirely sufficient condition for determining subsequent behavior or change in the personality. From context to context, the degree of PA effectively present may vary. Percept unassimilability causes an interruption of behavior; the individual does not know what to do, and feels helpless and anxious. The impact of percept assimilability/unassimilability may or may not involve conscious representation depending on the directional properties awarded the incoming percepts and on other characteristics of the personality system at the time.

As in the distinction made earlier between drive and tension, the degree of percept assimilability or percept unstructure may be considered as reflecting the "directingness" or familiarity of the individual's situation, as it registers on the individual. It is degree of PA that demands specific and immediate reaction within the personality system, which inexorably must be dealt with and integrated into the ongoing transactions of the individual. External AA, on the other hand, represents the "potential" impact issuing from the outside world, the environment as it "should" be seen by the individual. Of course, there may be, and usually is, important correspondence between degree of AA and degree of PA. But often enough there is not, and the discrepancies between AA and PA are of great interest and consequence. Autochthonous assimilability/unassimilability influences behavior only via its transmutation, more or less faithfully, into percept assimilability/unassimilability. The extent to which the degree of PA mirrors the degree of AA is to be understood as solely a function of the perceptualizing apparatus.

THE CONCEPT OF THE PERCEPTUALIZING APPARATUS

The perceptualizing apparatus is the second construct introduced to subserve the concept of ego. Traditionally, in psychoanalytic discussions of the ego, there has been talk of the ego as "executive" or as the "do-er" and the ego as "perceiver" or "reflector." The ego has been described as the agent that monitors the "forces from within" and, conjointly, the "forces from without." The ego as an executive controlling the "forces from within" I have attempted to encompass in the preceding chapter by the notion of the control apparatus. The perceptualizing apparatus is brought forward now to incorporate that sense of the ego system concept wherein it functions as a "perceiver," a defender against and adapter to the "forces from without."

The *perceptualizing apparatus* is meant here as a relatively enduring, partly genetically intrinsic, but mostly experientially evolved subsystem or structure existing within the larger personality system. It is posited that AA becomes PA and is thus in a position to shape perceptions only by virtue of being modulated and modified by the perceptualizing apparatus. The perceptualizing apparatus is not a contentual or phenotypical construct; it is a metapsychological and genotypical one. It is not motivational in nature; it is structural in its operation and thus influences the fate of motivations. Although the perceptualizing apparatus is partly intrinsically given and partly life-evolved, it functions contemporaneously in later life.

As with the concept of the control apparatus, the several dimensional characteristics of the perceptualizing apparatus must be specified if the notion is to achieve a systematic status. It has seemed cognitively economical but also theoretically fruitful to characterize the perceptualizing apparatus in terms analogous to and formally identical with those used earlier in defining the control apparatus. Accordingly, the perceptualizing apparatus is posited as having the dimensional properties of (a) degree of articulation (or differentiation); (b) of modal threshold for the activation of perceptualization (or permeability); and (c) of resilience (or elasticity), the capacity for (temporary) change from and return to the modal level of permeability of the perceptualizing apparatus.

By the articulation or differentiation of a perceptualizing apparatus, I refer to the complexity or primitiveness of the perceptual alternatives available to the individual. From a differentiated perceptualizing apparatus, a large number of perceptual possibilities and discriminations may issue—given, of course, the appropriate other conditions. By contrast, a relatively undifferentiated perceptualizing apparatus can offer only a few perceptual guides or sets for behavior. A person with a differentiated perceptualizing apparatus has the potential (not necessarily realized) of perceiving a multifaceted, articulated, particularized "splitting" environment. By comparison, a relatively undifferentiated perceptualizing apparatus imposes simplistic, highly general, "lumping" categories upon the environmental flux.[3] Perceptual differentiation, like behavioral differentiation, provides a basis for what is often but too simplistically called intelligence. That is, it functions as a necessary but not sufficient condition of intelligence in its larger meaning. Like differentiation of the control apparatus, perceptual differentiation is what is often called a form of crystallized intelligence.

A decisive property of the notion of articulation of the perceptualizing apparatus is its dependence on the ease of perceptual learning during development and through experience. Articulation of the perceptualizing apparatus primarily occurs over time, with rather little occurring within the contemporaneous moment.

The differentiation level achieved by the individual is a factor influencing perception contemporaneously. However, it should be noted that the diversity of perception deriving from perceptual spontaneity or perceptual changeableness per se does not imply perceptual differentiation. Impromptu perceptual flexibility or spontaneous, creatively rich percepts due to personally original and new conceptions of the world are differently based. They are the basis of serious art. Perceptual differentiation instead always implies the invocation of prior cultiva-

---

[3]There can be dedifferentiation (also known as perceptual regression or primitivization) as well, reducing perceived environmental complexity and fostering assimilability.

tion or evolvement of ways of seeing, of the learning of gestalts or to resist gestalts, of perceptual skills and knowledge, of a sheer variety of perceptual alternatives. It refers to temporally evolved structural change in "percepts ... over time by progressive elaboration of qualities, features, and dimensions of variation .... Perceptual learning ... consists of responding to variables of physical[4] stimulation not previously responded to" (J. J. Gibson & Gibson, 1955a, p. 34).

For example, an unschooled visitor to an art museum may have spontaneous, personally valid esthetic reactions, but it is likely that he or she will fail to perceive many of the nuances and significances of a masterwork. Given a genuine course in what unfortunately has been labeled "art appreciation," the student now will be able to see in the painting many qualities and facets which earlier had not been noticed. It is by such means—but usually of a less formal kind—that differentiation of the perceptualizing apparatus evolves.

There is a difficulty in enforcing operationally a separateness between a differentiation of the control apparatus and a differentiation of the perceptualizing apparatus. Positivistically, perceptions are known only through the criterion of a behavioral response—creating an ambiguity as to where the property of differentiation resides, at the informational, intake side or at the behavioral, output side. Although phenomenological report might be acceptable as supportive of a distinction between perceptual differentiation and response differentiation, few of these introspections relate to "pure" perceptual experience (but see Brunswik, 1956). Rather, the reports are of mentations, which might seem to partake simultaneously of both perceptions and response.

Nevertheless, I am willing to posit for conceptual purposes a distinction between perceptual differentiation and response (i.e., control apparatus) differentiation. The distinction advocated has had some prior intuitive appeal, (e.g., J. J. Gibson & Gibson, 1955b; Tighe & Tighe, 1966), although an arduous research road still must be traversed before these intuitions fully earn their consensual validation. The reader concerned about the logical and psychological status of the differentiation property as it applies to the perceptualizing apparatus may find it instructive to refer to Gibson and Gibson's (1955a) work, the critique by Postman (1955) of this position, and the rebuttal by Gibson and Gibson (1955b). Wohlwill's (1958) contribution brings a further clarity to the debate.

The meaning of the differentiation property as it applies to the perceptualizing apparatus can be conveyed most readily by illustration

---

[4] I would add variables of social stimulation as well.

and by suggesting ways of operationalizing the notion. The key feature of the notion is the element of *perceptual learning*. Differentiated perceptualizers are perceptually informed, practiced, and able to take many different stances in visualizing their world. Perceptually undifferentiated individuals have less resolving power as they opt their environment; their intakes make only coarse distinctions, and their visual alternatives are few.

Perceptual differentiation might be operationalized by an object-sorting task, by one of the extant measures of breadth and articulation of categorizations, or by the Rorschach technique, scored for the individual's diversity or range of response. In the more classical experimental vein, Wohlwill (1958) suggested a number of different tasks wherein, if learning occurs, the operations warrant the presumption of perceptual differentiation. Reliable individual differences within these experimental situations would provide another kind of index of differentiation of the perceptualizing apparatus. Further manifestations of the individual's level of perceptual differentiation might be sought in literary style, the usualness or unusualness of metaphor, the sophistication and references of associations to a particular environmental context, or the dimensionality of interpersonal or object perceptions as measured by factor analyzing the individual's semantic differential or Q-sort personality descriptions. Without minimizing the attendant difficulties, it seems reasonable to presume that individuals may be ordered with respect to a conceptually valid notion of perceptual articulation or versatility.

By the degree of perceptualizing or degree of permeability of the perceptual apparatus,[5] I mean the modal or characteristic threshold of the individual's perceptual apparatus for allowing in and reacting to the surrounding environmental situation. It is assumed that, regardless of their specific content or nature, the environmental characteristics potentially presentable to an individual become presentable subjectively or effective personally only when a characteristic perceptualizing "restraining tendency" in the individual is exceeded.

A permeable perceptualizing apparatus is one that permits the environmental press to register relatively immediately and directly. Individuals characterized by a relatively permeable perceptualizing apparatus may be called "underperceptualizers"—they tend to see the raw, naked world in all its infinite, intrinsic, and undeniable unstructure. Underper-

---

[5]The terms perceptualizing and permeability with respect to the perceptual apparatus are used interchangeably throughout.

ceptualizers are relatively unable to establish assimilations or new accommodations to organize what has come through to them.

An impermeable perceptualizing apparatus is one that permits the environmental press to register relatively slowly, along established perceptual routes, and indirectly. Individuals with a relatively impermeable perceptualizing apparatus may be called "overperceptualizers"— they tend to perceive a world as already familiar or in procrustean ways they create a world for themselves that has organization and is not personally troublesome or threatening. Ceteris paribus, overperceptualizers tend to invoke established assimilations to constrain, exclude, or impose strong structure on the intruding environmental press; they tend not to attempt restructuring efforts at accommodation.

Observationally, underperceptualizers tend to be at the mercy of their environment, which floods in on them without selectivity or surcease. In Goldstein's phrase, underperceptualizers are relatively "stimulus-bound" but are also highly distractible serially because of an inability to exclude enough features of the environment to permit directed activity consequently to take place. They are overly inclusive in what they attend to, seeing more features of their environment than is usual. For underperceptualizers, the world is likely to be more like the great "blooming, buzzing confusion" ascribed by James (1890) to infancy. It is not that, in William Blake's metaphor, "the doors of perception" have been "cleansed." Rather, they have not been sullied or rutted or organized by experience; in the underperceptualizer there is an absence of the schemata that, although helpfully preventing a perceptual overload of the individual, also serves to deprive the individual of the infinite richness and complexity of the raw world.

Observationally, overperceptualizers appear to exclude much that is potentially available for effective attention. Where underperceptualizers have an excessively "wide-angle" attentional field, overperceptualizers use "tunnel (or even, funnel) vision." They are not distractible and not "open to experience" or environmental absorption. The assumptive world that overperceptualizers construct for themselves is a stable, categorical, highly organized one that offers the possibility of habituating or "automatizing" subsequent responses. (Seeming) perceptual irrelevancies are excluded, and concentration is on the selected essentials that prior experience has sharpened into focus. At best, when overperceptualizers are well attuned to their special world, they function readily, efficiently, and with great psychological economy in the service of their ends. They have "a place for everything and everything in its place." But at worst, in a fluctuating or radically changing environment, insulated overperceptualizers bring now inappropriate schemata to what are new adaptive problems, with ineffectual and possibly disastrous results. The overperceptualizer is made uneasy by and is therefore avoidant of ambiguous or inconsistent situations and is not exploratory.

The permeability property of the perceptualizing apparatus has usually not been studied under the banner of this label and, indeed, it has not been so well experimented on as the permeability concept of over- and undercontrol. It has seemed to me that much of the research by Klein and his coworkers (1953; 1958), by Witkin and his group (1954), and by Frenkel-Brunswik (1951) can be so subsumed.

Converging from very different directions and in resonant support of the presently suggested dimension of the perceptualizing apparatus has come research and interpretation from Lacey (1959), Bruner (1957), and Rogers (1963). Lacey (1959), in interpreting some ingenious experimentation, suggested that measures of autonomic responsivity can reflect the moments when the individual "is 'open to his environment' and ready to react to it, or conversely, when an individual is not 'open', and indeed, instrumentally 'rejects' the environment" (p. 205). Bruner, in his masterful review of "perceptual readiness," integrated an outpouring of neurophysiological findings in support of his view that environmental stimuli are monitored or filtered by certain highly complex and still unspecifiable "sensory-gating processes" (could this be "ego" again?). Rogers, from his own concerns with the nature of psychotherapy and an anchorage for the concept of adjustment, placed high emphasis on the dimension of "openness to experience," the extent to which the individual permits and even welcomes environmental influx. For Rogers (1963), the less-than-optimal personality is, to greater or lesser degree, closed off from fresh perceptions, from the essence of immediate and ongoing experience, from a smelling of the flowers. Instead, the maladapted person is "living his life in terms of rigid personal constructs, based on the ways he has construed experience in the past" (p. 24). Surely, this is our overperceptualizer.

In contrast, the excessive underperceptualizer is *not* coincident with Rogers' adjusted person. Radical underperceptualizers certainly do not exclude their world. Rather, they go to the opposite extreme; they submit to and are submerged by their impinging world. To meet the criterion of adjustment held by Rogers, an individual must be an underperceptualizer in the sense that he or she must not deny the encroaching world but also, and conjointly, must have mastery and integration of the richness of his or her resulting experience. The Rogerian conception of adjustment thus is seen to be a complex conjunction of a number of dimensions that, from a systematic point of view, might better be identified in terms of ego-resiliency, discussed later.

Tellegen and Atkinson (1974), coming from a different conceptual direction, developed an inventory scale that reflects "absorption," a close relative of under- and overperceptualization. More recently, Mc-Crae (1993) conceptually and empirically argued for the importance of what he also termed "openness to experience" and measures with a scale correlating well with the earlier one of Tellegen and Atkinson. Both of these emphases and efforts connect intrinsically with what I have called perceptual permeability. Many necessary studies loom ahead, but the behavioral significance of the dimension seems indisputable, and no insurmountable problems would appear to exist in ordering individuals along an underperceptualizing versus overperceptualizing dimension.

In order to further operationalize the permeability of the perceptual apparatus, presume that the environmental context is not massively directive or compelling and registers equivalently on all its experiencers. Presume too that for all individuals the level of tension or motivational impetus is constant. Whereupon, operationally, the permeability–impermeability aspect of the perceptualizing apparatus may be indexed by measures, for example, of incidental learning, distractibility, the influence of one's immediate surround in determining free associations (Mann, 1956), and the independence by the individual from the misleading perceptual field in determining the true vertical (Witkin et al., 1954). Stimulus generalization—the same response but to many stimuli as in reacting to peripheral light as well as the central target light—is a valuable marker of permeability of perception as well as is adaptation-level speed. Further ways proposed for operationalizing perceptualizing permeability are the individual's preference for complex or simple geometric figures, the nature of musical preferences, the number and unusualness of the Rorschach responses emitted, the extent to which he or she conforms to or deviates from a fixed day-to-day schedule, the ease or difficulty of hypnosis, the susceptibility to perceptions of pain, and the frequency with which novelty and freshness is perceived in the world. Underlying behavior in all of these proposed procedures is something akin to the breadth or narrowness of the perceptual field effectively impinging on the individual, what has been called the individual's openness or closedness to experience.

Superficially, one may confuse permeability and the differentiation of the perceptualizing apparatus. A permeable perceptualizing apparatus may issue perceptual responses that seem based on perceptual differentiation, and vice versa. It is necessary to hold perceptual differentiation constant to see the pure effects of perceptual permeability, and vice versa. Special circumstances or special manipulations will permit the disentangling of the two perceptual constructs.

By the resilience or functional elasticity of a perceptualizing apparatus is meant the range of permeability variation available to it within the personality system as it pursues its adaptive bent. Although, as just posited, the perceptualizing apparatus possesses a characteristic level of permeability or modal threshold for perceptualization, it also has the potentiality of varying about this characteristic mode. When the personality system is stressed, the permeability of the perceptualizing apparatus may increase or decrease as ways of regaining a psychologically tenable state. A generally low threshold for perceptualizing may be heightened so that an underperceptualizer temporarily takes on the characteristics of an overperceptualizer. Or a typically high threshold for perceptualization may be lowered, permitting the usual overperceptualizer to temporarily function as an underperceptualizing person.

The perceptual resilience or elasticity parameter thus specifies the extent to which an alteration in the individual's perceptualization threshold may be called upon in the system surge for a viable tenable state. If resilience or elasticity of the perceptualizing apparatus is low, then little variation of the perceptual permeability property is available, and changes in perceptualization threshold cannot provide a major basis for readapting or system survival. If perceptual elasticity or perceptual resilience is great, then changes in the perceptualizing permeability can be a ready and continuing equilibrating mechanism.

Operationally, resilience of the perceptualizing apparatus can be evaluated—not easily—in a number of ways. In one possible procedure, incidental learning under natural conditions would be contrasted with incidental learning under the set to intentionally learn. If a normally widely ranging incidental learner focuses efficiently on his or her assigned task to the exclusion of the usually attended to but currently extraneous environmental field, then that individual may be considered elastic or resilient in this one direction. If the usually poor incidental learner can enlarge the angle of apprehending when the situation, by its objective or assigned characteristics, calls for this change, as in a problem-solving situation, then resilience in the direction of increased perceptual permeability (i.e., lessened utilization of existing schemata) may be presumed. Certain of the resiliency experiments in earlier work (J. H. Block & Block, 1980) were based on this reasoning.

Another means of operationalizing perceptual resilience might be to press the individual, for example, to try to give as many Rorschach responses as possible, having first responded to the inkblots in a natural way. After proper correction of this deliberate Rorschach numerosity to exclude responses that are not meaningfully different, the relation between the number of natural and attainable responses can be seen to fit the paradigm of perceptualizing elasticity. An analogous operational possibility may be found by use of a fluctuating figure. The relation between the individual's natural rate of perceptual reversal and the rate of perceptual reversal when instructed to prevent reversal of the fluctuating figure could prove to be another means of translating the concept. All proposed measures of resilience of the perceptual apparatus will have to derive from the relation of two observations, one that manifests the individual's normal or natural or spontaneous or preferred orientation toward inputs from the environment and one that indexes the individual's range of accommodation when pressed to orient differently toward the attentional world. Wallace's point on the distinction between capability and predisposition again seems relevant here to establishing the elasticity of the perceptual apparatus.

The resilience property of the perceptualization apparatus presently is a relatively abstract concept. Its empirical basis lies largely in the future. Its virtues in the present formulation stem from considerations of theoretical symmetry, introspective data, and some occasional observations that accord with the premise. We all know individuals who can become attentionally immersed in their work to the literal exclusion of the everyday world. Known too is the individual who enlarges or reduces his or her perceptivities under certain motivational conditions. Observations of this order suggest a sufficient empirical basis for perceptualizing resilience may yet be won.

Chapter 8

Closing the Ring

It is apparent, when one contemplates personality functioning, that the personality system operates in interactive, sequential, ultimately organized ways. As Simon (1994) remarked,

> natural selection (in an organism that had to satisfy some needs in serial, one-at-a-time fashion) developed motivational mechanisms for signaling current urgencies among its many needs, noticing mechanisms for detecting and learning information of future interest to goals not currently active, and an interrupt mechanism to set aside currently active goals for more urgent or advantageous ones." (1994, p. 12)

What happens in one part of the personality system affects the functioning—perhaps with a lag time—in another part of the system, all organized and sequenced by what I have called the ego and, by others, the executive. It behooves a serious effort at even a limited personality system to attempt to state, specifically if insufficiently, the rules of mutual influence of subsystems within the larger, organized personality. One cannot go far, of course, before matters become so complex and daunting that more thinking and knowledge advance become absolutely necessary. However, there are some simple but still consequential rules that theorizing and observation suggest.

THE CORRESPONDENCE BETWEEN
PERCEPTUALIZING AND CONTROL APPARATUSES

The qualities of the control (or perceptualizing) apparatus are posited as tending to go along, often but generally imperfectly, with the qualities of the perceptualizing (or control) apparatus. Thus, underdifferentiators of the perceptual apparatus tend to be underdifferentiators of the control apparatus, overdifferentiators of the perceptual apparatus tend to be overdifferentiators of the control apparatus, and vice versa. Undercontrollers tend to be underperceptualizers, overcontrollers tend to be overperceptualizers, and vice versa. Perceptually inelastic or unresilient individuals tend to have inelastic or unresilient control apparatuses, individuals resilient in their perceptual modes tend to be resilient or elastic in their control modes, and vice versa.

However, the generally positive relation between the control and perceptual apparatuses should be recognized only as an overall, not wrong statement. Particular individuals may or may not display the general, population-wide tendency of homologous apparatus qualities to covary. Thus, the absence of a total connection requires the separate recognition of two ego apparatuses rather than one coalesced ego apparatus. The conceptual separation, of course, sets the stage for the delineation of various adaptive mechanisms—effective and ineffective—held by individuals.

Within each property of ego apparatuses, one may inquire; What about the domains of experience to which they apply? For instance, are there people who are perceptually differentiated in some domains but not in others? Are individuals permeable or resilient in some areas but not in others? Certainly, domains of differentiation exist, but properly contextualized, a differentiated farmer would be conceptualized similarly to a differentiated art critic—they differ in the content of what they are differentiated about, but their level of differentiation may well be equivalent. Moreover, I hazard the suggestion that only an idiot savant is so disparate in his or her domains of differentiation as to starkly question the presumption of the broad consistency or applicability of the theoretical properties specified. In the discussion of far-removed issues—politics or computers or life experience in general—the farmer and the art critic may show equal articulateness or inarticulateness.

With respect to permeability and resilience, similar—perhaps easier—arguments can be made. Although there may be situations especially encouraging of undercontrol versus overcontrol or underperceptualization versus overperceptualization, I suggest that, overall, individuals when broadly viewed are remarkably consistent in the way they express themselves or see the world around them. In chapter 2, I suggest why seeming inconsistency of personality is frequently seen or frequently argued—especially by those observing psychopathology. Even if my conceptual explanations in chapter 2 are deemed empirically insufficient by some, it seems to me that a good bit of consistency in an individual's action and perceptual style is to be readily seen with close and long evaluation of the person. Much the same applies to resiliency: Some individuals are consensually evaluated, overall, as resilient and some are not, even controlling for narrowly defined IQ (J. Block & Kremen, 1996). Close and long evaluation can reliably identify those who are consistently adaptively versatile and those who are consistently adaptively ineffective in responding to their ever-changing circumstances.

An especially implicative set of recent analyses distinguishes resiliency from IQ, as evaluated by the differentiation-emphasizing Wechsler Intelligence Scales. Ego resilience and IQ are somewhat positively correlated, certainly as they conceptually should be, but ego resilience alone proves to be associated with adaptive engagement with the world whereas IQ alone often is effective only in narrow, rigid ways. Ego-resiliency is, adaptively, especially better than IQ in "fuzzy" environments, as most situations are. Gender differences in modes of ego-resiliency are also important to recognize; resilient girls are less overcontrolled whereas resilient boys are less undercontrolled (J. Block & Kremen, 1996).

THE CUMULATIVENESS OF TENSION AND DRIVES, OF AA, AND PERCEPTS

Although mentioned incidentally earlier, it is expressly posited that various multiple inputs from outside or action tendencies from within arising simultaneously or in close sequence from different sources may cumulate or cancel as the case may be. Thus, small or numerous additional autochthonous inputs or tensional outputs may have large consequences as their addition of psychological loads finally uses up available resiliency resources. The elastic reserve of the relevant apparatus having been exhausted, shattering or crossing the threshold occurs. Later and further stress has its effect from a different, already used-up system position.

Resiliency bounds, if reached, may then cause an extreme reaction, even a shattering of the personality system. The proverbial straw that broke the camel's back or the uncontrolled kicking of the cat causing one to stumble (when one already is heavily burdened by pressures) are instances of the effects of cumulation, the phenomenon of small additional inputs having large consequences. A further (even small) stress, imposed upon an already used-up system margin may introduce a seemingly unwarranted perception or behavior, or it may influence a radical shift to another psycho-logic of adaptation (discussed later). Conversely, the input of autochthonous situations or action tendencies that are variously anxiety-opposing may summate and operate to lessen anxiety-causing tendencies, thus reducing the overall level of the person's anxiety. Being loved conjoined with having an interesting, secure job is more anxiety-lessening than either one separately. And, of course, a simultaneous medley of anxiety-causing and anxiety-opposing factors when processed by the commensurate-making personality system may leave the individual in a tumultuous but not extreme state.

THE PREVIOUSLY POSTULATED RELATIONS WITHIN EGO SUBSYSTEMS

I have postulated two ego or executive subsystems of the larger personality system. One deals with the flow of surgency within the organism and how this vital force is mediated. The second is concerned with the outside world and how it registers or is perceived by the individual in situ. The constructs and relations within each subsystem have been posited. Thus, to briefly remind:

1. There is tension—high to low. Tension is modulated by a control apparatus with various characteristics—differentiation, permeability, and elasticity—to produce what is called drive.
2. There is assimilability of externally autochthonous environments—high to low. AA is modulated by a perceptual apparatus with various characteristics—differentiation, permeability, and elasticity—to produce PA.

THE DYNAMIC RELATIONS BETWEEN THE CONTROL AND PERCEPTUAL APPARATUSES

To account for intraindividual personality dynamics, there is the further necessity of stating the relations between the subsystems. By closing the intraindividual ring, the collection of constructs takes on larger, total system properties and indicates a set of feedback relations that, staying within boundary conditions, presumably ensures the continuity of the system and, correspondingly, the psychological viability of the individual.

It is reasonable to suggest that the relations between the two kinds of ego apparatuses—control and perceptual—vary as a function of how close the elasticity of each is to its bound or limit on change. As an ego subsystem comes closer to its elastic limit, further change toward the limit is posited as becoming increasingly difficult and even impossible if the total system is to be maintained. When the elastic bound on change of one apparatus is reached, or more likely when the apparatus comes close to its bound, the generally positive relation between change in the one apparatus and change in the other may become lowered. It may become nonexistent and perhaps may even become reversed in direction. For adaptive purposes, a variable of the other ego-subsystem may come into play and begin to function to lessen a system anxiety where previously that ego apparatus was irrelevant or only slightly related to the way anxiety initially had been generated.

POSITED RELATIONS BETWEEN AA, DRIVE LEVEL, AND THE PERCEPTUAL APPARATUS

1. Holding objective or external AA to a relatively low level, as drive is varied from low to high levels, the perceptual apparatus varies from a state of usual or relative permeability to a state of relative impermeability (to the limits set by the elasticity or resilience parameter of the perceptual apparatus).

In alternative, more colloquial terms, when the autochthonous or objective psychological environment is relatively unstructured (perhaps, only moderately structured) but there is increasing drive level, the perceptual filter operates, to the extent it is able, to increasingly "process" the unstructured autochthonous environment so as to exclude ambiguity and present to the individual a perceived-as-more-structured environment. By so doing—providing psychologically to the individual a seemingly structured environment—the individual's drive may find a personally tolerable behavioral expression. Thus, the individual receives a narrower, objectively distorted, but experientially nonthreatening or acceptable percept. Behavior takes on an inflexible aspect affectively eased by categorical understanding of the situation. The individual has shifted, perhaps progressively and perhaps discretely, from puzzlement and curiosity when confronted by the unassimilable autochthonous environment to what has been called "intolerance of ambiguity," a latently desperate protective response dealing with the problem of arising unreleasable and potentially uncontrollable drive. Thus, too much drive is posited as initiating changes in the perceptual apparatus in the direction of a narrower, categorical, and approvable percept.

2. Holding autochthonous assimilability to a relatively high level, as drive is varied from low to high levels, the perceptual apparatus does not change its essential structural characteristics. The registered percept remains a relatively direct and faithful function of the autochthonous or objective environment and does not vary as drive changes. Behavior shifts, under the dominating influence of the varying drive, from quiescence when there is insufficient energizing drive present to urgent, automatic, unvarying, usually effective, even "flowing" response when drive is high.[1]

In summary, the perceptual apparatus operates when drive is (relatively) high, to increase the subjectively apparent organizability or structure of the autochthonous situation from low levels to high levels. Otherwise, within the person, the perceptual apparatus does not appreciably modulate the relation between the autochthonous situation and the perceived situation.

POSITED RELATIONS BETWEEN TENSION, PA, AND THE CONTROL APPARATUS

1. Holding tension constant at a relatively high level, as PA is varied from high to low levels, the control apparatus varies from a state of usual or relative permeability to a state of relative impermeability (within the bound set by the elasticity or resilience parameter of the control apparatus).

That is, as an objective or external situation is increasingly perceived subjectively as unstructured, uncertain, or ambiguous, tension is contained by an increasing impermeability of the control apparatus and is not manifested or dealt with as drive. Impulses or urges are withheld or

---

[1]Sometimes autochthonous structure may be high but provides a directive of behavior incompatible with the individual's high drive. Unceasing clashing of drive with the autochthonous environment may ensue unless the drive level is changed suddenly or slowly or, when control resilience bounds have been reached, perceptual assimilability is radically and suddenly redirected by changes in the perceptual apparatus.

increasingly constrained from behavioral expression in the presence of seeming (perhaps actual) chaos or ambiguity and are held to a low level or only indirect and slowly increasing or diffuse expression. Only where a perceptual alternative is recognized as assimilable and thus becomes behaviorally directive do urges receive release and the personality achieve a tenable system resolution. Thus, where external, encompassible order or assimilability registers so subjectively, tension is vented easily and directly via its expression as drive. Increasing received percept unassimilability or unstructure is posited as initiating changes in the individual's control apparatus in the direction of behavioral constraint and caution.

2. Holding tension constant at a relatively low level, as PA is varied from high to low levels, the control apparatus does not change its essential characteristics. Tension is not contained beyond the level ordinarily imposed by the intrinsic or modal permeability of the control apparatus. Consequently, drive level is in close (albeit perhaps discontinuous and temporally lagging) correspondence with tension level. Under the dominating influence of the received PA variable, behavior shifts from bored quiescence when AA is high but no energizing drive is present to become, when AA is low, curiosity and an intrinsic life-ordained accommodative perceptualizing.

In summary, the control apparatus operates to contain tension when it is high, and the autochthonous situation is (relatively) unorganizable or unstructured. Otherwise, within the person, the control apparatus does not modulate the tension and drive relation.

DYNAMIC IMPLICATIONS OF PERCEPTUAL AND CONTROL APPARATUS INTERACTIONS

By the changes in the perceptual apparatus and in the control apparatus caused, respectively, by excessive drive and excessive percept unassimilability, there arises the possibility of accounting dynamically for the various adaptive mechanisms that an individual employs.

Thus, as tension and therefore drive increase, the structure of the perceived environment may be increased. Drive activation in the individual will influence subservience of his or her perceptual apparatus to be sensitive or attentionally vigilant to alleviating possibilities in the AA. However, as drive continues to be high or to further increase, the perceptual elasticity of the individual may reach its limit of search in the autochthonous situation to achieve an assimilable percept. At this juncture, the perceptual apparatus may take over adaptive primacy and function to distort and even deny resolution of the previously activated drive; tension remains as a "psychological load" on the system.

Alternatively, an incessant and intense unassimilability may cause the personality system to exhaust its perceptual elasticity with the subsequent invocation of an impermeable control apparatus to limit the behavioral expression of tension and thus enhance system adaptation; a stiff caution ensues.

EVOLUTION AND DIFFERENTIATION, PERMEABILITY, AND RESILIENCE

A decent theoretical approach should be sensibly relatable, without artifice, to the evolutionary principle of reproductive fitness. That is, the theoretical principles should have implication for long-term adaptation and its evolutionary implication.

Viewed in this connection, the several theoretical constructs—differentiation, permeability, and resiliency—would seem to apply easily.

Differentiation reflects the ability to discriminate, to make close contingency recognitions. Of course, the ability to discriminate can lead to excessive discrimination when instead the circumstances call for an overall, more abstract and less detailing generalization. Both discrimination and generalization serve evolution. But discrimination must precede generalization, and so may be favored adaptively early in development although not in a later phase of problem-solving life (J. Block & Gjerde, 1986a).

Ego permeability reflects the modal level of perception–behavior manifested by the individual. The person is in a rut or not in a rut; perseveration or unorganized, transient variability is manifested according to the level of ego permeability. Depending on the ecosystem, both extremes of permeability may at times be adaptive and hence some kind of balance ultimately is struck. To explore a country (e.g., the Far West or the Australia of 200 years ago), relatively permeable individuals are required—they are the risk-takers. For stably settling a country, relatively impermeable individuals are useful—they tend to be more risk-averse and their steadiness can be salutary. Both permeability and impermeability can thus serve evolution and societal change.

Ego-resiliency reflects the capacity to adaptively change or not change characteristic modes of permeability–impermeability, to invoke perseveration or variability as required or evoked by the situation. The resilient person anticipates wisely when to stop something unfruitful (like repetitively hitting a large boulder with a tiny hammer) or to continue something that may ultimately prove fruitful (like shattering a small boulder with a repetitive sledge hammer). In its adaptiveness, resiliency well serves evolution.

A CONDENSED STATEMENT OF THE PRESENT PERSONALITY SYSTEM

It is useful to bring together into one place the various aspects of the present theory. By this redundant summary, the reader can better reflect on the system's sufficiency. The presentation is a skeletal one, to be fleshed out by memory or a re-reading of earlier chapters.

1. Naturally, by virtue of the life force itself, the individual takes in information and seeks to organize it. By so doing, the long-term viability of the individual is enhanced.
2. This long-term orientation may be pre-empted by the occurrence in the individual of anxiety, a psychological warning of dangers to short-term viability.
3. Anxiety is caused by excessive drive, the perception of excessive unstructuredness of the environment, or both.
4. The individual seeks to lessen his or her level of anxiety by reducing its causes, discussed earlier.
5. Drive is caused by tension as modulated by the control apparatus.
6. Perceived unstructuredness is caused by the degree of structuredness in the autochthonous environment as modulated by the perceptual apparatus.
7. Tension is created by psychological urges or impulses, which sometimes may be of biological origin.
8. Degree of structuredness in the autochthonous environment is a function of its affordances, as created by the operation of evolved universal neurology, past life experience, and by cultural inculcation.
9. The modulating control apparatus is characterized by differentiation, permeability, and elasticity.
10. The modulating perceptual apparatus is likewise characterized by its differentiation, permeability, and elasticity.
11. Differentiation refers to the degree of articulation (of the control or perceptual apparatus).
12. Permeability refers to the modal degree of expression (via the control apparatus) or the modal degree of impression (as received via the perceptual apparatus).

13. Elasticity refers to the capacity of the control apparatus, the perceptual apparatus, or both, to shift from its modal degree of permeability to another level—up or down.

14. When the elasticity of an ego apparatus—be it the control apparatus or the perceptual apparatus—is exceeded, the other ego apparatus may come into play to help achieve a psychologically sufficient adaptation.

15. Elasticity of the control or perceptual apparatuses, or both, provides a way of adaptively responding to internally or externally arising demands, thus functioning to reduce anxiety.

ANALOG MODELS VERSUS DIGITAL MODELS OF PERSONALITY FUNCTIONING

It is thought-inducing and provocative to consider the personality system in terms of the distinction between an analog computer and a digital computer (e.g., von Neuman, 1958).

In an analog computer, variables are numerically represented along a continuum. In specified or predetermined interaction, earlier or independent variables issue or derive a later or dependent variable (e.g., as a nonpsychological example, the independent variable, water pressure, and the independent variable, pipe diameter, together influence the subsequent dependent variable, rate of water flow). Analog devices refer ultimately to an output in "energic" form (e.g., amount of voltage or current flow).

The contemporaneous model of personality presented here is primarily an analog model. Anxiety wells up and diminishes, emotions surge and abate, there is a rise time in the experience of an emotion and a delay in return from that emotion to one's modal affective level. System changes occur, by and large, in continuous ways as functions change their values. As permeability of the control and perceptual apparatuses increases or decreases, and as the personality system functions to minimize the state of anxiety, anxiety rises and falls.

In many ways, the present system is similar to ancient metaphors used in psychodynamics, of a "hydraulic" model or of advancing "armies" that leave many of their troops behind. Of course, such metaphors soon enough are unhelpful, but also they often resonate intuitively with certain aspects of human psychic experience. Such resonance for the present model is all that is hoped for here.

A digital computer operates and calculates on "markers" of information, each two-valued marker indicating the presence or absence of something. (As a nonpsychological example, digital information may be expressed by presence or absence of a particular pulse or voltage or current). Applied to psychological functioning, much of what is called information processing in cognitive science seems to me to be digital in nature. Perhaps distinct step by distinct step, a perception is or is not made by the person, something is or is not recognized, something is or is not done. Information is not phenomenal in analog, continuistic terms. As so often characterized, information processing is studied as a digital happening but is not viewed as affectively motivated. However, with its emphasis on the processing of information per se and its uninterest in "hot" emotion, the digital or cognitive model may not be a sufficient model for much of human behavior. Similarly, I must acknowledge that preoccupation only with an analog or affective model may also be insufficient to encompass all behavior.

Thus, to respond to the insufficiencies of both the analog and digital systems when applied to personality study, the rules of the personality system may ultimately have to refer to what von Neuman called a "mixed system," with both analog and digital features. In placing primacy on the affect of anxiety and the personality system's ways of lessening anxiety, it should be recognized that the personality system is also digitally responsive. Experientially, although the affective system seems to function as an analog system, it is influenced in its ultimate function by digital (i.e., discrete) happenings. As a function of information processing, there may be an abrupt change—up or down—in registered drives or registrations of the perceived environment thus causing motivational changes—up or down—in anxiety. An unacceptable awareness may suddenly intrude and cause panic, or a pride may suddenly be felt and cause sublime contentment; an instantaneous and unexpected external danger may appear, or a massive threat may vanish.

The distinction between analog and digital informational approaches becomes very complicated as messages change their character—perhaps repeatedly—from digital to analog and from analog to digital. Digital messages arise in the human being from the course of mentation. Their variety perhaps is noticed initially as an unordered listing. But continued mentation soon enough recognizes a vague constellation or ordering of the digital information. When this constellation becomes perceived—validly or not—as coherent, then affect-serving perception and action may occur. Thus, a person may receive all sorts of cues, each digitally recorded, but not assimilable by existing schema. When the set of cues coherently gel, then one is affect-driven—positively or negatively—to organizing subsequent perceptions and behaviors.

Much more thinking is needed here.

SYMMETRY IN THEORY CONSTRUCTION

Having elaborated the constructs of the control and perceptual apparatus, partitioning them each into several components or dimensions, it will have been observed that in a number of ways I have chosen to develop the respective notions along parallel lines. This theoretical isomorphism is by no means required, of course. But I like to think that this symmetry in theorizing is perhaps more than a matter of personal convenience or procrusteanism. If the parallels in development do not seem especially forced ones, and the resultant constructs perform well their assigned functions, then in some vague but satisfying way, a kind of esthetic economy has been achieved in the formulation.

The esthetic properties of a theory are a fuzzy and disputable criterion. Idiosyncrasies in taste cannot be stilled or averaged, and accordingly a much more workable basis for judging a theory is simply how well it integrates and predicts the behavior falling under its compass. A conglomeration or hodge-podge of variables wired together by a Rube Goldberg is a better theory if it works than a beautifully spare set of variables linked by a system of differential equations that does not apply well to its chosen domain.

All other things being equal, though, there is an elegance in the economy a theory achieves by symmetry or isomorphism or analogy or parallelism. Historically, this has seemed to be true of good theories, that they show an order in their structure. In the present formulation, the desire has been to encourage a parallelism in the concepts constructed. Within the confines set by this theory, the symmetry of concepts and also of their interrelations, which it has seemed useful to maintain, is often impressive to me. How persuasive or how delusory this appearance of "simple structure" may be the reader will have to decide as we go along.

Chapter 9

Clinical Implications

It is worthwhile to consider just what the offered set of concepts and the posited relations entail or suggest and how they may apply dynamically or speak to observable psychological realities. I have alluded to some of these entailments before but bring them forward again in a more explicit and discursive way. Other theoretical implications I call attention to for the first time. It should be noted that the discussion or illustrations presented are derivative from or influenced by the theorizing that has gone before; they are not simply eclectically selected, atheoretical instances.

GENERAL CONSIDERATIONS

Regarding the Revealing of Personality Processes

The mechanisms of personality processes are discernable not only in motivationally intense, destructured social situations; they are to be seen as well in unstructured, nondirective settings wherein the individual is not caught up by externally elicited motivations but, rather, is bored or subject to operant impulses and schematized ways of perceiving and responding. When motivation is very low, as well as when motivation is very high, the essential structures of personality will tend to be revealed. What is crucial is that in both extremes of these motivational circumstances, the situation registering on the individual must be unstructured, ambiguous, alternatively definable, and nondirecting. In most psychotherapeutic circumstances, this is the context sought.

Regarding the Role of Anxiety

As has already been noted, anxiety is a sign of disadaptation. Also, although as previously posited, anxiety may have no conscious representation, it often does. Anxiety may have many perceptual–behavioral manifestations and may by its subsequent implications lead to an awareness in the individual of itself and its associated contexts. "We only become conscious in proportion to our disadaptation" (Piaget, 1928, p. 213). Mandler (1980) and J. Block (1982) have offered similar recognitions. A general goal of psychotherapy is the patient's conscious awareness of the roots of his or her disadaptation.

Anxiety is beneficial if well regulated so as to prompt the individual to soon enough or acceptably escape threatening situations. Insufficient anxiety, due perhaps to simple stupidity or to impulse-driven misperception of environmental risks, may lead to undue and even unaware incaution that lessens the probability of the individual's continued existence. Too often, such risk-taking individuals may not come to the attention of mental health professionals because risk-takers are usually subjectively at ease with themselves (and may die earlier).

It is important to distinguish between primary anxiety per se and a generalized susceptibility or predisposition to anxiety. In the latter, a continuous, implicitly looming threat of primary anxiety serves to elicit what is frequently called secondary anxiety. Primary anxiety is a relatively transient "state" if only because it would be unendurable if truly inexhaustibly present. Secondary anxiety is a "trait," a manifestation of an individual's relatively enduring structural personality characteristic that causes him or her to always be aware of a potentially impending primary anxiety. This generalized susceptibility to anxiety does not preclude an individual from having a sufficient lifetime if the environmental situation is a secure and placid one, but the individual latently remains always relatively vulnerable and insecure. Unless the individual has been fortunate in niche-picking a benign environment in which to comfortably wallow, he or she will frequently encounter (perhaps even create) anxiety-causing situations.

The distinction between anxiety as a state and anxiety as a trait vanishes when the individual is so exquisitely susceptible to potential anxiety that a heightened state signaling primary anxiety is omnipresent. At anything less than this extreme, the distinction is necessary for bringing order into a diversity of findings and recognitions. Very often, anxiety as state and anxiety as trait will offer the same predictions, but it usually is important to make the distinction between the two. For example, a generally unanxious individual thrown out of an airplane without a parachute may experience a panic; an anxiety-susceptible person awaiting a bus that happens to be late may also experience a panic. But for the first individual, the panic reflects a state; for the second person, the panic derives from a trait.

Regarding the Broad[1] Conceptual Property of Resiliency

As earlier characterized, resiliency is adaptively responsive variability. It involves situationally effective response, the ability to change as the context requires, a tolerant handling of frustration, a rapidity of affective recoverability from stress. It is "a complex system of potential ranges of behavior that may be evoked (within the limits of possibility for the person) by the various physical, social, and cultural conditions that surround him at any given time" (G. W. Allport, 1961, p. 181).[2]

Resiliency may be conjectured to reflect the existence of an inborn capacity evolutionarily evolved but experientially matured and influenced, that can bring together and integrate diverse and simultaneous inputs. To invoke role-definition terms, resilience means being able to meet well all the demands placed on one by the multiplicity of roles the variety of social situations encountered place on one.

Conceptually, there cannot be "overresilience" as, psychologically, there can be excessive ego strength. The latter is conceptually no more than an overcontrol, perhaps somewhat fused or confounded with resilience. Resilience is a form of deep and often practical integrated intelligence (not IQ points, per se!). Something akin to resilience has been informally witnessed by observers, noted formally, educed from factor analyses of many kinds of data, and evidenced in experimental studies (see chap. 1). In addition to being termed elasticity herein, it may be called "range of threshold shift" or the "first derivative of permeability."

---

[1]By *broad*, I mean to include together both resiliency of the ego-control apparatus and resiliency of the ego-perceptual apparatus.

[2]Ancient references are deliberately used (as well as current ones) to indicate these ideas are not new and connect with earlier observations.

The concept of resiliency may also be linked to what has been called "control theory" by Carver and Scheier (1998). They discussed negative feedback processes that reduce the discrepancy between a present state and a standard or desired state. But the notion of homeostasis or "set points" they put forward may be too static in conception to sufficiently describe a personality system that is continually acting and reacting so as to keep certain system parameter values within bounds. The term, "allostasis" (Sterling & Eyer, 1988) may better characterize the incessant system readjustment of the personality system to its changing environmental circumstances as compared with the homeostasis or set points achieved reflexively by context-ignoring negative feedback mechanisms. Although resiliency implies change in either direction, change may be easier in one direction than the other because of intrapersonal "ceiling effects" or "floor effects." These, if operative, may increasingly slow but otherwise not limit further change toward boundary conditions. The direction of resiliency change usually depends on where the individual happens to be at the particular time vis-à-vis the boundary conditions.

For an individual who is ordinarily or at the moment an undercontroller or underperceiver, resiliency toward but not necessarily reaching overcontrol or overperception is adaptively attractive. One can move away from undercontrol or underperception without necessarily becoming an overcontroller or overperceiver. This is an adaptive change often observed to characterize the development of boys in an ultimately shaping society.

For an individual who is ordinarily or at the moment an overcontroller or overperceiver, resiliency toward but not necessarily reaching undercontrol or underperception is also adaptively attractive. One can move away from overcontrol or overperception without necessarily becoming an undercontroller or underperceiver. This is an adaptive change often observed to characterize the development of girls able to seek vistas beyond what the society usually provides.

In the clinical literature, one frequently finds a distinction made between so-called "coping" or "defense" patterns. However, viewed functionally, coping mechanisms are identical to defense mechanisms. In effect, when an adaptively intended mechanism or technique adaptively works, it is labeled a coping mechanism; when an adaptively intended mechanism or technique does not adaptively work, it is called a defense mechanism. A more compelling view of defense per se and accounting for its absolute rigidity is that it refers to the last adaptively intended mechanism used, whether in a long or short series of such mechanisms. Beyond this last effort at adaptation—after its exhaustion or demonstrated insufficiency—there lies only the extreme of anxiety and personality "crackup."

By definition, the resilient person will have multiple adaptive techniques available, the unresilient person will have relatively few. More specifically, the elasticity or resilience–brittleness property of the ego-control and ego-perception apparatuses offers the possibility of encompassing a variety of adaptive (coping or defense) mechanisms. The potential sequences of coping and defense invocation are almost infinitely rich and extend well beyond what the present theoretical effort can attempt to delineate and connect with human twistings. But a limited interpretation of some personality mechanisms, attempted later, can convey some of the conceptually ordained psychodynamics that may underlie their interjection into perceptualization and behavior, and perhaps their change over time.

Thus, when an individual's elastic limit for change in the ego-control apparatus has been reached, and system stress still exists at an activating (i.e., unendurable) level, then, short of personal disintegration, another component of the personality system must perforce come into play. The perceptualizing apparatus by its available elasticity or resilience may provide the further possibility of encompassing a variety of perceptual coping or defense mechanisms.

When an individual's elastic limit for change in the ego-perceptual apparatus has been reached, and system stress still exists at an activating (i.e., unendurable) level, then short of psychological shattering, another component of the personality system must become invoked. The available elasticity or resilience of the control apparatus may offer further possibilities of encompassing a variety of controlled coping or defense mechanisms.

A person with an inelastic ego-control or perceptual apparatus is one who perseverates with his first or an early adaptive mode. However, the firmly inelastic person ultimately must resolve system disequilibriums, if at all, by other than what has caused and continues the psychic disequilibrium.

To provide an illustration of this, it is posited by the present theory that an individual with starkly unassimilable external inputs will, under system stress, move toward impermeability of the perceptual apparatus—operating the clinical mechanism of "denial." If the perceptual apparatus permits changes toward highly selective permeability, the resultant subjective perception may result in what is termed clinically as "sensitization"—a preoccupying hyperfocus on a limited area of attention. When an individual's elastic limit for change in the perceptualizing apparatus has been reached, and system stress still exists at an activating (i.e., unendurable) level, then another component of the personality system—the ego-control apparatus—becomes operative. It introduces an increase of behavior control to counter personal acknowledgment of existence of the perceptual denial or to limit the impact of incessant sensitization.

Regarding the Broad Conceptual Property of Permeability

In economic terms, permeability differences may be said to eventuate in individuals organized to maximizing gains versus minimizing regrets; to adapt to a disturbed equilibrium quickly or slowly; to require little or much information in so doing; to optimize (aim for the best) or to satisfice (have enough but not aspire to more than enough). There is more than a little connection of permeability differences to Gray's (1987) speculations regarding a Behavioral Approach System and a Behavioral Inhibition System.

In the natural world, widely to be observed are two quite different modes of behaviorally and perceptually managing anxiety—the suppressive mode and the expressive mode. In the suppressive mode, there is at most indirect, somewhat hidden external evidence of the subjective experience of anxiety. There is perseverative perception and consequent perseverative behavior. In contrast, in the expressive mode, the individual's subjectively experienced anxiety is unable to be hidden from the outside observer; it is directly, manifestly, to be seen. There is erratic, diffuse, transient apprehension of a situation with resultant erratic, diffuse, unsustained behavior. In both modes there is an underlying conflict of pushes and pulls. But in the suppressive mode, there is an immobilization (matched pushes or pulls) as compared with the expressive mode wherein the individual, also conflicted, oscillates among alternatives in a transient and unstable fashion. The first, suppressive approach to anxiety management derives from overcontrol; the second, expressive approach derives from undercontrol.

Both suppressive and expressive reactions to trivial stimuli are exaggerated, but the suppressive individual may also appear especially overresponsive to slight situations because learning that safeguarding behavior in reaction to repeated false alarms may cost less than a single failure to respond when danger is great (Marks, 1987). There may develop a nonparticipation in—even avoidance of—what previously has been quite usual for the individual to experience.

Conceptually, the psychopathological expression of impulse may derive either from the individual's failure to developmentally form a societally and personally attuned mode of perceiving–behaving or from a decompensation or regression of previously achieved inhibitory development. These are two very different routes to unrestrained impulse expression: The developmentally based absence or insufficiency of inhibition is not conceptually the same as the release or decompensation of previously attained inhibition that itself may derive from or imply an earlier pathologic development. These two psychodynamically different routes to unconstrained expression should not be terminologically conflated (see, e.g., Nigg, 2000; Pickering & Gray, 1999; Watson & Clark, 1993); uninhibition is not the same as disinhibition

Psychopathological inhibition of impulse may derive from either the individual's developmentally forming a societally attuned but personally unsatisfying mode of inhibited perceiving–behaving or it may derive from an abrupt percept–behaving compensation or exclusion— adaptively intended but crudely formed—to inhibitively respond to the sudden subjective experience of anxiety. These are two very different routes to overrestrained impulse expression: The developmentally based stylistic mode of inhibition is not conceptually the same as the sudden characterological shift from relative spontaneity to intense inhibition, a compensation that may be based on an earlier pathologic progression.

Regarding the Broad Conceptual Property of Differentiation

The property of differentiation is rarely studied in psychology, if only because it is omnipresent under a variety of often not quite sufficient labels and is therefore not centered on. However, various investigations of what is called "complexity" (Linville, 1987) but perhaps is better called "complicatingness," sorting and categorizing proclivities (Murdock & Van Bruggen, 1970), and size of vocabulary or amount of general information (Gough, 1954), all connote and seem to approximately operationalize this property.

The question arises: How should the conceptual property of differentiation be fitted into a personality-adaptive framework? Certainly, one can think meaningfully of an individual who is insufficiently differentiated perceptually or behaviorally. Such persons are crude in their perceptions and unskilled in their behaviors. But can one conceive sensibly of an individual who is excessively differentiated? Can one conceive of a person who is too complicating, makes too many sorting categories, knows too many obscure words, or has too great an amount of often specious information?

It is easy enough intuitively to view excessive complicativeness or obsessive particularization of sorting categories as overdifferentiation. But if differentiation is thought of alternatively, can a person who has a very large vocabulary or is a polymath be viewed as an overdifferentiator? In frequent circumstances, yes. My own resolution of this question is predicated on a simple recognition I wish to put forward.

An infinite number of distinctions in perception and behavior can always be made. And this infinity can innumerably grow. But in any infinitely expansive circumstance in a finite world, a simplification or a refusal to complicate further or an ability to generalize becomes necessary. Otherwise, one is stultified forever (perhaps comfortably so). Obsessive, overcontrolled individuals in effect counter their anxieties by eternally extending complications and without the courage of necessary arbitrariness. Adaptively, one always needs the courage to stop reading, to learn no more beyond a certain point, in order to get on with pressing necessities—to organize and therefore simplify previously collected information. It follows then that, for example, a large vocabulary that simply further enlarges but cannot be resourcefully used is only pedantry; encyclopedic knowledge that is unorganized and not put to use is a sign, often pretentious, of dilettantism. Differentiation without an ultimate integration, I suggest, conceptually may be viewed as overdifferentiation and a defense against something more than itself, that is, the intrusion of a fundamental anxiety. This is not to say that extreme differentiation is always defensively predicated—it may well be organized. However, its basis must be clarified.

With these several general considerations in mind, I turn now to discuss (a) kinds of psychotherapy consequent upon the sources of anxiety; (b) some coping and defensive adaptive orientations individuals may establish; (c) the essence of what is called attention deficit-hyperactivity disorder (ADHD); (d) the source and immediate catalyst of antisocial behavior; and (e) how the effects of drugs, by themselves and in combination, may be said to derive from the personality conceptualization offered. Finally, some diverse observations are recounted that relate directly or indirectly to the theoretical stance adopted herein.

COMING TO PSYCHOTHERAPY AND BENEFITING FROM PSYCHOTHERAPY

People encounter psychotherapy for various particular reasons, but all come to diminish their personal discomfort with the lives they are leading and to escape an anxiety perhaps only dimly recognized. For certain individuals, discomfort and anxiety have become an acute and incessant presence, intolerable, both innervating and enervating, a shattering influence.

The present personality theory suggests four prime ways in which acute discomfort and anxiety may be incremented in life and lessened subsequently by psychotherapy. Modes of psychotherapy have previously evolved pragmatically, and too often they tend to be unconceptual, without a unifying conceptual system that prescribes different courses of action according to the individual's deep reason for entering therapy.[3] The present theory offers a conceptual scheme indicating how the need for psychotherapy comes about and the kind of psychotherapy therefore required.

In the first acute instance, an objectively chaotic or unstructurable environment will create discomfort and anxiety. An illustration might be an intrinsically orderless situation that cannot be mastered or assimilated or accommodated to by any human being, regardless of the individual's talents and proclivities. The realities of a particular anarchic, traumatic situation or an imposed, unsought, disarranged life situation too often are of this nature.

In psychotherapeutic response to this circumstance, such destabilized individuals may be moved into or surrounded by an objective psychological environment that is orderly, structurable, manageable, predictable. An example might be placement of a child—formerly overwhelmed by too stimulating and inconsistent, therefore unstructurable an environment—into a lower key or masterable situation. Such change in the environment has frequently been called "milieu therapy." Other similar situations from the clinical arena are the use of highly structured inpatient facilities for people undergoing psychotic breaks or the way individuals who are having a "bad drug trip" are calmed down by providing a calm, structured, low-intensity environment. Although desirable behavioral change certainly may ensue as the objective situation is changed, it should be noted that little or no enduring character change is involved in the person helped by being moved from one circumstance to another. But the move into a better niche still has psychotherapeutic implication for the individual involved.

In the second acute instance, transient excessive internal tension, however occurring, will create discomfort and anxiety. An example

---

[3]The reasons for entering psychotherapy may have to be uncovered to the patient although they may be recognized by the therapist.

might be deeply felt, introspection-based fear—for example, a remembered experience of extreme stress happening in a wartime circumstance or another "near-death" experience. What is remembered, although the experience is no longer present, operates memorially in the here-and-now to vividly contribute to an acute, unmanageable, inescapable anxiety.

In psychotherapeutic response to this circumstance, such individuals may achieve surcease from previously experienced but no longer continuing trauma by abreaction or societally acceptable expression of the tension-causing anxiety, in the context of interpersonal support. An example might be catharsis in reaction to having been under personal threat in a school shooting and having seen a close friend suddenly and shockingly killed at random. Generally, what has been called "Post-Traumatic Stress Disorder" (PTSD) involves relatively normal individuals burdened by an unfortunate, deeply apprehended, vivid experience of the past that recurrently has entered memory and causes deep personal anguish and stress. Psychotherapy generally consists simply of led abreaction, guided tumultuous expression, and a protected reliving of the torment-causing experience. The release of feeling and memory that occurs in abreaction psychotherapy, although it may influence subsequent positive behavioral change, does not involve serious and enduring characterological change in the person experiencing release of earlier anguishing experiences. The absence of genuine character change is, of course, no hindrance if the source of unresolved tension is not repeated and the experience is attenuated to below a threshold of intrusive awareness.

The two remaining reasons for entering psychotherapy do involve fundamental character change.

In a third acute—but personality-structure-based—instance, an overly permeable perceptualizing apparatus will create discomfort and anxiety. The external world ceaselessly and overwhelmingly subjectively afflicts the individual. An example might be the individual who is "stimulus bound," at the mercy of the infinity of subjective perceptual possibilities always present, of the endless ways of personally seeing things, of subjectively feeling assailed and overwhelmed by the great "blooming, buzzing confusion" out there.

In psychotherapeutic response to this circumstance, such individuals may achieve a lessening of perceptual permeability or a reorganization of perceptual inputs so that what from the outside was previously apprehended as overwhelming is now internally assimilated or capable of being internally accommodated. In effect, the individual must build up a revamped internal experience of the world that is structurable. Such individuals require the development of attentional focus, of ability to resist attentional interference. He or she must develop the ability to impose an acceptably revised new and different structure on the environment as subjectively received, achieve the courage to be perceptually decisively arbitrary, learn to adopt different perceptual premises. The therapeutically necessary change in received inputs is uncertain and generally slow to occur, even perhaps impossible to achieve for temperamental or irretrievably established learned reasons. When change has been successful, the sequence requires being led gradually by a psychotherapist to greater or differently based perceptual control and filtering and a greater structure or reorganization of what has impinged subjectively upon the individual. Significant and enduring character change is involved in modifying the perceptual apparatus toward greater and more selective impermeability–permeability so that perceptual change occurs.

In the fourth—personality-structure-based—instance, an overly permeable control apparatus will create discomfort and anxiety. All tensions immediately, directly, and fully are expressed in behavior. An example might be the individual who is "response bound," at the mercy or under the influence of particular arising strong urges or impulses. Tension is inexorably, fitfully activated and inexorably, fitfully released as drive, with perhaps an ultimate consequence of adverse societal aftermath or subsequent guilt or self-unacceptance.

In psychotherapeutic response to this circumstance, individuals with an overly permeable control apparatus require a lessening of this permeability or a reorganization of behavioral outputs so that what is actually emitted is more modulated or redirected so as to be societally or personally acceptable. Such individuals require development of the ability to control and direct behavioral impulses in societally or subjectively acceptable ways, to monitor urges, to delay gratification, to advance beyond behavioral diffuseness. This change is uncertain and generally slow to occur, even perhaps impossible to achieve for temperamental or irretrievably established learned reasons. There is often no or insufficient separation of subject and object, an insufficient ability to distinguish between them, a failure to discern a difference between impulses and, separately, feelings. Syncretism must be carefully left behind, symbolization and distinctions between symbols must be developed. When change has been successful, the revamped sequence requires being conducted gradually by a psychotherapist to a greater impulse control and a greater modulation of what actions are emitted by the individual. Significant and enduring character change is involved in modifying the permeability of the behavioral control apparatus toward greater and more selective impermeability–permeability, and behavioral change is a consequence.

In noting each of the four conditions of urgent anxiety, it should be remembered that these conditions can be conjoint and were posited earlier as cumulating anxiety level. The ultimate personal experience of anxiety can come about when all four contributors are present. However, such an extreme condition is psychologically intolerable (and, ultimately, biologically intolerable) to the person. Panic would result were all four factors to be prolongedly present simultaneously. Typically, only one or two or perhaps three anxiety contributors are present, and so only an intermediate but still importantly uncomfortable level of anxiety may be present.

Similarly, in cataloging the different kinds of psychotherapies, it should be recognized that they may be brought into play conjointly. An individual may experience one, two, or three, even all four of these approaches to psychotherapy. It also follows—importantly—that an anxiety may be lessened or dealt with by the individual or by the individual's psychotherapist in ways different from the way in which the anxiety initially came about. The conceptual system leading in manifold ways to the experience of anxiety also sets the stage for the manifold ways of reducing anxiety.

There are also less acute—but finally confronting—reasons for coming into long-term psychotherapy. One may have a sense that life is passing one by, one is not partaking of life's possibilities. One's tensions are not expressed for such reasons as an uncomfortableness with expressiveness, a lack of knowledge as to how to express tensions that inevitably arise, a prior conviction that a drive is not releasable, a view of a self that is not efficacious.[4] Many people lead such (societally untroublesome) lives of "quiet desperation." This latent basis for seeking psychotherapy stems from a successful warding off of acutely felt anxiety but at a subjectively recognized personal cost of unrelieved, omnipresent, often only vaguely recognized control of accumulated tension.

---

[4]Shyness, popularly and interestingly discussed by Zimbardo (1977), is really one kind of caution against expressiveness used as an adaptive mechanism when there is "response uncertainty"; the individual simply does not know what to do in an uncertain situation. Over time and context, when the situation typically presumes a competence in responding to the situation and the person continues to be unsure what to do, this uncertainty troubles the person who may then suffer a loss of self-esteem.

During the actual process of psychotherapy for such individuals, expressivity usually creates appreciable insecurity and anxiety. Successful psychotherapy, if incurred, must deal with this exacerbation of acute anxiety during the therapeutic process as the individual, via destructuring long-established controls, experiences self-recognitions previously screened off. Subsequently, he or she may learn to effectively—usually expressively—deal with new recognitions and establish new structures. Freudian therapy initially primarily dealt with the kind of personal unhappiness caused by overcontrol of action in the context of unreal or unnecessary percepts. Such overcontrol still remains a frequent problem seen in psychotherapy. The psychotherapeutic achievement, when it occurs, is in the direction of a change in the way the social world is perceived and a reduction in the individual's life-unwarranted delay of gratifications.

Another perhaps not-so-common reason for psychotherapy is that an individual is scattered or erratic in perceptions and impulsive and shortsighted in behaviors. In developmental time, there may come a self-recognition of failures to lead a meaningful and cumulative life and thus becoming a contributing member of society. Sometimes, there is not a self-recognition of these failures; instead, there is such a societal or social recognition by others, and psychotherapy is compelled rather than freely sought. The psychotherapy of Mowrer (1950) sought to deal with this kind of, often unaware, problem resulting from undercontrol of behavior. But often psychotherapy to steady and firm up behavioral control proves unavailing; such individuals are usually sorry candidates for improvement.

A remark by Cloninger and his colleagues (Cloninger, Surakic, & Przybeck, 1993) is pertinent here because of its aptness in regard to the third and fourth ways—perceptual revamping and behavior altering—through which meaningful structure-changing psychotherapy seems to occur; The occurrence of "insight involves the conceptual organization of perception and is defined as the apprehension of relationships. Insight learning involves the development of a new adaptive response as a result of a sudden conceptual reorganization of experience" (p. 978). By such means may personal distress be alleviated.

The difference between intellectual and emotional insight and the need for working through resides here. That is, intellectual insight (so-called) is unemotional, recitable, almost rote learning; emotional insight is the reorganization or re-cognition or new accommodation of a variety of old experiences and thoughts that have been vague or conflicting because not previously unified or perceived as subsumed by a common principle. These, theoretically, are in the preconscious, clanking around, just as problems may be reacted to via unconscious inference accurately or semiaccurately, although the precise principle cannot yet be formulated by the individual. The role of interpretation in therapy is to help the patient coalesce by reorganization a variety of phenomena under one rubric, to help the patient get the principle underlying the problem but not to tell him or her the principle. Piaget (1970) and Wertheimer provided quite relevant analogs of how one helps children and apes to understand for themselves and in usable ways the principles underlying solution of a problem. The therapist adds a little bit more—not too much (Fenichel, 1945) so that the patient solves the problem—and in the process learns to learn and learns to learn to learn.

REGARDING DESCRIBING THE INDIVIDUAL'S EFFORTS AT EMOTIONAL REGULATION

It is interesting to relate the preceding discussion of theoretically ordained psychodynamics with a recent effort (Gross, 1999) to descriptively list some of what individuals recursively tend to do, as "self-psychotherapy," in implementing what falls under the broad rubric of "emotional regulation."

In what Gross (1999) overall called a "process-oriented organization," he recognized a distinction between antecedent-focused and response-focused emotion regulation. Antecedent-focused emotion regulation focuses on the psychological "input" to the individual. It seems to me to be essentially mediated by attention deployment—the individual's direction and breadth of attention—and would seem to require the existence of something like the earlier described perceptualizing apparatus. Response-focused emotion regulation centers on the psychological "output" of the individual. It seems to me to be essentially mediated by response modulation—the individual's direction and containment–expression of motivation—and would seem to require the existence of something like the earlier described control apparatus.

Beyond the broadly relevant regulatory processes of attentional deployment and response modulation, Gross mentioned several additional, more specific descriptive processes, but I suggest these additional processes still fall within the nominal rubric of attentional deployment and response modulation and their interplay. "Situational selection" represents the avoidance or seeking of certain input situations (e.g., choosing an emotionally positive rather than an emotionally negative situation). "Situational modification" represents the changing of certain input situations (e.g., construing a situation in alternative but personally nonemotional terms). Both processes create change in the registered milieu. However, the change is initiated by the person capably involved rather than by an external agent (see the earlier discussion of the first psychotherapeutic means of anxiety-reduction). The emotional regulation process of "cognitive change" means the individual has, out of desperation or resiliency, imbued a different, likely more adaptive possible meaning to the situation registering on him or her and thus has positively regulated his or her emotional state (see the third psychotherapeutic route to anxiety-reduction). "Response modulation" involves the individual's compensatory reaction after emotion has occurred—the direct influencing of one's behavior, of experience, and of one's physiology. There may be emotion containment or expression (e.g., suppression or affective spontaneity). If contained, and as also indicated by the present theoretical formulation, there may be continued tensional experience and a physiological cost.

ADAPTIVE ORIENTATIONS—COPING AND DEFENSIVE—AVAILABLE TO INDIVIDUALS

As posited in the previous chapter, there is appreciable similarity between the two subsystems with regard to their respective levels of differentiation, permeability, and elasticity. However, the relations between the two subsystems, although posited as generally appreciable within a sample, may be far from perfect in the individual instance.

A lack of correspondence between the control and perceptual apparatuses in effect permits the existence of different system personality patterns that come about as the individual seeks to contain anxiety within bounds. Parameter variations of posited theoretical concepts issue different characteristic personality patterns. The usefulness of the present abstract, content-free personality theory may be evaluated by considering how these patterns connect with what has been observed in the clinical situation. Of particular relevance are the various "neurotic styles" noted by the acutely observant clinician, Shapiro (1965).

Thus, consider an individual who, by theory, is generally differentiated, generally inelastic, overcontrolling but also somewhat underperceptualizing. Such an individual by derivation from present theory is cautious, constrained, obsessive, and unresilient in his behavior. He is overwhelmed by the subjective situation in which he perceives himself and therefore seeks out simple or simplifiable situations. His stimulus-bindedness means he has little other recourse available for managing anxiety but to be overcontrolling of his actions. By narrowing and constraining his behaviors, he may avoid getting into intolerable trouble.

As a consequence of his character structure, such an individual finds it difficult to straightforwardly express his human emotional needs. For example, he tends to marry later or not at all, as noted by J. Block (1971, chap. 8); he is continually afflicted by a pleasure deficiency. His life is complicated rather than complex; he is unready for flexible reaction. Although perhaps having a somewhat superior IQ and a good memory for factual details, given the overcontrolled organization of his life he is relatively slow to appreciate the exuberant shock of humor or to be highly original. His orderliness per se may bring him a clarity, his perseverance may lead to success, his checking for correctness may lead to virtuous avoidance of errors, and he may be oriented toward conscientiously achieving an ideal standard. But also he is too meticulous, pedantic, and indecisive; he is conceptually underinclusive, making distinctions that for many others would not seem to be worthwhile, his perseverance in the wrong situation can be stupid, his ideal standard may doom him to personal failure or a false arrogance and an overstrong moral rage toward deficient others. His problems may gradually gather and may become more overpowering than they should be. He is a worry-wart and uses excessive structure and safe-keeping rituals for worry control, seeking to restrictively shape the received environment. Indeed, he is seeking an ultimate (i.e., safe) articulation and to minimize regrets. These are personal characteristics, all of which limit his resourceful adaptiveness.

This adaptive pattern corresponds, I suggest, to the obsessive neurotic style described by Shapiro (1965) in his superb clinical analysis of years ago.

Now, consider again this individual (still defined theoretically as generally differentiated, generally inelastic, overcontrolling but also somewhat underperceptualizing). However, this individual becomes further stressed and moves to the end of his personal tether of differentiation and limited elasticity. He must adaptively change if his anxiety level is to be better managed. Simple continuation of obsessivity has become insufficient.

As Shapiro (1965) noted, there is a close affinity between obsessive and paranoid states: "Often the premorbid background of a paranoid decompensation will turn out to be … an obsessional character" (p. 104). However, as compared with the obsessive, the subsequent paranoid is much narrower in his perception, is tied to specific biases and suspicious suppositions, and lacks a sense of proportion.

Although this posited individual has been diligently applying his constricted personality capacities for adaptive ends, he has become excessively and uncomfortably tight in his accommodations to life. Tensions and insupportable drives have accumulated in this inelastically overcontrolling individual and may be leaking through. Such leakage results in the erratic manifestation of undeniably unacceptable impulsive behavior in the midst of generally well-controlled behaviors. Sequentially, intensification of internal tension has placed additional strain on the personality system, and a stylistically rigid person has become even more rigid until his personal elastic limit is reached. However, the passive surrendering to internal urges would create, by boundary constraints, a shattering, unmanageable, and intolerable anxiety.

Psychodynamically, by the presently posited theory, the individual may now adaptively shift to using an external solution to what had earlier been an incrementing and intolerable internal problem. From his prior obsessive state, he converts to what is called a paranoid state, relying on overperceptualization to provide a subjective psychological environment leading to a more tenable anxiety state of the personality system.

The paranoid solution involves imposing a new and stark—but opportune and adaptively sufficient—subjective structure on what previously has been a relatively reality-attuned, field-cognizant, quite different perceived structure of the external environment. By so doing, the individual's internal tensions can be psychologically redirected and ascribed to an external source, lessening internally based anxiety. Thus, his tension level is alternatively construable as a drive of different origins and becomes self-tenable. The paranoid individual subsequently may manifest appropriate behavior control and even appear phenotypically to be relaxed. However, he becomes energized in certain narrow contexts and is sharp-eyed, anticipating and interpreting possible, often strangely defined threats, without a self-acknowledged sense of personal vulnerability.

Thus, this further pressed and stressed, overextended obsessive moves into a paranoia. His newly asserted subjective perceptual structure does not brook disturbance. He repetitively, continuously, closely directs attentional search and scans incessantly for what his new subjective structure targets him to see. He is troubled by surprise, the unusual, the unexpected because it may break through the particular rigidly firm perceptual structure he has created. In a kind of adaptivity, the unexpected is triumphantly declared to be expected and is easily assimilated without disruption of the individual's evolved narrow and distorted perceptual structure. Whatever remains unusual must be intensely scrutinized and fitted into perhaps recent but now existing structures to dissipate its potential for threat.

Disconcertment—a personally recognized inability to assimilate—is what makes the paranoid most apprehensive. What has happened is projection, a cognitively distorted interpretation of apparent reality, "a process by which an internal tension may be (advantageously) transformed by a certain psychological organization into an external one" (Shapiro, 1965, p. 89). The paranoid, having settled on one restrictive, distorting, dominant hypothesis, then "excludes whatever he cannot handle regardless of its importance. In extreme instances the multidimensional becomes unidimensional: everything that can be made congruent gets absorbed into … the developing delusional system, even though this system may not correspond with social fact" (Cameron, 1951, p. 304). He cannot be spontaneous nor does he attribute spontaneity to others (who are viewed as sneakily planful). He is prudently aware of power, of rank, and has a pecking order mentality—obsequious or arrogant, depending on where he places himself vis-à-vis others. But within his paranoid mode, he is uncomfortable with his deepest self, graceless, too tense to be a good dancer or to be otherwise esthetic.

When the paranoid individual's control of his perceptual schemata is assailed or demonstrated to be faulty, his emotional equanimity is lost. His initially disturbing thematic internal problem may reassert itself, and personal fragmentation or uncontrolled, usually aggressive behavior may result.

This sequence of adaptations and the adaptive pattern attained corresponds, I suggest, to the paranoid neurotic style described by Shapiro.

Consider now an individual who, by theory, is conceived as somewhat differentiated, generally inelastic (unresilient), undercontrolling but also somewhat underperceptualizing. Such an individual by derivation from the present theory is regularly risk-taking, expansive, loosely organized, careless, speedy, with low frustration tolerance, and societally ineffective in structured, contextually demanding circumstances. He is influenced by his environment in whimsical, arbitrary, impressionistic ways and cannot receive or impose stable structures for the situation in which he finds himself—there simply are too many possibilities to attend to in the world. But also, many internal urges beset him.

Anxiety may rear its ugly head, but if the situation permits, it is quickly reduced by urge expression that does not receive negative reinforcement or is otherwise tolerated. So the individual may lead a perceptually impulsive, behaviorally impulsive, unintrospective, sensuous, self-gratifying life. There is little reason for restraint. Little long-range planning is required, little intentionality beyond immediate importunate wanting is involved. Wants are limitless, arise abruptly, are transient, fortuitously capture the individual, and sought to be maximized. He is emotionally expansive, pleasure-oriented, flexible to an extreme degree, smart enough but not seriously or sustainedly analytical. He is both receptive to unsubtle humor and creative of unsubtle humor, relativistic in the way he views the world and hence permissive. He is carefree, an insufficient anticipatory worrier and therefore taking little time between thought and decisive, often too quick, action. He is over-inclusive in his generalizations and insufficiently persevering. These personal characteristics all limit the effectiveness of his adaptiveness in a structured world expecting expectancy and conformance. But such individuals can be original in strange and sometimes quite advancing ways. They often have a certain canny, perceptive, manipulative intelligence in achieving their immediate goals; they selfishly but not selflessly can take the role of the other (e.g., consider the view often held of car salesmen).

This adaptive pattern corresponds, I suggest, to the impulsive neurotic style described by Shapiro.

Consider now the individual who remains generally undifferentiated, is generally inelastic (i.e., unresilient), undercontrolling and overperceptualizing. Such a theoretical individual in growing up has earlier experienced stress by virtue of her flamboyant impulsivity. Being undifferentiated, she is unanalytical, uninformed, forgetful, and surprisingly untaught. She is a reader of headlines rather than a concentrator on the specifics of information; she shrinks from focusing on what disrupts her. Instead, she accepts or constructs a narrowed, overly simplified, field-dependent structure from the surrounding world that, although excluding much, is sufficient for forming impressions. In her conjoined impulsivity, inelasticity, and naivete, she is unaware of the generally held implications of her excitable, sometimes narcissistic behaviors. She responds quickly to the obvious but often cannot rationally explain her actions; her hunches become final decisions. She romanticizes excessively and becomes excessively revulsed by the unpleasant. She does not understand and is often astonished when others so often misperceive her, especially in nonpermissive social situations. But she is not prolongedly perturbed nor does she learn from experience and change.

Potentially intolerable anxiety looms ahead for this essentially undercontrolling, overperceptualizing individual. With further stress, she experiences but cannot prevent the breaking through of strong, consciously unacknowledged, anxiety-threatening perceptual recognitions. When the limit on the elasticity of her ego-perceptual apparatus has been reached; no further adaptive compensation is available by further increasing her restrictive structure of perceptualization. In psychodynamic adaptation, according to the present theory, she therefore moves toward certain containment of her ego-control impulses that, if vented, would confront her with unacceptable personal recognitions. Her ego-control threshold changes abruptly toward overcontrol, and categorically, because of her inelasticity. She continues a repression or denial of her perceptual evocations by invoking an ego control that is massive and primitive (viz., *la belle indifference*). In order to deal in a self-evading rather than self-confronting way with implicit perceptually precipitated realizations, she has become overcontrolling of her action impulses thus permitting her to continue to subjectively assert (and believe) her situation is safely simple. What has happened is conversion hysteria, based on a mentation-distorted restriction of behavioral impulse; an initially external problem has been advantageously resolved, at least temporarily, by an internal solution.

This adaptive pattern corresponds, I suggest, to the hysteric neurotic style described by Shapiro.

Both the paranoid style and the hysteric style are examples of what I earlier have termed bimodals—individuals who conjointly are both inhibited and impulsive. The paranoid style is at first inhibited but in certain areas and under certain conditions becomes aggressively impulsive; the hysteric style is at first flamboyantly impulsive but in certain areas and under certain conditions becomes repressively inhibited. Extreme psychiatric patients are rather frequently bimodal personalities; the more ordinary person, even if seeking psychotherapy, tends to be system-coherent rather than bimodal.

REGARDING THE DIAGNOSIS AND CONCEPTUALIZATION OF ADHD

A surprising number of young children have received the popular psychiatric or school diagnosis of Attention Deficit-Hyperactive Disorder (ADHD). Current understanding of this diagnosis is well conveyed by

Barkley (1997), Hinshaw (1994), and E. Taylor (1994). Thus, the diagnosis is viewed as including attention deficit, hyperactivity, and also impulsiveness. The label is applied variously in different cultures or subcultures, but all depends on the definition of the categorical diagnosis and how the definition is interpreted. Various frequencies of incidence are reported in different parts of the world. *DSM–IV* estimates that in the United States about 3–5% of children are clinically estimated to have ADHD, but empirical studies have reported frequencies as high as 19%. In England, however, the comparable rate is about 1%. Taylor suggested the diagnosed rates are overinclusive—too many children are so labeled by their teachers, parents, or mental health workers. Boys more than girls are so diagnosed (about 4 to 1).

Applying the medical model, ADHD has frequently been conjectured to be due to "minimal brain damage" (MBD) or "neurological immaturity." However, frequent and diverse efforts to reveal specific neurological signs have issued failed or confusing findings. However, some genetic basis for ADHD may have been established. Medication (e.g., an amphetamine such as ritalin) is frequently administered for ADHD and has become increasingly controversial as a specific ADHD alleviator. The nonspecificity of amphetamine medication for ADHD is indicated by recent studies demonstrating that, for normal individuals as well as ADHD individuals, amphetamine enhances stimulus evaluations (slowing them) and response processes (speeding them; e.g., Peloquin & Klorman, 1986; Sostek, Buchsbaum, & Rapoport, 1980; Zahn, Rapoport, & Thompson, 1980).

The diagnosis of ADHD in children is often taken to be a risk factor for the subsequent psychiatric label of conduct disorder in adolescence and maladaptiveness in adulthood. However, Taylor noted that in England ADHD in childhood turns out to have little pathological implication for adulthood. It is fair to say that the diagnosis of ADHD in childhood, recognized as personally, familially, and societally important, is not clearly understood biologically or psychosocially.

How shall one try to understand ADHD in personality terms, in particular the terms of the present theoretical rationale?

First of all, it should be noted that E. Taylor (1998), an important and insightful clinical researcher on hyperactivity, has defined the term as a personality organization "continuously distributed in the population: an enduring disposition to behave in a restless, inattentive, impulsive and disorganized fashion" (p. 15). Barkley (1997), another central clinical researcher, also takes a dimensional view of ADHD as representing the extreme end of a personality continuum. As Barkley views the concept, it refers to a continuum of psychiatric relevance rather than a diagnostic category per se. By this conception, there are interindividual differences along a continuum, with children relatively extreme at one end being arbitrarily labeled or categorized as having ADHD.

Second, the quality of impulsivity, presented as a defining feature of ADHD, need not be attached solely to hyperactivity per se, as seems to be the frequent definitional practice. Certainly, impulsivity of behavior is to be seen in many ways in children identified as having ADHD. Also to be seen in children identified as having ADHD, however, is distractability, inability to sustain attention (what Barkley calls a deficiency of "interference control"), a changing from one activity to another, a rapid satiation of boring activities—these are all manifestations that appear to indicate an impulsivity of perception as well. So, impulsivity appears to exist at the intake side as well as the output side of psychological functioning, at the reaction side as well as the response side of experience

Third, the psychiatric continuum involved is conceptually conflated, combining attention deficit (perceptual impulsivity) on the one hand with hyperactivity (behavioral impulsivity) on the other. It is true that attention deficit frequently goes along with hyperactivity and so the assumed conjunction of attention deficit with hyperactivity has not posed serious workaday problems in the usual practice of usual psychiatry. But as has been noted by various investigators, there are some children who manifest attention deficit but not hyperactivity[5] and some children who manifest hyperactivity but not attention deficit. Conceptually, therefore, this distinction requires theoretical attention. One must conclude that, within the grand label of ADHD, there are reliably different subgroups with one reflecting attentional dysfunction, a second reflecting response dysfunction, and a third reflecting the conjoint presence of attention and response dysfunction.

Given these recognitions, I suggest that ADHD readily falls within the conception of ego-control and ego-perceptual apparatuses earlier described. The permeability of the ego-control apparatus, if extreme, can be viewed as explaining hyperactivity—the uninhibited, unslowed expression of arising tensions. The permeability of the ego-perceptual apparatus, if extreme, can be viewed as explaining attention deficit—the uninhibited, unslowed reaction to the immense variety of perceptual inputs. Slowing down confusing reactions and responses

---

[5]It has been well established that learning disabilities do not explain the children manifesting only attention deficit.

provides the possibility of using both perception and actions purposefully and in an organized way. The posited positive (but not complete) relation between the characteristic of the two ego apparatuses fits well with the indisputable finding of subtypes of ADHD but also their frequent conjunction. By placing ADHD within the present theoretical framework, the diagnosis is given a larger context and the variety of findings and expectations elsewhere surrounding ego control and ego perception become applicable as well to ADHD.

Further, it follows from definitions of elasticity or resiliency, as these apply to both ego-control and ego-perceptual apparatuses, that ADHD children with insufficient personal resources of resiliency will, by their behavior, inevitably cause unacceptable societal problems and may often be characterized as being "delinquent," as having a "conduct disorder." They will be erratic attenders of school, will blaze with anger, will manifest an unfocused attention, will be educationally unprepared for the flux of life, and will be identified as intellectually compromised, ineffective individuals (Block, 1995b). However, the ADHD person who is sufficiently resilient and only playfully undercontrolled, underperceiving, or both will be viewed as interestingly energetic and an unusual perceiver. It can be expected that, over time, he will constructively outgrow his problem of excessiveness, carrying over no especial life-altering deficits.

Phrased succinctly and perhaps simplistically, undercontrol and underperceptualization may well get one into societal trouble. Ego resilience can get one out of trouble; its absence will keep one in difficulty.

THE PROBLEM OF CONDUCT AND ANTISOCIAL DISORDER OR DELINQUENT BEHAVIOR

Conduct disorder and delinquent behavior seem to arise also for reasons other than ADHD, and the contributing factors are a problem of great practical societal concern. Much attention has been directed toward discerning and disentangling those influences that, separately and conjointly, lead to behavior societally identified at various ages as wrongdoing. Studies abound, stemming from diverse viewpoints.

To date, there does not appear to be a reliable neurophysiological indicator of a deficit in complexly adaptive integrated behavior that leads to societally unacceptable functioning. Such a deficit has been conjectured, presumed to exist, and frequently sought, but as yet no dependable neurophysiological diagnostic avails. Thus, injury to the prefrontal cortex seems to be well related to subsequent impulsivity of behavior, but impulsivity of behavior does not seem, in reverse, to indicate an identifiable deficit in the prefrontal cortex.

Sometimes, IQ per se has been posited as an indicator of neuropsychological function and the cause, when IQ is relatively low, of delinquency (e.g., Lynam, Moffitt, & Stouthamer-Loeber, 1993). The relation between IQ and delinquency, after arguable statistical analysis, has been presented as evidence for this view.

Certainly, a lower verbal IQ tends to characterize delinquents. However, this lower verbal IQ can as readily be viewed as a consequence rather than as a cause of the behavior viewed as antisocial or delinquent. Typically, such individuals are undercontrolled and also unresilient individuals by virtue of their upbringing (conjoined perhaps with their genetic lineage).

In the immediate context of intelligence testing, it should be remembered that effective performance involves constrained, slowed, reflective behavior. Such behavior is less likely to occur with impulsive, unresilient children and adolescents who are unable to modulate their actions and reactions. So some lowering of their achieved IQ is not surprising (Block, 1995b). Further, in the longer developmental context, learning in life occurs on a day-by-day and year-by-year basis. It involves focused attention and prolonged concentration by the child and adolescent within structured educative settings. During their education, undercontrolled unresilient children, because of their personal qualities, may cumulatively register less of the information and reasoning logic on which IQ scores depend and, in addition, they will often tend to miss a good deal of school. Indeed, Ceci (1991), summarizing a host of evidence, noted that "children begin school with average or near average IQs and, over time, their IQs decline as they miss more and more school" (p. 706). For these reasons also, when confronted by an intelligence test, they will be less prepared and their IQ scores accordingly will suffer. Thus, the causal "flow" underlying the undoubted relation between IQ and conduct disorder or delinquency may be from the latter to the former rather than from IQ to delinquency, as often concluded.

Separately, it is also worthwhile to consider phenomenologically those life circumstances wherein an individual—already undercontrolled and unresilient—may be prone to display unacceptable conduct or delinquent behavior. The individual frequently will encounter frustrating situational conditions and will not have the required adaptive knowledge to manage or circumvent the problem. He or she simply will not know what to do next (i.e., will be unresilient). Constrained by the recognition of inadequate adaptive routes but still pulled or pushed by desires or unwanted pressures, he or she will tend toward local, immediate, unplanned, explosive, prepotent behaviors such as stealing, striking out at others. Usually, these behaviors are perceived (properly) by the larger society as unacceptable and therefore maladaptive. Such behaviors by the individual, repeated by him or her, and repeatedly reacted to and remembered by the established environment, will soon enough create a reputation of uncivilized conduct. Society must indeed respond, but response too often is only punitive rather than understanding and creating of the environmental conditions promoting of character change toward more resilience and control. Forgotten by most is the recognition that conduct disorder and antisocial personality are ultimately dependent variables, not independent variables. They are consequences rather than causes.

CHANGING EGO STRUCTURES VIA DRUGS— AN UNCERTAIN CONJECTURE

Referring to pharmaceutical recognitions and to lay knowledge as well, it is widely known that the imbibing of alcohol (e.g., via cocktails, wine, whiskey, or beer) causes the individual to loosen ordinarily held behavioral restraints, to express previously contained impulses, and in my terms to become more undercontrolled. A deep or prolonged alcohol state may lead to a crazy impulsivity, hurtful and dangerous to others and to self.

It is also well known that psychedelic drugs (e.g., mescaline, LSD, psilocybin), in William Blake's terms, "cleanse the doors of perception," destructure the ordinarily received environment, and cause the individual to see things ordinarily unseen. Indeed, the mescaline experience is often unstructurable. In my own terms, individuals become very underperceptualizing. Indeed, a deep and prolonged or unsupportive psychedelic experience often leads to an experience of being perceptually overwhelmed. But often too, the refulgent freshness of a psychedelic experience is perceptually transporting.

It is further known that the amphetamines when first imbibed often create a focusing of activity, a directed usage of energy, a concerting of effort—what I term an increase in overcontrol. Caffeine, because of its ubiquitous availability, is also frequently taken for similar reasons. Deep or prolonged usage of amphetamines or coffee ("caffeine jags") tends to elicit an excessive overcontrol—first an obsessive–compulsiveness wherein little real, integrated work gets done, only little things, and then often to rageful, hypervigilant paranoia.

Finally, it is well known that tranquilizers (e.g., Reserpine, Miltown, Xanex), paraphrasing Blake, dull the doors of perception, fog the perceived environment to reduce what is attended to or noticed, cause the individual to become much more of an overperceptualizer. Deep and prolonged usage of anxiolytic tranquilizers can produce an individual manifesting little psychological energy or interest in the experience of life. Such drugs may well deal with the immediate or presenting anxiety problem of the individual, but by virtue of the apathy or experiential dullness they create, they may make the person deficient in other respects.

When an individual has imbibed a psychedelic (moving an individual toward underperceptualizing) and enters what proves to be a "bad trip," tranquilizers (moving the individual toward overperceptualizing) are known to return the individual to his psychic home base. It has not been studied, to my knowledge, whether taking LSD will negate or reverse the effects of a tranquilizer.

Although common student folklore testifies to the effects of amphetamines and caffeine in opposing alcohol effects, it has not been studied, to my knowledge, whether taking whiskey will cancel out the effects of amphetamine or caffeine.

During the strange cultural times of the 1960s and 1970s, there was a great deal of drug usage. Some of these drugs were societally sanctioned or were socially tolerated; others were unlawfully imbibed and strictly discouraged. The drinking of alcohol was not prohibited and was generally (and still is) put up with. It was (and still is) not unusual for tranquilizers and amphetamines to be alternated, as deemed needed by the imbiber, without askance being too vocally raised. But psychedelic drugs were and generally still are societally unacceptable and even frightening in anticipation to laypeople.

Although experienced too often in uncontrolled circumstances, extensive early drug usage nevertheless offered many insights into drug effects and their interaction. A number of interesting anecdotal observations relating to drug imbibement accumulated.

Thus it was observed by the California highway patrol that some individuals driving in a clearly drunken, impulsive fashion nevertheless had relatively low blood alcohol levels and hence could not be legally charged as drunk while driving. On interrogation, these individuals acknowledged the immediately prior usage of tranquilizers. It appeared that tranquilizers, themselves considered rather innocuously deadening, seemed to potentiate the effects of alcohol. This observation has subsequently become a well-documented scientific recognition. In terms of the present personality schema, the tranquilizers apparently functioned to make the ego-perceptual apparatus relatively impermeable or unappreciated, thus clouding the doors of perception. Such clouding apparently helped to open the gates of impulsivity. It was as if when the intake from the external world is restricted or de-emphasized, then internal influences are released and seem exaggerated.

Separately, it was observed by street chemists that when psychedelic drugs were in short supply, the mingling of some amphetamine with tiny and otherwise insufficient amounts of psychedelics caused the psychedelics to have a greater experiential effect. It appeared that amphetamines seemed to potentiate the effects of psychedelics. In terms of the present personality schema, the amphetamine apparently functioned to make the ego-control apparatus relatively impermeable and uninfluential, thus diminishing its directive role. Such diminishing of behavioral influence apparently helped allow an overwhelming of previously established perceptions via the ego-perceptual apparatus. It was as if when output from the internal world is restricted, then external influences are exaggerated.

These relationships have a loose, perhaps even a tight connection with Rapaport's (1958) speculations about ego autonomy. Therein, he talks of "drive slavery" perhaps occurring when "external stimulation" is reduced. In parallel, he views "stimulus slavery" as perhaps occurring when "id derivatives" (drives?) are withheld from expression.

Thus, the effect of the drugs singly and in complex interaction appear to change ego structure temporarily with the changes observed being in some accord with the system of personality herein being described. As a bit of a joke, in order to submit the present theory to crucial test (and to horrify a university Human Subjects Committee), one might simultaneously administer to a participant pharmacologically equivalent amounts of all four types of drugs—bourbon, Reserpine, amphetamine, and LSD. If the theory is indeed correct, nothing should happen to the participant—he or she should be unchanged in personality! I leave it to others to assay this theoretical conjecture.

SOME DIVERSE OBSERVATIONS AND ASIDES

The term "psychopathy," is often used confusingly because for many it is interpreted as psychopathology in the general sense rather than as a specific kind of psychopathology. True psychopathy is based on the self-percept not being activated in situations when for most people it is. By not introspecting when normatively one should, the true psychopath is without shame or remorse or anticipated guilt or loyalties or a sense of personal responsibility. For this reason, it is probably better to use the term "sociopath," to describe the true psychopath. When the option for psychotherapy is available, the sociopath is usually without a genuine wish for psychological treatment.

Another kind of behavior, also casually called "psychopathic," is sometimes seen in adolescence or in young adulthood. It derives from a manicky despair, a sense of anomie and meaninglessness, excessive introspection, a self-percept that is too often, even incessantly present. Such individuals may react to their anomie and despair by being shocking, startling, and deliberately outrageous. But they are false psychopaths, with motivations and perceptions quite unlike those of true psychopaths with whom they should not be confused. Both kinds of character structure may frequently be in societal trouble because both are undercontrolled and may or may not be unresilient. But only the false psychopath is a self-watcher and may be intrinsically experientially disturbed.

A further useful distinction, perhaps too infrequently made, is to recognize what are called "dissocial" individuals. Dissocials are individuals who, although disregarding usual social mores, have strong loyalties to a group largely in conflict with or disregarded by society. They are not asocial like the true psychopath, although like the true psychopath, they may behave in ways conventionally judged as antisocial. The dissocials are differently social; they react—perhaps quite strictly—in terms of their own culturally deviant moral code.

It is also useful to distinguish between "acting-out" and "acting-up." The term acting-out is too often used incorrectly and without knowledge of the origins and meaning of the psychoanalytic phrase. Acting-out means the symbolic expression, via behavior, of the individual's conflicts and internal psychodynamics. It often but not necessarily involves impulsive behavior (Frosch, 1977). In referring solely to expressively impulsive behavior, the term acting-up may be more denotative.

Chapter 10

Connections to Theoretical Alternatives

Given the theoretical conceptualization offered in previous chapters, one needs to consider some alternative approaches to many of the same theoretical goals to see their connection, divergence, and relative merit. Two of these, although themselves radically opposite to each other, will illustrate some major new efforts to treat personality—the five-factor approach of Costa and McCrae to personality and the so-cial–cognitive approach of Mischel to personality. Considering them in their own right and in their connection to the viewpoint presented herein cannot but be perspective-inducing.

THE FIVE-FACTOR APPROACH OF COSTA AND McCRAE

A Short History of a Still Unsettled Approach

A currently popular pursuit, vigorously, resourcefully, and encom-passingly advanced by Costa and McCrae (e.g., Costa & McCrae, 1992a), has proposed that what we call personality can be well and suffi-ciently expressed by means of five robust factor dimensions universally found by various factor analyses of a number of self- and peer question-naires, parent ratings, and behavioral scores. The five orthogonal fac-tors widely proposed have been named Neuroticism, Extraversion,

Openness to Experience, Agreeableness, and Conscientiousness. This set of factors has been christened by Costa and McCrae as "the five-factor model." Alternatively, and confusably, there is the psycholexical Big Five of Goldberg (1993).

It has been said that the model's five factors "are both necessary and reasonably sufficient for describing at a global level the major features of personality" (McCrae & Costa, 1986); "the five-factor model developed in studies of normal personality is fully adequate to account for the dimensions of abnormal personality as well" (Costa & McCrae, 1992a, p. 347).

Why are there five and only five factors? Five-factor protagonists say, "we believe it is an empirical fact, like the fact that there are seven continents on earth or eight American Presidents from Virginia" [McCrae & John, 1992, p. 194). The contention is that, via the mathematical method of factor analysis, the basic dimensions of personality have been "discovered." I would prefer to say, instead, that these factors were conceptually constructed.

Recent chapters favorably recounting the background of the five-factor model are to be found in John and Srivastava (1999) and McCrae and Costa (1999). A less favorable telling of the history and logic of the five-factor approach was presented some years ago by Block (1995a). A chapter by Butcher and Rouse (1996) focuses on insufficiencies of the five-factor model when used in clinical assessment.

Taking a historical view, Digman and Takemoto-Chock (1981) early remarked that the five-factor approach only represents "domains of research effort and theoretical concern which have long been of interest to psychologists" (p. 149). In recent years, given the vogue of the five-factor model conveniently exemplified by its questionnaire expressions, it is frequently used by many individuals far from the field of personality psychology. If only because it is an unthinking research task, the personality inventories designed for the five given factors have been related to any available criterion. Accordingly, a plethora of dissertations, minor research, and perhaps some useful research under the five-factor banner now floods the literature with correlates. Looking (in February 2000) at the most recent 50 PsycINFO references to the five-factor model, 25 prove to be doctoral dissertations, 21 are studies of the five-factor model in relation to such topics as compulsive buying, media use, computer stress, the Rorschach, exercise, multiple sclerosis, personnel selection, degree of intellectual engagement, spinal injury, expatriate selection, and so on. This is a hodge-podge of reports, signifying almost nothing of central importance to the study of personality. Four references are to substantial efforts, the two 1999 chapters already mentioned and two *Journal of Personality and Social Psychology* articles.

In my view, many five-factor research findings were similarly and earlier available from the host of studies using such inventories as the Minnesota Multiphasic Personality Inventory (MMPI), the Guilford–Zimmerman Temperament Survey, the Eysenck inventories, Jackson's Personality Research Form, Cattell's 16 PF Inventory, Gough's California Psychological Inventory, the Multiple Personality Questionnaire of Tellegen, sundry other inventories, and a variety of personality scales.

Thus, originally, as acknowledged by them, the Neuroticism and Extroversion scales of Costa and McCrae were constructed to psychologically duplicate Eysenck's long work, itself dependent on previous efforts. The Openness to Experience scale of Costa and McCrae does not go beyond the prior and purer Absorption scale of Tellegen and Atkinson (1974). The Conscientousness scale of Costa and McCrae has long been understood to represent a fusion or confound of what is called resiliency and overcontrol, previously indexed.

In the ahistoric field that personality psychology has become, the perspective afforded by previous research requires remembrance if we are to be cumulative in our efforts and to recognize new advances. Only occasionally and selectively is this history recalled.

Unresolved Issues

Leaving aside historical matters, some earlier noted problems still besetting the five-factor approach but not yet answered require mention here.

In the method of factor analysis, many procedures and criteria conventionally used at various steps in the factoring sequence produce questionable results (Fabrigar, Wegener, MacCallum, & Strahan, 1999). Inspection of the five-factor literature, "rooted" (McCrae & Costa, 1989) in factor analysis, indicates many of the reported findings have been based on less than adequate methodology.

As P. Meehl (1992, p. 152) has remarked, "no statistical procedure should be treated as a mechanical truth generator." Separately, H. J. Eysenck (1998) has commented that "factor analysis is a good servant, but a bad master!" (p. 79). Psychological results always require a psychological interpretation; they do not exist by themselves. It is widely accepted that "the 'true' number of dimensions of human personality is a metaphysical rather than a scientific question" (Costa & McCrae, 1980, p. 69).

Despite these recognitions, analyses sometimes and in an unacknowledged way have shaped the supposed findings because of a precommitment to a particular number and particular structure of factors. Thus, in an analysis by McCrae, Costa, and Busch (1986), the scree test used as a guide to the number of factors indicated that seven or nine factors exist, but the authors settled on eight "along with *versions* [italics added]" of the five they emphasized. The tenor of their paper and subsequent references to it is that only five confirming factors resulted.

It is widely recognized, and also acknowledged by five-factor propagators (e.g., Costa & McCrae, 1992b; Goldberg, 1993) that there is a crucial influence in factor solutions of the particular set of measures used, a problem not yet sufficiently faced. It is also the case that the nature of the sample used and various matters influencing the computed correlation coefficients subsequently factor-analyzed affect the results subsequently achieved. The downstream findings issued by factor analysis thus may be fundamentally affected by often unevaluated upstream influences.

Also remaining to be settled is the substantive meaning of the—always five—factors; the sense of the factors differs according to the investigator. Thus, for example, one principal interpretation places impulsivity as within Extraversion, another principal interpretation places it under Neuroticism conjoined with anxiety and depression. Thus, there is agreement on the number of factors but not on what they psychologically mean.

Moreover, it is also not clear how the five-factor approach would be progressively scientifically improved upon. Has our science achieved a final and absolute way of looking at personality, or is there a way to further improve on our conceptualization? In the article by Costa and McCrae (1997) foretelling the changes in their inventory, the NEO-PI(R), to be expected in the new millennium, they anticipate there will be only minor wording modifications and some simplification for those of lower reading levels. So, it looks as if the five-factor approach is viewed by its primary advocates as a final or almost final achievement in personality psychology.

Some Recent Five-Factor Findings

In the time elapsing since my last worried review of the five-factor approach, further problems have emerged. An admittedly incomplete and unsystematic sampling of some developments over the last half dozen years may cast some additional light on the conceptual and empirical problems besetting the five-factor approach.

Among those depending on the method of factor analysis, research on broad item pools often finds it necessary to consider factors beyond those contained in the five-factor model (e.g., Ashton, Jackson, Helmes, & Paunonen, 1998; Benet-Martinez & Waller, 1997; Caprara, Barbaranelli, & Comrey, 1995; Church & Burke, 1994; Jackson, Paunonen, Fraboni, & Goffin, 1996; Paunonen & Jackson, 1996; Waller & Zavala, 1993; Yik & Bond, 1993). These findings are of a kind and number requiring consideration; they may not be ignored.

Ashton et al. (1998) reported that the five-factor scales, acknowledged to be broad and sweeping, are substantially less incisively valid than their constituent facet scales. This point previously has been made by Wiggins (1992), McAdams (1992), and Costa & McCrae (1995), among others.

In regard to the personality disorders covered by the *DSM–III-R*, Coolidge et al. (1994) demonstrate the limited discriminatory value of the five-factor approach in the clinical field, its assignment incorrectly of equal explanatory weight to each factor although it is Neuroticism and Extraversion (the old "Big Two") that contribute the most to understanding personality disorders, and also note that more than five factors are required for describing psychiatric symptoms (see also Livesley, Jackson, & Schroeder, 1989, 1992; Schroeder, Wormworth, & John, 1992).

It has been noted that the fifth factor of Openness to Experience is often confused and confusing and too often does not reliably emerge (De Raad, 1998).

Paunonen and Jackson (1996) have contended the Conscientious factor lacks coherence and is better partitioned into three separate dimensions: methodical and orderly (e.g., Adolf Eichmann), dependable and reliable (e.g., Jimmy Carter), and ambitious and driven (e.g., Richard Nixon). Loevinger (1994) further argued the Conscientious factor, as currently operationalized by the five-factor model, no longer reflects a moral nature.

Although Costa and McCrae consider their descriptive approach to apply uniformly to all adult ages, Mroczek, Ozer, Spiro, and Kaiser (1998) found substantial differences between the factor structures emerging from older men as compared with undergraduate students.

One study (Sneed, McCrae, & Funder, 1998) reported that the five-factor model is imbedded in the associative memories of undergraduates, but another study (Dabady, Bell, & Kihlstrom, 1999) found that undergraduates do not organize their associative memories as five-factor clusters.

Viswesvaran and Ones (1999) reported that the status of individuals on each of the five factors can readily be faked.

Clearly, much clarification of these unexpected and troubling findings is needed.

Higher-Order Factor Analysis of the Five Factors

Deeper analyses of the five-factor approach have begun. Theoretically, factors exist at different hierarchical levels. Besides the efforts demonstrating or arguing for dimensions at a more specific, narrower level of understanding, there have been efforts going the other way—to create higher order, more abstract factors. Some higher order analyses of the five factors by Digman (1997), separately extended by Carroll (in press), are of especial interest and warrant presentation here.

Digman recognized that the supposed orthogonality of the five factors was apparent rather than real; such orthogonality had been imposed by the use of a particular method of factor analysis and rotation. Factor dimensions ordinarily are not orthogonal, and they should not truly be expected to be. If extracted by a mathematical, psychologically innocent method, orthogonality may be assured, but it is quickly lost when the mathematical abstractions are given psychological content, typically implemented by inventory item summations selected to represent the factors. Although factor dimensional scores have to be conceptually fully separable, empirically they often are not. It is not surprising to find that each five-factor dimension is correlationally linked to the other four (of the five) factor dimensions. This condition immediately suggests the relevance and perhaps usefulness of a higher order factor analysis.

Digman took 14 correlation matrices all showing five-factor solutions. In various, reasonable ways, he allowed the five factors of each matrix to be nonorthogonal (i.e., correlated): Sometimes he computed factor scores by factor loading weightings, sometimes he took the intercosines of axes from a nonorthogonal (promax) rotational solution, often he took the correlations among trait scales designed to reflect the five factors, and so on. The data he used were diverse: Sometimes trait ratings by teachers of children, sometimes self-report or peer-reports on differently authored scales intended to reflect the five factors; the samples were of different ages and culture.

Digman's analysis of these 14 correlation matrices—each one based on the correlations among the five nonorthogonal factors—was interpreted by him as suggesting the existence of two robust higher order factors. His results repay consideration.

His first higher order factor was suggested as representing the socialization process and was interpreted as concerned with impulse restraint
(versus its absence), conscientiousness, and the reduction of aggression
in socially unapproved ways.

Digman interpreted his second higher-order factor in more uncertain, groping terms: personal growth, Tellegen's Positive Emotionality,
a venturesome encountering of life, surgent imaginativeness. Other
characterizations of this factor were also provided.

A severe problem with Digman's interesting and only partially successful effort to seek higher order factors is that he was limited to analysis of the already created five-factor matrices. He was unable to return
to bedrock data—the characteristics of the individuals subsequently
scoring differentially on his higher order factors.

However, Carroll (in press), a well-respected, technically versed
factor analyst, recently worked through a hierarchical analysis of a
data set containing individual personality characteristics. His analysis is therefore especially implicative to consider here. The analytical
approach of Carroll was superior to that of Digman methodologically and, most important, it permitted identification directly of the
personality characteristics associated with the resultant higher order
factors.

Carroll used teacher ratings provided by Digman and Inouye (1986)
of 43 characteristics rated on 499 early adolescents and submitted the
data to hierarchical analysis (via the Schmid–Leiman procedure). This
set of data apparently was not included in the Digman higher order
analyses. In Carroll's analysis of these data, the initial, first-order personality characteristics of the participants became five second-order
but not orthogonal factors and these five factors in turn warranted going on to two higher order "superfactors."

Interestingly, these "superfactors" explained far more common factor variance than the "standard" five factors together with their constituent items (.74 vs .26). Further, the nature of these two orthogonal
superfactors can clearly be seen by inspecting the characteristics of individuals scoring high on each superfactor.

The first half dozen attributes defining one Carroll Superfactor are
"not impulsive," "not restless," "not rude," "not fidgety," "not spite-
ful," and "not outspoken." The attributes associated with this
Superfactor would appear to suggest something akin to the construct
of overcontrol (as compared with undercontrol) and is like the first
higher order factor of self-restraint and aggression socialization interpreted earlier by Digman.

The first half dozen attributes defining the other Carroll Superfactor are "socially confident," "adaptableness," "perceptiveness," "verbalness," "originality," and "sensible." The attributes associated with this Superfactor would appear, in my view, to connote something much like the dynamic construct of ego-resiliency (as compared with ego brittleness), of being adaptively tuned to the surrounding world.

These higher order analyses of the five ordained factors open up the possibility for future research along these lines to better see what the several levels of personality abstraction may be and to compare their relative conceptual and empirical fruitfulness.

Certainly, other relevant correlation matrices should be more deeply evaluated to see how the five factors place within this higher order context. In the meanwhile, I suggest the Carroll analysis may indicate how the five-factor approach may be fitted into the personality system presented in previous chapters.

The Five-Factor Model as the Five-Factor Theory

Recently, the five-factor model has been further formulated as a theory (McCrae & Costa, 1999). Sixteen five-factor theory postulates, arranged in six groups, are offered. This set of five-factor theory postulates, in its entirety, impresses me as inclusive of widespread, certainly not wrong, broad recognitions. However, there is no serious approach to the study of personality and development that would not subscribe to these background tenets. In this age of psychological science, it should be recognized that these orienting postulates do not function as a committed, implicative theory. No specific theoretical consequences are entailed by the five-factor postulates; no sense is provided of the specific dynamics of personality. It is not a theory in the sense of an interpreted deductive system.

However, McCrae and Costa performed a valuable service in characterizing in broad terms how their five factor-traits have a biological basis, influence styles of adaptation, and how these styles are further affected by external influences such as cultural norms and life events.

Evaluative Remarks

"Most psychologists regard 'outer' (behavioral) traits as descriptions that need explanation and they assume that 'inner' (emotional and cognitive) traits generate and therefore explain outer traits" (Johnson, 1997, p. 79). The five-factor descriptive model, relying primarily and necessarily on outer, seeming frankness of self-report or lay-report of behaviors, does not appear to attempt sufficiently a dynamic elucidation of the inner, often unreported motivations sequentially influencing perception and behavior. A remark by Wold (1956) is pertinent here: "A frequent situation is that description serves to maintain some modus vivendi … , whereas explanation serves the purpose of *reform* …. Description is employed as an aid to human adjustment to conditions, while explanation is a vehicle for ascendancy over the environment." (p.29)

If the five-factor model descriptively applies everywhere, then it should be recognized that it offers little help in directing nontautological efforts at personality understanding. In contrast, the present personality theoretical system attempts to offer entailed rules—perhaps and even likely empirically incorrect—governing its elements and their conjunction. Further, it should be noted that the theoretical effort described in earlier chapters was theoretically driven and long preceded currently popular data-driven factor analyses of questionnaires.

Although little truly new conceptual information may as yet have been fostered by the five-factor approach, it does not follow that the approach has not been, in its way, beneficial to the inchoate personality field. The widespread use of the same (or almost the same) questionnaire in a variety of contexts has permitted the linking, in—commensurate terms—of a host of previously unconnected empirical findings. However, all in all, it seems to me wisest still to be ambivalent about the current five-factor fashion as THE way to study personality until its definitional and empirical perplexities are resolved.

MISCHEL'S APPROACH, PAST AND PRESENT, TO UNDERSTANDING PERSONALITY

Some History and Orienting Remarks

A third of a century ago, Mischel (1968) came forward with a forceful, pessimistic, and remarkably influential volume proposing that the study of personality qualities is scientifically unsustainable. Personality psychology was said by him to call for consistent cross-situational behaviors, to be exemplified in the form of high correlations between conceptually related variables. However, his review of the research literature concluded that individuals empirically display poorly correlated behaviors and, therefore, that "the concept of personality traits as broad response dispositions is … untenable" (p. 146). In effect, he suggested that personality psychology could not be presumed to have the possibilities of a science.

I have commented earlier (J. Block, 1977) on some of the evidential and statistical reasons by which Mischel's adverse review of cross-situational findings may be questioned. For a close analysis of Mischel's logomachy, the reader may wish to consult that still-relevant discussion. However, because Mischel's critical conclusions continue to have enduring influence, it still remains worth remarking on them and their basis.

There is much to question regarding Mischel's (1968) "empirically based" claim. First, note that he discussed only very briefly and selectively the grand issue of the consistency and specificity of behavior relating to personality (in only about 5,500 words and 16 pages, pp. 20–36). Within these few pages, he touched on such deep matters as attitudes toward authority and peers, moral behavior, sexual identification, dependency and aggression, rigidity and tolerance for ambiguity, cognitive avoidance, conditionability, moderator variables, and the temporal instability of personality (an estimated 612 words only, per topic).

To illustrate the scholarly scantiness of Mischel's capsule review, consider that his remarks on the major psychological topic of aggression were limited to but 6 lines, referring to an unpublished progress report by Bandura (see Mischel, 1968, p. 28). In contrast, for example, Feshbach (1970) also evaluating the conceptualization and empiricism surrounding aggression devoted 101 pages to a similar review; Olweus (1979) required 23 journal pages to review a developmental aspect of aggression.

Also, Mischel seemed often to be methodologically unversed and, to many, conceptually inappropriate. For example, he did not recognize that all psychological measures are psychometrically subject to attenuation, and therefore the possibility of finding consistency when the measures used happen to be unreliable may be vitiated. Thus, poorly executed research—and there is much research that can be so described—inadvertently supported Mischel's views. Also contributing to the low correlations he cited are the logical (lowered) limits placed on their values by the discordant shapes of the distributions being related (cf. Carroll, 1961), the operation of multiple influences on behavior that thus dilute the obtainable size of the particular correlation focused on (cf. Ahadi & Diener, 1989), the conceptual question of when to square the obtained correlation coefficient and when one should not (cf. Ozer, 1985), range restriction effects (cf. McNemar, 1964), the need to trim or "Winsorize" distributions to lessen the undue effects of maverick or outlying observations on empirical relations (Mosteller & Tukey, 1977), the usage of methods such as the varimax rotational method in factor analysis that were guaranteed to preclude positive coherence findings (cf. Harman, 1967), and the often unasked but absolutely crucial conceptual question, Should the operational measures being used theoretically relate?[1]

Thus, as an example of Mischel's then-conceptual framework, the aggressive behavior of a juvenile delinquent with his schoolmates and the submissive behavior of the same individual when with his aggressive father was interpreted as denying the existence of a generalizing personality concept (Mischel, 1968, p. 28). Many would say instead that these divergent behaviors bear witness to a deeper generalizability and coherence of behavior.

Finally, I must mention that a further reason why the correlation between conceptually related behaviors may be low is because the behaviors involved are truly functionally equivalent; we are perhaps correlating alternative behavioral manifestations of the same motiva-

---

[1]It is useful (perhaps belaboring, perhaps illustrative) to consider a deeper methodological look at the Hartshorne and May studies of grade-school children, invoked early and still lauded as a prime illustration of the behavioral inconsistency or specificity of moral conduct (see Mischel, 1968, 1999; Mischel & Shoda, 1999).

First, be it noted that in the original study, reliabilities varied widely, and their substantial attenuating influence was not considered. Further, the differences between the shapes of score distributions were not provided, and so their correlation-lowering effects were also not evaluated and allowed for. Notwithstanding these important psychometric considerations, and in contrast to the conventional reception in psychology of the Hartshorne studies, a strong common factor nevertheless was found among the various ethical measures (Burton, 1963). Maller (1934) earlier had found similar indications of a general consistency of behavior. Moreover, as initially reported by Hartshorne and May, honesty was relative to the situation and this relativity proved to be ordered rather than chaotically distributed (May & Hartshorne, 1926). Webb, Campbell, Schwartz, and Sechrest (1966), in their volume on unobtrusive measures, reported that May and Hartshorne found cheating opportunities formed a unidimensional scale, with a Guttman reproducibility coefficient of .96 and a scale reliability of .84! As Burton reminds us, multiple other psychological influences on behavior also were present, thus further lessening the particular obtained correlations generally focused on. And finally, Ozer (1985) commented that Mischel misstated his trait model, neglecting a latent variable that theoretically was involved. Therefore, the obtained correlation coefficients of about .40 did not warrant Mischel's further squaring but should have been interpreted directly in percentage terms. So, the oft-cited and quite ancient Hartshorne and May studies, when evaluated more closely, appear to not justify their often-invoked summary.

tion. If one manifestation occurs, then no other manifestation of the same motivation need arise. For example, if one chooses to satisfy hunger by selecting one entree from a menu, this choice is usually—because of appetite constraints—not positively related with one's concomitant selection of a second entree. One—any one—of the entrees will be sufficient to assuage hunger. And so, overall and depending on the mix of individuals and the psychological setting, food choices may be reciprocally related or unrelated or positively related; of course the correlations will be low.

To psychologically exemplify the point, one can be dependent in a number of ways. For some or many persons, any way of dependency may be quite sufficient, and therefore of sometime correlation with alternative manifestations of the same motivation. One has to consider whether, for an individual, one form of dependency sufficiently serves his or her motivation or whether multiple forms of dependency are psychologically necessary.

I therefore suggest that if the research litter-ature is of poor quality—without regard for ascertaining construct validity, psychometric limitations, or a relevant method of data analysis—one can readily fail to reject the null hypothesis resoundingly enough. It is only by implicitly accepting the null hypothesis that one can conclude the empirical findings seemingly demonstrate no or too little behavioral coherence. However, as one learns early in the study of logic, the uninteresting null hypothesis cannot be proven. To the extent many readers of Mischel's judgment of disappointing findings thought that he was suggesting the demonstration of null findings, they were in logical error. And why were Mischel's conclusions so eagerly accepted? It seems to me that they fitted in with the arch-situationist temper of the period, still erratically continuing despite the many newer and improved conceptualizations of personality in situ.

Mischel (1968) further remarked that it "may be futile to seek common underlying dimensions of similarity or generalization on the basis of which diverse events come to evoke a similar response pattern for all persons" (p. 190; see also Mischel, 1973, p. 265). Individuals were said to respond to situations differently and in idioms not structurable in common or commensurate ways. Extrapolating from his 1968 evaluation, Mischel opined that generalizations regarding behavior prediction likely were eternally unachievable. For him, the individual's situation was exquisitely idiosyncratic and adventitious, knowable only dimly through the individual's report. But by implication, given the (often-undeniable) inadequacy of personality-based predictions, and given inattention to the fundamental vitiating role of error variance, he and others (e.g., cf. Nisbett & Ross, 1980; Ross & Nisbett, 1991) inclined to the position that with personality so unpredictive, the person's situation was the major source of behavioral variation. Ironically, when later evaluated, the situational context proved to explain no more of behavior variance than did personality dispositions (Funder & Ozer, 1983); error seemed to explain the unassigned variance.

Mischel's Current View Regarding the Status of Personality Consistency

More recently, in closing out the century, Mischel has offered a rather different, more complicated view of personality. His recent chapter (Mischel & Shoda, 1999) provides a good statement of these more current conceptions regarding personality. It is useful to evaluate Mischel's contemporary orientation compared with his earlier stance and to offer some comment on their relation to the conception offered herein.

Mischel still maintains that his early characterization of the field was not overstated despite the many detailed responses to his contentions that have appeared (e.g., Jackson and Paunonen, 1985; J. Block, 1977; Funder, 1991; Kenrick & Funder, 1988; Olweus, 1979, 1980; Epstein, 1979; Rushton, Brainerd, & Pressley, 1983; among many others). He continues with his assumption that what he chooses to label as "situation-free" personality constructs necessarily call for an "empirically unviable" personality consistency (Mischel & Shoda, 1999, p. 214).

However, Mischel has himself reported the enduring and consequential effects of early personality configurations (instantiated by delay of gratification at age 4) on scholastic performance a decade later (Mischel, Shoda, & Peake, 1988). It seems to me that a child of four and the same child as an adolescent are living in very different environments or behavioral settings. If so, then such evidence of temporal consistency—and there has long existed much such evidence—necessarily implies important cross-situational consistency. Indeed, on reflection it should be clear that all cross-situational consistency is really cross-temporal consistency—with the always present time interval being variably long or short.

Mischel's Current Theoretical Conceptualization

In the last number of years, Mischel has evolved a theoretical approach labeled the Cognitive–Affective Personality System (CAPS). It reflects a cognitive–social orientation wherein personality functioning is to be understood by reference to the interactions between cognitive processes and social contexts. These cognitive mediators are characterized in capacious categorical terms rather than being specifically defined and circumscribed. It is by means of these cognitive structural establishments and their unspecified but assumed dynamic interconnections that personality behavior is predicated to respond adaptively to the situational context.

Mischel went on to contrast what he calls "the dispositional or trait" approach to personality, viewed by him as concerned with stable, broad, "context-free" person characteristics, with his preferred "processing" approach—the internal mediating units expressly responsive to the particular situation and their interaction.

In what may be a change from his earlier views, Mischel now does not deny that consistent internal qualities and consistent behaviors characterize different individuals (Mischel, 1999). However, his thinking and research still center primarily on the cognitive–social processes that, responding to situational contexts, give rise to the individual's experience and behavioral manifestations. He views his personality conceptualization as unifying both the dispositional approach and the psychological processes approach.[2] His work is thoughtful, elegantly stated, and requires sober appreciation.

In greater detail, Mischel offers what he calls cognitive–affective units (CAUs), all posited as dynamic rather than static and all stated as reciprocally interconnected, for understanding the basic psychological processes underlying experience and subsequent behavior. His five proposed CAUs (really psychological categories rather than "units") are encodings, expectancies and beliefs, affects, goals and values, and competencies together with self-regulatory plans. The description of these CAUs seems only slightly restated from the five "cognitive social learning person variables" offered earlier (Mischel, 1973). The change in terminology may reflect a recognition that the earlier "person variables" described by him were, except for one (construction competency), not psychological variables in the usual sense of implying differential position of individuals on a specified continuum.

Mischel goes on to assume that there are individual differences in the "chronic accessibility" of CAUs, the ease with which separately and to-

---

[2]Interestingly, Cervone and Shoda (1999, pp. 10–11), intellectual descendants of Mischel, take a diametrical view and "explicitly reject" the position Mischel now takes of uniting the trait view of personality and the social–cognitive approach.

gether they are activated to influence behavior. In addition, Mischel further assumes there are distinctive differences between individuals in their organization of the CAUs. Although each individual has a personal and relatively stable organization of CAUs, from individual to individual there exist distinctive differences in the way CAUs are organized. It is these dissimilarly organized but individually stable complexes of CAUs, together with the situational differences encountered, that allow for the existence of personality differences in experience and behavior. By his posits, Mischel allows for individual differences in the ease or fluidity of access to the CAUs and further allows for individual differences in the organization of underlying CAUs.

With regard to situations, Mischel and Shoda make a further crucial distinction, between the nominal situation and what they call the situation's "active ingredients" or psychological features (Shoda, Mischel, & Wright, 1994). Nominal situations are descriptions of life events expressed in concretistic, unpsychological terms. Thus, fishing, trampoline activity, a library reserve room, a dormitory room—all are instances of nominal situations (Shoda et al., 1994). The active ingredients of a situation are those of distinctive psychological relevance for each experiencing individual. "These psychologically active features of situations constitute a main part of the individual's personal experience and 'life space' " (Shoda et al., 1994, p. 684).

It follows from the Mischel and Shoda distinction (and also the physicalistic, concretely described situation described earlier), that the individual's responses to nominally the same situation have limited cross-situational implication. Nominally the same situations or unpsychologized environments each ultimately have different active ingredients as subjectively experienced, per individual. Therefore, disparate behaviors in response to nominal or concretely described situations are readily to be seen, and little cross-situational consistency of individual behavior is to be observed.

Mischel posits that for each situation in a set of situations there are idiosyncratic active ingredients characteristic of each individual. Within that subsequent complicativeness, Mischel suggests that the behavior of each individual becomes fully predictable, dependent on the active ingredients of the enveloping particular situation for that individual. There is behavioral change by the person from encountered situation to encountered situation, but the change for each person is posited as individually and differently lawful, not random in occurring.

From this viewpoint, each individual may be said to have a "behavioral signature," uniquely responsive to and evolved from the set of particular life situations previously encountered. For each individual confronting a range of situations, there is a distinctive, exquisitely discriminating, and personally stable set of context-responsive behavioral if–then reactions. However, from individual to individual, there are other, differently distinctive, exquisitely discriminating, and context-responsive sets of behavioral reactions. Given a particular situation, the particular individual responds in a singular but personally consistent way. The identical behavior is emitted by the particular person whenever the identical active ingredients again impinge on that person; with a different particular situation, the individual manifests a different particular behavior.

Each individual is thus said to have a characteristic and distinctive set of conditional if–then relations or personal procedural rules shaping variations in his or her behavior as a function of the situation's active ingredients.

In précis, according to Mischel, when the person is confronted by one situation (the "if" or "when"), a certain behavior follows (the "then"); if the person is confronted with a different situation, then another quite different behavior lawfully follows. The singular behavior of the individual reflects the established qualities of the person as further influenced by the active ingredients of the particular situation experienced, a theoretically attractive conceptualization.

Because Mischel presumes each individual is distinctively fully consistent personally in his or her behavior, the subsequent variety of behavioral profiles from one individual to another means that for a sample of individuals taken as a whole, overall personality consistency in the sense of appreciable cross-situational correlations may not be expected to exist. Thus, Mischel still currently preserves—but now on a more articulated basis—his earlier position of limited behavioral cross-situational consistency.

As noted earlier, when considering the practice of personality psychologists of calculating a behavioral score summed over all behaviors, Mischel has spoken against the idea of placing a person on a personality dimension when the person's behavioral signature is ignored. If individual CAUs vary so idiosyncratically and situations are so diverse in their active ingredients, he suggests the procedure of aggregating systematically removes the situation and limits the very process of personality understanding and the effort for specific prediction (Mischel, 1999).

Such an aggregating approach Mischel views as in violation of existing, stable, behavioral discriminations; it removes the many situations in order to find broad behavioral dispositions. It treats the variability of an individual across situations as error, ignoring context-responsiveness. For him, it is precisely the distinctive patterns of the person's behavior over diverse situations that should instead be focused on.

Mischel's Hot–Cool System Proposal

In a recent further theoretical development, Mischel (with Metcalfe, 1999, p. 39) has introduced the notion of "hot" and "cool" subsystems of personality in order "to incorporate the long-neglected but crucial role of emotion in the personality system" (see also Mischel & Shoda, 1999, p. 203; Metcalfe & Mischel, 1999). Mischel views the posited hot subsystem as functioning immediately, automatically, emotionally, and virtually reflexively; he labels it as the "go" system. Elsewhere, he additionally characterizes the hot subsystem as "unconscious," "emotional," and "impulsive" (Mischel, 1999, p. 46). In still another article, the "hot" system is said to be the source of fears and passions, influencing the individual to be unable to delay gratification and undermining self-control so that "stimulus control" predominates (Metcalfe & Mischel, 1999).

The cool subsystem is described as highly mediated, reflective, involving higher order cognitive processes such as "effortful control" to prevent impetuous responses; he labels it the "know" system. Elsewhere, Mischel (1999) goes on to characterize the cool subsystem as "conscious," "cognitive," and "rational" (p. 46). Metcalfe and Mischel (1999) further described the cool system as "contemplative," "flexible," "integrated," "slow," "monitoring," and "strategic." "Cognitive rumination is a hallmark of this system" (p. 6). It enables self-regulation and self-control (i.e., "willpower"), fostering delay of gratification (Metcalfe & Mischel, 1999).

There appears to be an uncertainty regarding how the hot–cool systems should be instantiated. There are mentions of the neuroscience basis of the two systems, but in the main, the two systems are conjectured in the framework of "contextualized social–personality interaction analysis" (Metcalfe & Mischel, 1999, p. 6) rather than seriously provided with neural origin.

The dynamics of hot and cool interactions are most interestingly proposed and discussed in terms of hot and cool nodes, their separateness and interconnection, hot and cool stimulus coding, priming, and "the learning algorithm" of Hebb.

A variety of predictions are offered based on the posited characteristics of the hot–cool systems. Thus, when the hot system is said to be dominant because the cool system is not yet well developed or is dysfunctional, it is predicted that exposure of a hot stimulus will tend to elicit impulsive response. It is further predicted that when the hot stimulus is not saliently exposed, a child's ability to delay of gratification is facilitated. Avoiding attending to a hot stimulus will diminish its eliciting power. Concurrent exposure to another nonrelevant stimulus (i.e., distraction) or the individual's deliberate focus on nonrelevant topics will weaken the effect of a hot stimulus. When a representation of a hot stimulus is presented rather than the hot stimulus itself, cool-system control is enhanced. Thinking about the cool properties of a stimulus rather than its hot properties will increase delay behavior. With increasing age, because the cool system develops more slowly, self-control will increase. With increase of stress or chronic stress, dominance should increasingly shift from the cool system to impulsive behavior. So far, these are the predictions offered by the hot–cool system proposal.

Evaluative Remarks

I have devoted so many words to the concepts and approach of Mischel because his work seems to me to have been central in psychology's efforts to better conceptualize personality. And I have learned much from his writings, directly and also from the necessity of finding a countering response to his conclusions and assertions I believed to be inappropriate. With this acknowledgment, it behooves me to mention some apposite but also some critical aspects of the Mischelian approach to the position adopted herein.

In apposition, the presentation and elaboration of the "hot" and "cool" systems may well be viewed as suggesting some of the needed grounding for much that is insufficiently discussed in my earlier chapters. Using a different metaphoric root, the characterizations of the hot and cool seem to be appreciably relatable to the conception offered earlier with one crucial difference to be brought forward when conceptual differences are noted.

Mischel's (1999) "psychological processing" approach, to the extent it recognizes the existence of common human motivations and common cultural shaping circumstances (p. 200), appears to permit the existence of individual differences fully equivalent to those studied by so-called dispositional psychologists. If so, the now understood contrast between dispositional approaches and Mischel disappears.

The view of Mischel and Shoda regarding situations seems to partially connect with the one offered earlier in chapter 3 (see also J. Block,

1950; J. H. Block, 1951). Whereas they limit themselves to distinguishing the "nominal" situation from the "active ingredients" of the situation (which I prefer to call the subjective psychological environment), I go further and place between their two situations the situation as it ought to be construed by the culturally normative individual—the normative objective psychological environment. I believe the active ingredients of the situation as perceived by the individual and how the situation should be construed are both psychologically important and are much the same.

I might also mention the deep connection of the hot–cool distinction with the work of Epstein (1993; 1994) on cognitive and experiential systems and their interconnection. The two systems conjectured by Metcalf and Mischel impress me as reminiscent of Epstein's distinctions. When Epstein lists the attributes of cognitive and experiential processing, they appear to be most similar to the hot–cool distinction.

In opposition, Mischel's approach, in its emphasis on cognition as primary, seems to me to subordinate basic affect—which I believe is primary and precedent—to subsequently established cognitive mechanisms rather than the other way around. In what I suggest is more than a trivial change in emphasis, the present theoretical effort awards priority to affective motivations and looks on subsequently evolved and applied cognitive mediators or processing as in the service of affectively adaptive ends. The present approach, by its emphasis on the primacy of affect, subordinates cognition in its various forms to the task of keeping affect within bounds.

In regard to the conceptual contrast Mischel offers between the dispositional approach and processing dynamics, it needs to be recalled that dispositions from their inception have never been conveyed as context-free (e.g., G. W. Allport, 1937; Cattell, 1957; Guilford, 1959; Lewin, 1935, 1946; Murray, 1938). Certainly, situations may not have been conceptualized adequately, but in principle and in small practice, the recognition of the influence of behavioral setting was unquestionably held. In the field of practice, clinical psychologists are oriented to take into account the situation surrounding the individual and its possible influence. Admittedly, the use of personality questionnaires only vaguely recognizing contextual variation by the use of such item qualifiers as "sometimes," "frequently," or "tends to" was and is insufficient. So, acknowledging historical inadequacy by all—social psychologists as well as personality psychologists—in close, serious conceptualizing of environments, it may be excessive to unqualifiedly consider the dispositional approach to personality as being without recognition of differences in the evocativeness of a situation, as being "context-free."

It is true that the specific content of the immediate stimulus situation was generally (but not always, see e.g., Endler, 1982) left incompletely stated by personality psychologists. However, it was widely recognized that behavior was a function of the individual's dispositional tendency in reaction to the dispositional evocativeness of the particular situation.

Although the five CAUs are astutely selected to be involved in the functioning of personality and its expressions, it should be noted that each CAU is presently characterizable only in broad, sweeping terms—as names for mental domain categories. Further, there is no theoretical rule of how CAUs, separately and in dynamic connection, specifically should influence the individual's experience and subsequent behavior. No maximizing or optimizing function is offered by Mischel that might bring integration to his theory. Thus, the conceptualization offers limited predictability. After the fact of behavior, it may be helpful to interpret an experience or behavior in terms of CAUs, but in anticipation, CAUs offer only a characterization, in social learning terms, of cognitive domains that generally may be involved in personality functioning.

The distinction between the "nominal situation" and the "active ingredients" of the situation seems to be partially reminiscent of the distinction made in earlier chapters. Expressed in previous terms, the Mischelian nominal situation may be viewed as existing in physicalistic, "geographic," unstructured terms, and the Mischelian active ingredients situation may be viewed as the "subjective psychological environment" impinging on the individual. The usefulness of conceptualizing the objective psychological environment—which attempts to rise above the nominal but psychologically irrelevant situation to achieve a generally held or normative or "canonical" sense of the demand quality of the situation—does not seem to have been considered or thought to be of import.

However, not uniquely, it is not immediately apparent how, a priori, it is possible to specify what are the subjectively operative active ingredients of situations. It appears that one can only resort to ascertaining post hoc what the particular individual found relevant. If so, troublesome uncertainties and even tautology may arise, as mentioned in chapter 3.

In a relatively unelaborated supplementation to the idea of individual behavioral signatures, the existence of group-characteristic or type-characteristic behavioral signatures is acknowledged—that is, there can be group-common or type-common organization of CAUs and their if–then procedural rules so that situational reactions can be common (Mischel & Shoda, 1999, p. 209; Shoda et al., 1994). It is not indicated, conceptually or empirically, to what extent behavioral signatures may be relatively common. I believe that if there can be a commonality of behavioral signatures, its degree must be empirically assessed to see to what extent the emphasized idea of individual distinctiveness indeed holds and shapes behavior.

Mischel does not explain the basis for the high reliabilities usually surrounding aggregated scores nor the many, many demonstrations of a construct validity for such scores. Indeed, in what can only be regarded with perplexity, he "recognizes the existence of broad overall average individual differences at the aggregate level with regard to which most people can be compared on most dimensions" (Shoda et al., 1994, p. 684). How this recognition of "overall average individual differences" can be reconciled with an emphasis on the distinctiveness of individual behavioral signatures is difficult to comprehend.

In a fundamental sense, the if–then approach of Mischel and the still traditional dispositional (I prefer the term, "structural") approach to personality may be viewed as differing in regard to the breadth (narrow or wide) of the behavioral setting deemed psychologically relevant. As Rosch (1978) has cogently noted in regard to "basic objects" in the natural structure of the environment: "In the perceived world, information-rich bundles of perceptual and functional attributes occur that form natural discontinuities [and] basic cuts in categorization are made at these discontinuities" (p. 31). The Roschian view applies, it seems to me, not only to categories of objects but also to categories of concepts, categories of interpersonal relationships, and categories of situations.

In regard to the Mischelian view of distinctive individual–situation relations, one must ask whether an approach in terms of idiosyncratic if–then understanding represents a basic cut of the individual's situational universe or whether broader and more humanly common situation categories would cut or function empirically better, as being more basic and certainly easier to consider, even in regard to the individual involved. It merits remembrance that, as G. W. Allport (1937) noted, traits (or personality structures) "render many stimuli functionally equivalent, and … initiate and guide consistent (equivalent) forms of adaptive and expressive behavior" (p. 295). So, conjointly with the ability to make "exquisite discriminations" among situations as emphasized by Mischel, there remains a remarkable ability to make deep generalizations about situations.

The current Mischelian approach takes the position that if–then understandings are correctly narrow and therefore are individually distinctive in specifying reactions to the particular situation. The structural approach takes the view that certain environments as subjectively perceived by all commonly acculturated individuals bear a broad family resemblance to each other. Which conceptualization is correct or more correct? Or, phrased perhaps better, which conceptualization logically should be exhausted first before going on to the other?

Mischel in his idiographic focus suggested that analysis of intraindividual organization and regularities of individual functioning should come first. Only subsequently should personality psychologists seek pattern features common to groups or types or other categories of people (Shoda et al., 1994). I contend that the scientific pursuit of full idiographic understanding is certainly slow and laborious, even an infinite task, resulting only in a surfeit of phenomenologies.

Instead, I will wager that broader if–then dimensions or generalized schemas of understanding will prove to be seen as more information-rich and as more likely to represent the underlying basic units of personality behavior. Indeed, the recent recognition by Mischel of the existence of if–then relations common to groups and types seems to be a chink in the claim of idiosyncrasy and uniqueness. It is of further interest to note that Wright, early involved in proposing the conditional, if–then approach, while still attending trenchantly to contextual considerations, now takes a broader, more common orientation on the different situational reactions and responses of three differently diagnosed but all maladaptive child groups (Wright, Zakriski, & Drinkwater, 1999). These three groups each have what is recognizable as a distinctive contextual pattern. Of even further interest, there often seem to be further if–then clusterings in a group already diagnostically split off from the larger undifferentiated sample. For example, there seem to be two different kinds of if–then patternings within a group already grossly labeled as "externalizing" (Wright & Zakriski, in press). If so (and likely so), "one might begin to bridge the existing gap between syndromal assessment tools [i.e., involving the aggregation approach]—which are efficient but contextually insensitive—and fine-grained case-specific functional analyses—which are contextually sensitive but often laborious, idiosyncratic, and difficult to compare" (Wright & Zakriski, in press, p. 27). Bridging the gap would seem to require keener and therefore narrower but not yet narrow definitions of still too broad constructs. By proceeding from this direction, more acutely based aggregations should be more contextually responsive but without achieving the complete idiosyncrasy that perhaps may represent ultimate truth (or perhaps only ultimate unreliability). By improved conceptual or empirically based groupings, a more context-responsive aggregation approach may much improve to the point where a full idiosyncratic effort would add little but an endless phenomenology.

A strong point made by Funder (2001) impresses me. He commented that although much attention is addressed to the "if" of the if–then conjunction, little attention has been directed toward the "then" consequent. Just as we have to think about and conceptualize the stimulus, equal thought must approach just what is meant by the idea of behavior.

A final crucial difference is in the way delay of gratification is viewed by Mischel and by me. Mischel, in his early work and in his current conceptualization, considers delay of gratification as an unalloyed achievement, as signifying "maturity" and "willpower."[3] However, I believe there is more to life than delay of gratification, per se. From my theoretical (and experiential) perspective, I believe it is conceptually advantageous to separate impulse control from adaptation. Certainly, the degree of delay between urge and action is usually a sign of psychosocial adaptation. But it is also the case that the degree of delay imposed between urge and action may itself often be maladaptive (cf., e.g., J. H. Block & Block, 1980; Dickman, 1990; King, 1996). In other words, overcontrol may lead to personal immobilization and adaptive rigidity. And undercontrol, if not too extreme, can have adaptive implications by contributing to spontaneity and warmth, creativity, and the seizing of opportunities lost if unclaimed.

Metcalfe and Mischel do not take their thinking so far as to consider the possibility of excessive delay of gratification, an indicator of overcontrol. If overcontrol is accepted as an indubitable and appreciable way individuals may develop (as I have attempted to argue in preceding chapters), the account of Mischel and Metcalfe seems incomplete. They only offer a theoretical rationale for the hot undercontroller moving toward cool resilience. They do not recognize the existence of personality overcontrol. Further, they do not recognize that developmentally a new child advances from undercontrol to overcontrol and only then to resilience. Mischel and Metcalfe combine and confound the last two of these steps. Although undercontrol may be seen as hot, the other extreme— overcontrol—should be viewed as a problem of unexpressivity, reten-

---

[3]It may be the case that for a canny lower-class kid living in a poor and chancy world, immediate accepting of a chocolate bar from a foreign stranger may not imply inability to delay awaiting a larger chocolate bar sometime in the unpredictable future from the unknown person. Rather, the kid may simply be opting for a bird in the hand rather than two in an unknown bush.

tiveness, and interpersonal unease. The psychopathology of overcontrol is not especially talked about by Mischel but is essentially submerged without acknowledgement within the cool concept. I would suggest instead that overcontrol warrants being perceived as behaviorally cold.

The particular hot–cool predictions Metcalfe and Mischel offer seem to fall within what is generally understood in developmental and personality psychology. These predictions receive their major support from the research program of Mischel a quarter century ago. There is something outworn in these predictions, I suggest, as we face a new millennium.

Chapter 11

Prescript: Developmental Aspects of Ego Control and Ego-Resiliency

It devolves, as an intellectual responsibility, to attempt a developmental analysis of our theoretical concepts. Under different terminology, it seems to me that various antecedent aspects of articulation, ego-permeability vis-à-vis tension and vis-à-vis the stimulus environment, and resiliency affecting both impulses and percepts have been offered by various writers. In the field of developmental psychology, these various writings often center on what has been called "regulation," a global term that connotatively encompasses important adaptive phenomena but not in a specific, unifying way. The term requires closer and more analytic consideration than it has sometimes received.

GENERAL CONSIDERATIONS

The Conception of Regulation

Definitionally, the term regulation, by dictionary and thesaurus, carries such meanings as "adjusting," "synchronizing," "coordinating," "managing," "phasing," "ordering." It means *adaptive modulation*. Thought of as applying to an adaptively governed mechanical system (e.g., a motor or engine), the term means responsively speeding up as necessary but also responsively slowing down as necessary. Thought of in psychological terms, it should be remembered it does not mean increasing containment of action or perception per se. Besides the possibility of adaptively requiring an increase of behavioral or perceptual restriction, the idea of regulation also means the possibility of adaptively decreased behavioral or perceptual restriction—either direction of change can mean regulation, depending on the larger situational context.

In personality development, all regulation depends on context, especially on age-relevant pushes and pulls and on quotidian rhythms of environment and person. Psychologists have, in my view, focused one-sidedly on the regulation term as seeming, and necessarily, to imply an increase in containment. There has been a neglect of its further included meaning—regulation also implies, if circumstance or possibility warrants, a lessening of directive perceptual and behavioral management. A drink before dinner after a hard-working day, viewing an interesting movie in an evening, convivial times with friends; taking a holiday—these as well are instances of regulation per se. Thought of in this larger sense, regulation means what has in this book been called resiliency.

Regarding Genetics and Personality

One cannot begin a discussion of experiential development without considering those aspects of development contingent upon intrinsic personal qualities existing prior to experience. Overall, the empirical literature on genetics and socialization (e.g., Loehlin, 1998; Plomin & Caspi, 1998; Plomin & Caspi, 1999) suggests to me that something akin to the constructs of ego control and ego perceptualization can be discerned in the diverse studies and findings reported. Although not specifically studied as such in genetics research, they would seem to be importantly (albeit not completely) temperamental, appreciably a function of inborn genes and perhaps irreversible congenital (perinatal or neonatal) influences. Longitudinal study of three decades regarding ego control supports this view (J. Block, 1993). With respect to ego resilience, the genetic evidence seems to be somewhat obscure and may be gender-linked. The actualization of differentiation, although experientially based, likely is constrained more than a little by intrinsic genetic capacity.

However, many anomalies remain. Molecular findings seeking to relate one of the dopamine receptors to novelty-seeking (under- control and underperception) remain uncertain and premature (Plomin & Caspi, 1998). An attention-gaining finding by Lesch et al. (1996) connecting serotonin transporter gene polymorphism to anxiety has failed numerous efforts at replication (e.g., Ebstein, Gritsenko, & Nemanov, 1997; Flory et al., 1999; Gelernter, Kranzler, Coccaro, Siever, & New, 1998; Greenberg, McMahon, & Murphy, 1998). We cannot comfortably explain why almost no heritabilities are found in an adoptive study but are substantial in twin studies (Plomin, Corley, Caspi, & Fulker, 1998). There appear to be important differences in heritability as a function of gender (Jang, Livesley, & Vernon, 1998), an unexpected result. Surprisingly, great differences in heritability are reported across age cohorts (Pedersen & Reynolds, 1998). The meta-analytic finding that monozygotic and dizygotic twins both diverge with the passage of time evidences the diminishing influence of genes with age and an increasing influence of the nonshared environment (McCartney, Harris, & Bernieri, 1990). The frequent finding of the variance unimportance of the "shared family environment" seems based on neglect of the unique place the individual usually has within (and without) the particular family context and otherwise requires further theoretical, methodological, and meta-analytic evaluation (Turkheimer & Waldron, 2000).

All in all, I think it wisest for now to delay close conclusions regarding the role of genetics in personality. Further reflection on the logic of whether genes and the environment truly can be separately estimated would be salutary. As Gottlieb (1996, p. 92) remarked:

> The procedures of quantitative behavior genetics deal with "how much" and not with how. It assumes gene and environment contributions are additive and not interactive, as developmentally we know them to be. The size of heritabilities varies as a result of different ages or stages of development. And the heritabilities apply to populations (whose parameters can be various or wittingly changed) and do not apply to individuals.

If the effects of genes and the environment are inextricably fused—as I believe—can the interaction of genes and environment be evaluated when the very term "interaction," presumes the prior separation of genes and environment? We should keep abreast of the import of genetic research for psychology but we should resist "geneticization—thinking of ourselves as readouts of our genes" (Hubbard, 1995, p. 10). As Marks and Nesse (1994) reminded us, "our nervous system is neither a tabula rasa nor a clockwork machine" (p. 256). Genes provide "recipes," not "blueprints" for subsequent behaviors.

So much for genetics, at least here.

The Basic Dilemma of Ego Development

There are inevitable problems besetting a starting human being in forming a modus vivendi and these problems may be broadly characterized in terms of ego development.[1]

If the infant beginning life is to become adaptively attuned to the surrounding psychosocial environment, perceptual and behavioral impulse cannot indefinitely be allowed free rein. The immediate and societal environments inevitably will find and declare unrestrained impulse expression is intolerable. The capacity to regulate or modulate impulse must be developed by the child to avoid societal dysfunction. Adaptive perceptions and behaviors consequently arise or are shaped by the surround. By these developments, the potentially dangerous and also potentially enticing world existing beyond the child becomes less fearsome and more controllable. Adverse consequences remain untriggered while pleasing consequences become more likely by the judicious invocation of behavioral and perceptual impulse modulation. Such impulse modulation develops over time via the maturation and experientially derived construction of various personality structures or substructures.

Many of these maturations or invocations involve a strong, affectively directed cognitive component. In psychoanalytic terminology, these personality structures serve to bring the individual, otherwise bent on maximizing the "pleasure principle," reluctantly under the governance of the preemptive "reality principle." There is a "hedonism of the future" (Freud, 1950) wherein anticipations of possible or likely pleasure are tempered by anticipations of possible or likely pain. To cite Freud (1966), "our total mental activity is directed toward achieving pleasure and avoiding unpleasure …. It is automatically regulated by the pleasure principle." (p. 443)

In the terms set forth in this book, it can be said that the human goal is to be as undercontrolled as possible and as overcontrolled as necessary. When one is more undercontrolled than is adaptively effective or more overcontrolled than is adaptively required, one is failing in life. The interrelated, sequentially organized set of personality structures is marshaled to give priority to avoidance of immediate threats to the viability of the individual. Within that overriding constraint, the personality system is further disposed so as to gratify the individual and to enhance long-term viability (e.g., reproductive fitness).

---

[1]Much of what immediately follows draws on Block and Kremen (1996).

This evolution-derived, dual, but hierarchically organized system attempts to resolve the contrary pulls of life and may be taken as what the term ego means in the present context. Phenomenologically, when the ego system is functioning well and the external surround is passably secure, the individual is zestful about life, takes in new knowledge, and experiences a sense of coherence and self-esteem. A sense of incoherence and an absence of self-esteem are subjective signs to the individual that the ego system is not working decently. When the ego system functions adaptively, the individual includes, among other qualities, affective awareness and responsivity and therefore has developed and now can count on enduring interpersonal relatedness (Epstein, 1994).

Ego Functioning Structures

Ego-functioning structures are orientations or premises implemented by behavioral routines or perceptualizing schematas; they are mental representations of or generalizations from interpersonal transactions; they are relational rules or scripts. These behavioral– perceptual principles include orientation to contextually warranted delay of gratification, rejection of contextually unwarranted delay of gratification, inhibition of aggression (which might elicit dangerous or unloving reactions from others), caution in unstructured situations, and playfully sentient experiencing of the environment. They may also include what attachment theory calls "internal working models" of relations oriented via evolution to effectively (i.e., affectively!) access the sense of secure love that prevents a feeling of abandonment (Bowlby, 1973). They may include what Freud called "experimental action" and Miller later called a "thought laboratory"—internal cognitive constructions and manipulations of anticipated, alternatively possible behaviors so as to foresee likely consequences—and so on.

The various ego structures involved in modulating perceptual and behavioral impulse are interrelated and auto-organized. Following dynamic system principles, these ego structures are invoked sequentially as the individual responds to and acts on the flux of experience, facing different contextual demands and different contextual opportunities. In psychology, these adaptive procedures are familiarly known as, for example, modules, mechanisms, routines, schemata, scripts, procedural rules, or production systems. Developmentally, motivational dynamics mold a usually only slowly changing personality system that, although it ultimately may be said to be unique, is much like other personality systems forged by facing equivalent adaptational problems. In many ways, we are all quite similar.

The interrelations and sequencing of evolved ego structures may be ineffective or effective in maintaining the personality system of the individual within the bounds of psychological viability. Psychological viability for the individual entails a tolerable anxiety level, a tolerable mesh with situational impingements, and a tolerable level of behavioral and perceptual impulse expression. If the evolved linkages of ego structures are relatively primitive and permit only one or two impulse routes, impulse—perceptual or behavioral—is responded to categorically, either with rather full expression or rather full containment. The behavioral and perceptual consequences of such limited alternatives are likely to be maladaptive. Societally or subjectively, the individual has too little or too much impulse modulation.

When the evolved linkages of ego structures are complex and permit multiple routes for impulse expression and containment, thus keeping the personality system within tenable bounds or permitting the finding again of psychologically tenable adaptational modes, the individual has evolved what herein has been called ego-resiliency of behavior and of perception. Many of the lower level mentational systems may be used by later evolved, more dynamic functional systems creating true regulation. Rothbart (1989) discussed ways in which impulse modulation (ego control) and ego-resiliency may share common precursors, especially in regard to various temperamental dimensions. Her later construct of effortful control (Ahadi & Rothbart, 1994) impresses me as largely similar to the construct of ego resilience.

As noted in chapter 2, the idea of resilience may be viewed as implying a characterological, "trait-like" quality of an individual. The term implies more than a highly specific, one-time behavior; it implies that the hallmark of psychological health is the individual's versatility in serving internal motivations and needs by a complementary coupling of external affordances with the contextual constraints and desires successively presenting themselves. Depending on impinging psychological presses, ego resilience implies the ability to change from and also return to the individual's characteristic level of ego modulation after temporary, accommodation-requiring stressing or pulling influences are no longer acutely present (J. Block, 1982). The problem of psychological development is to move toward resiliency or, less optimally, to find a life recess wherein resiliency is not seriously or continuously required.

The Beginning Neonate

Developmentally, regulative mechanisms and substructures maturate over time, with especially rapid change during the first several months and years of life. Initially, they reflect species-typical modal action and perceiving patterns (Barlow, 1977) adaptively designed for the evolutionarily expectable environment. These modal patterns may be further affected by individual temperamental proclivities and by developmentally relevant ecosystem constraints. And, further superimposed, there may be inborn, not genetically derived nor genetically transmissible, characteristics influencing the individual's regulation development.

The lower order patterns and individual components given by birth to the neonate immediately begin to be tempered by experience and the affordances provided by the actual physical and caretaker environment. Various skills evolve and come into play: for instance, perceptual control, object permanence, various forms of memory and their retrieval, intentionality, self–object differentiation, and categorization. Thus, the basic cognitive ingredients for a perceptual and behavioral control system are built up as the infant commences the ontological task of evolving specially tuned organizing or regulative principles—at first primitive—for expectancies and behavior regarding the received world.

The created primitive organizing principles are, in turn, themselves further organized, particularly when the mentation milestones of representational thinking and language acquisition are reached. Their complicated and even complex development allows the child to increasingly elaborate a model of self and its cognized relationships to others. In the same sense that individuals learn and then "learn to learn" (Bateson, 1942, 1951; Harlow, 1949), individuals after achieving proximate associative learning then learn to abstract from their variety of locally relevant mentations to form substructures of understandings and ultimately a higher order, affective–motivational "structure of structures." This structure of structures regularizes stable, long-range goals, a sense of self, values, identifications and interests, all of which are integral to modulation and regulation (Shapiro, 1965, 1996). The evolved time sense has special cognitive implications for both the frequent usefulness of a delaying of gratification and a compensating awareness that human time does not stretch on indefinitely and therefore does not warrant anticipation of an infinite future.

These higher order systems do not so much act "against" impulse as seek or provide organizing, motivating, and life-defining contexts within which the individual acts. It is through the direction provided by these ultimately affective internal considerations that a deep coherency is imposed on behavior, thus permitting the emergence and discernment of what is called character.

To the extent that the linkages within and among these systems—both lower and higher order—are responsive and flexible and allow anxiety to remain within tenable bounds, they will permit coherent, consistent, and sufficiently adaptive behavior in the encountered world (J. Block & Kremen, 1996). Motivational tension will be shaped, modified, or elaborated by established structures. Actions and construals will reflect these shapings and modifications, and behavior will appear well-modulated and appropriate to the situation.

But when the linkages of motivational tensions to established perceptual and action structures do not mesh because of inconsistent, conflictual, failed, or blocked connections within a personality system especially strongly committed to the avoidance of anxiety, overrestricted behavior can be expected to follow. Behavior and perception will appear overly modulated, and the expression of impulses or perceptions will be highly delayed, distorted, or absent. This attenuation of expression initially, and perhaps indefinitely, serves to limit anxiety by avoiding the potential dangers of adaptive uncertainty, by maintaining affectional support from others, or by the preservation of the person's own positive self-regard. With the passage of time, and the convenient mentational development of perceptual and behavioral automaticity, containment is often invoked reflexively, without introspective awareness of its deep affective basis.

Insufficient containment can be viewed as a function of poorly organized lower order or higher order ego systems. As noted earlier, these maturational deficits may be due to temperamental (i.e., inborn) givens limiting the development of attentional–behavioral subsystems and systems. Or there may be an absence of the usually provided normative experiential shapings that compose in the developing child both lower order attentional–behavioral substructures and the overarching higher ego systems. In individuals who are undercontrollers, activated motivations are relatively untempered and unmodulated and therefore will be expressed relatively immediately and directly in behavior.[2] Such behaviors are almost inevitably societally maladaptive if only because societies require certain conventions and structures for behavior.

---

[2]As previously noted, the absence of inhibition, or uninhibition, should be distinguished from the notion of disinhibition. Uninhibition is due to deficits in control structures and is manifested as undercontrol. In contrast, disinhibition refers to circumscribed failures of generally present inhibition. Disinhibition, occasionally manifested by some overcontrolled personalities, involves the abrupt, stark, and usually temporary cessation of usually quite-rigidly held controls. In a most useful paper, Frosch (1977) distinguished between "acting out" (disinhibition) and "acting up" (uninhibition).

A key aspect of development is the degree to which the individual is bound or committed to the elements of the higher order ego systems (see Shapiro, 1965, for a further discussion). Thus, when values, goals, identifications, self-concepts, and investments in others are rigidly held, there will be a higher likelihood for early conflict between a person's sense of real or ideal self and personally errant impulses. However, developmentally, there may be subsequently less subjectively experienced anxiety because rigid control permits forfending and foreclosing anticipations. Thus, although risky behaviors and disturbing feelings are avoided, little is ventured by the overcontainer.

At the other extreme, when values, goals, identifications, self-concepts, and investments in others are unarticulated, poorly formed, or tenuously held, the tendency will be for the individual to be expressive relatively immediately, directly, and primitively. There will be fewer internal resources for modulating or delaying urges to act, or for attenuating frustration. There often is little introspection in undercontainers or, where there is lengthy introspection, the introspection may suddenly be abandoned without clear recognition of the basis for the subsequent impulsive behavior. After the fact of emitted impulsive behavior, a consequence may be an increased vulnerability to anxiety (and guilt) because the person will so often be poorly prepared for the unforeseen consequences of these impulsive actions.

Gender Differences in Ego Control and Ego-Resiliency

Interactions between gender and parenting practices have often been noted in studies of the socialization of impulse (Brody & Shaffer, 1982; Grusec & Goodnow, 1994). These effects may be attributable to sex-linked differences in the effects and saliences of parental pressures on children. Numerous studies detail differential treatment of girls and boys by both parents and teachers (for a substantial review, see, e.g., J. Block, 1983).

Parenting practices may influence boys and girls differently because the organizational properties of gender-based self-structures such as identities, roles, values, orientations and the like may differentially mediate the effect of parental socialization behaviors. These self-structures themselves may also serve as higher order ego systems, leading the personality to be differentially organized as a function of gender. In particular, mothers' and fathers' behaviors may create in daughters and sons different affective relations between the generations involved, between same-sex and opposite-sex dyads.

There is a general trend, noted in the gender literature, for males to be undersocialized, leading to personality patterns emphasizing independence, autonomy and an agentic orientation. There is also a trend for females to be oversocialized, leading to personality patterns emphasizing obedience, caution, dependence, and a communal, interpersonal orientation (Bakan, 1966; J. H. Block, 1973, 1983).[3]

In abstract, Piagetian terms, boys are relatively accommodative and girls are relatively assimilative (Block, 1984, p. 206). This latter trend may well change, given recent cultural or subcultural shifts in women's roles, ambitions, and orientations to work and family. However, it is likely that many traditional orientations will continue to influence childrearing practices and the gender-linked messages received by children. These trends serve as background contexts perhaps altering the meanings and impacts of parenting behaviors for children's personality development, including their modal stage of ego control and ego resilience.

MOLDING PSYCHOLOGICAL DEVELOPMENT

The preceding theoretical characterization arises from a particular language system and seeks to paint the individual's formation of ego structure in broad and intrapersonal strokes. But many psychologists will prefer an alternative, less abstract, and more problem-oriented way of describing how resiliency or regulation are molded in the developing human.

To propose differently and more traditionally how regulatory skills develop or fail to develop in individuals, it is necessary to remember that development always occurs in a relational context. "Development is dialectical and not linear. What happens to a person all along the way, and what that person makes happen, will continuously affect her or his biological, psychological and social growth and development" (Hubbard, 1995, p. 8).

In folk culture and in formal psychology's short history, it has become recognized that children, through the interpersonal relations they experience, generally become socialized—they acquire capacities to regulate their own behavior in keeping with the prescriptions and proscriptions of the cultural group within which they are raised.

Accordingly, the socialization literature—oriented toward how the infant becomes functionally societal (and perhaps is also well served

---

[3]Girls do not learn to be helpless; rather, they do not learn how not to be helpless.

experientially)—has largely focused on the development of what is synonymously called self-control (e.g., Kanfer & Karoly, 1972), emotional control (e.g., Gross & John, 1997), self-regulation (e.g., Baumeister & Heatherton, 1996; Kopp, 1982), or emotional regulation (e.g., Kopp, 1989).[4] The rationale for such focus follows the widespread recognition that the capacity to delay responding to immediate environmental contingencies or to emotional or somatic pressures is a prerequisite for planful, organized, and directed adaptive responding.

In much of what follows, I lean heavily—both in apposition to and in augmentation of—Kopp's essays over the past 20 years (1982, 1989, 1997). She has presented some closely considered, comprehensive, and influential essays on how self-control, self-regulation, and emotional regulation come about.

In an early article, Kopp emphasized what she called self-control and later focused on the regulation of emotional distress. In her first account, self-control was viewed as becoming self-regulation when flexibility is added to the child's adaptational repertoire through modeling and incorporating the precepts of caregivers. Later, the necessary partnership of child and caregiver was viewed as promoting emotional regulation when the self-control regulatory rules catalyzed by the caregiver are assumed by the child. That is, a process of caregiver-assisted emotion regulation is presented as the route to self-control and then self-regulation; the intertwinings of caregiver–child suffice to explain, sequentially, the achievement of emotional regulation, self-control, and self-regulation.

Kopp's reasoning is integrative, and telling in many respects of contemporary socialization views. However, it merits mention that the descriptive perspective applied by Kopp is that of a cognitivist; she focuses on the cognitive requisites necessary as grundlage for the development of impulse-control in infancy and toddlerhood. She discusses changes over time in an infant's or child's behavior as due primarily to the formation of associative learnings, representations, recall memory, intentionality, goal-directedness, use of means, object constancy, and other cognitive achievements useful for socialization. The emotional impetus to such cognitive development is not sufficiently considered: "The rationale underlying the motive to obey parents ... is beyond the scope of this article." (Kopp, 1982, p. 204)

---

[4]It will be remembered that in chapter 2 I argued that the term "self" is a misnomer in this context because the sense of the word self as involving a sense of awareness is usually not intended. However, because of its ubiquitous invocation, I use the (uncertain) term here.

In my view, however, the omission of attempting to understand the child's deep and affective motivations importantly limits an effort to understand just what is going on psychologically in the child. In contrast to preoccupation with cognitive phenomena per se, some developmental and personality psychologists (e.g., J. Block, 1982; Izard, 1993; Malatesta, 1988; Zajonc, 1980, 1984) have suggested that matters of "hot" affect or emotion precede and dominate—directly or indirectly—supposedly "cool" and emotionally uninfluenced cognition. If so, the achievement of control of behavior cannot be sufficiently understood by focusing only on its cognitive requisites; the role of affect must be considered.

Regarding cognition and affect in the first couple of phases of neonate and infancy development toward self-regulation, there is not much that has been or can be said definitively about early ontogeny. These phases are undetailedly and uncontroversially pictured, if only because one is limited in describing an empirically unknown and unanalyzable time. Thus, a beginning phase of neurophysiological modulation is posited during the first several neonatal months. There is further nervous system maturation, reflex activity becomes more organized, discomforts become more soothable, there arises a wakefulness cycle in closer correspondence to the lightness of days and the darkness of nights.

A second phase involves sensorimotor modulation, the latter part of the first year. During this time, the infant learns certain simple voluntary acts in response to momentary motivations or intruding percepts. He or she experiences the feel of his or her own intentions and motor actions. In all societies the world over, infants at about the age of six months develop stranger anxiety as they start to crawl away from the mother and therefore encounter unassimilable strangers more often (Marks, 1987). Affectively, some interactions with caregivers, such as in the tempo of parental response to arousal, the availability of caregivers, and the emotional responsivity and tone of parents, may lead to early learnings that serve as precursors to higher order control structures important to later ego control. Theorists have speculated about global, affectively based, and primitive propositions evolved by infants, such as conceptions of the availability, dependability and trustworthiness of others (Emde, Biringen, Clyman, & Oppenheim, 1991; Erikson, 1950; Sroufe, 1979).

A major shift in parenting practices and in cognitive capacities occurs with the acquisition of language. With language, the child become open to the verbal regulation of behavior, with increasingly distal control by parents, increasingly precise and differentiated acquisition of knowledge, and increasing potential for influencing parents' behavior. Kopp (1982) described how the development of representational thought associated with this milestone leads to the use of internal language in impulse control.

A second development occurring at about the same period in childhood is the emergence of a concept of self, an awareness of one's person as an object (Harter, 1983). This achievement involves both a representational system for storing knowledge and a system for autoperspectivizing the individual as agent. Lewis (1991) discussed the role of self-awareness in the emergence of such emotions as shame, pride, and guilt. These emotions, which involve some reference to internal standards, may represent important motivators furthering the child's active collaboration in the socialization process. The organization of an autoperspectivizing system signifies a vast increase in the capacity of the child to acquire value-laden information and propositions about himself and his relations with others (Cooley, 1902; Mead, 1934; Sullivan, 1953). It is likely that this development sets the stage for the hierarchical elaboration of ego control and ego-resiliency, in which lower order perceptual, cognitive, and behavioral capacities are linked to higher order affective–motivational and goal-directed systems.

The proposition that ego regulation will increase as internal structures, both affective–motivational and cognitive, evolve leads to the question of what parenting behaviors will facilitate or impede structure development in offspring.

A central finding in the developmental literature on the optimal conditions for moral internalization is that affective arousal must be within an optimal range for effective learning to occur (Hoffman, 1977). In particular, the overarousal of negative affect occurring in conflicted parent–child relations or in chaotic homes may impede adequate development of internal structures. A second characteristic of parenting that may affect children's development of regulatory structures is the consistency or inconsistency by which parental messages and discipline are maintained.

Indeed, there is some evidence for a link between ego control and the degree of structure and predictability experienced in the family environment. Studying early parenting antecedents of ego control in adults, J. H. Block and Block (1972) divided participants into three groups: overcontrollers, undercontrollers, and appropriate or resilient controllers, separately by sex. They found evidence that overcontrollers had experienced families emphasizing structure and order, whereas the family backgrounds of undercontrollers were character-ized by conflict and a lack of structuring. Block and Block emphasized the affective climate of the household and the availability of parental figures for nurturance and modeling. In another study (J. H. Block, Block, & Morrison, 1981), complex relationships between ego control and an index of parental agreement on child-rearing were found. These relationships differed by sex: Parenting agreement was associ-ated with relative overcontrol and compliance in boys and relative undercontrol and assertiveness in girls.

Similar conclusions have been reached by workers investigating parenting effects on the development of aspects of self-control. For in-stance, Lytton (1977) found that the most important predictors of com-pliance were mother's consistency of rule enforcement, along with her encouragement of mature action, use of psychological rewards, and fre-quency of play with the child. He concluded that: "practices that lead to cognitive structure, generalization, and generally age-appropriate de-velopment … are the variables most strongly predictive of the develop-ment of compliance" (p. 249). In their investigation of the family correlates of aggression in boys, McCord, McCord, and Howard (1961) grouped individuals as nonaggressive, assertive, and aggressive. Al-though direct measures of ego control were not included, the nonaggressive group differed from the other two groups in being what appears to be relative overcontrol. As opposed to the other two groups, the nonaggressive boys had parents who "guided by a consistent set of controls [and] exposed [them] to examples of social conformity" (McCord et al., 1961, p. 92).

There are a number of developmental phases wherein clear differ-ences in caregiving can be expected to shape the child who evolves. Three of these molded manifestations are considered more closely here: compliance, aggression–prosocial behavior, and imitation–mod-eling. The conceptual issues surrounding socialization can be well rep-resented by considering these three domains of inquiry. They are not truly separate, of course, but each of them warrants specific attention. A full or sufficient literature review of these large topics is not presented; rather, a few comments and some points of difference from other view-points are offered.

Regarding Compliance

It is with the compliance phase (from 9–12 to 18 or more months) that interpretive complications arise. The child displays an appreciation of the social and task demands placed by caregivers and has a beginning ability to comply to commands, "to initiate, maintain, modulate, or cease physical acts, communications, and emotional signals" (Kopp, 1982, p. 204) to meet those demands. Such compliance "represents an important transition period along the path of self-regulation" (p. 204). From a related standpoint, it has been suggested that a toddler's disposition to obey adults who seek to inhibit socially unacceptable behavior is itself an indicator of adaptive behavior (Lytton, 1977; Matas, Arend, & Sroufe, 1978) or a child's commitment to become involved in a prosocial system (Richters & Waters, 1991).

Several aspects of this representation may warrant closer consideration. It needs to be recognized that the ability to comply often may not mean true agreement of the complier with the obedience-commander. Rather, compliance may mean subservience to or appeasement of another, a giving in, a toeing of the mark. Or it may mean polite or deceptive acquiescence. Compliance does not necessarily mean agreeing with the particular, perhaps arbitrary demand for compliance. Certainly, the ability of a child to comply may be a necessary developmental step to adaptively achieve, and it may—but also may not—augur the subsequent internal acceptance by the child of external rules and procedures. However, as first manifested, compliance represents an equivocal stage of development. What happens later developmentally is informing of the meaning of the earlier manifestation of compliance.

The psychological state of the child when compliance is first demanded needs to be considered. In the compliance situation, pressure is being or has been applied, the shape of the desired behavior is strongly suggested by the caregiver, fear of or affective reliance on the pressurer is heavily present. Under this circumstance, it is easy for a relating and therefore vulnerable child to emit the desired behavior. The child's immediate problem of what to do, of how to respond, is removed by simple compliance. If anger of the pressurer was presumed (correctly or incorrectly) by the child, it is deflected; if the loss of affectional sustenance was feared, then affection is continued. An otherwise consequential anxiety-inducing problem is avoided.

However, the attractively simple solution of compliance only means the replacement by the child of previous impulsive behavior with categorical control of impulse or expressivity. It is at this juncture that the nature of the caregiver becomes all-important in the kinds of transactions that ensue. Although obedient behavior by the child is constrained by the caretaker to occur, the resulting obedience may be usually so embraced and surrounded by a loving caregiver as to make compliance feel comfortable and even something affectionally to be sought by the child. Thus, the move to compliance for most children maintains or enhances the survival emotion of love and softens or distracts from potential organismic anxiety. As noted by Londerville and Main (1981), a child's close affective ties to its parents serves as a strong motivator for compliance. In this fashion, a well-reared, normatively compliant child experiences context-attuned responsiveness from caregivers, and the child's compliance may indeed represent a beginning progress toward internal control.

Subsequently, via the concomitance of maturation and experience in living, the child becomes more independent of the rearing surround and thus a more "difficult," less compliant, but more interesting organism. A developing sense of autonomy quickly enough causes automatic compliance per se to be superceded. As Kuczynski, Kochanska, Radke-Yarrow, and Girnius-Brown (1987) have noted, some forms of noncompliance prove to predict advances in social competence.

It is also to be noted that the caregiver-required obedience may sometimes only be a further resultant of a psychologically harsh, insensitive environment. In this not infrequent instance, compliance may derive from a fearful overmodulation of impulse, a restriction of child spontaneity that is the source of labile creativity and interpersonal connection. Crittenden and DiLalla (1988) called such behavior "compulsive compliance," a coping strategy to appease a cruel, unresponsive family environment. Unhappily, if the motivation for early compliance has only been parental mollification, when the compulsively compliant child becomes older he or she may continue into adolescence and beyond as an overcontained individual. Sometimes, during adolescence the child may discover the behavioral autonomy negligently provided by a lack of caregiver attention. The child then may abandon earlier inhibitions he or she felt had to be displayed as a child, especially toward aggressivity.

Thus, the child's learning of compliance, of behavioral inhibitions, of deference to external proscriptions and prescriptions is usually developmentally advancing for the child when it is motivated by lovingly attuned caretaker–child relations. Subsequently, much of this compliance may be differentially supplanted, an adaptive developmental move. Compliance for most is only a temporary and delimited developmental stage, and ideally it should be superceded by flexible, adjusting, context-attuned responsiveness developmentally. Adaptability in the long term requires more than the replacement of unbridled impulsivity with categorical, pervasive, rigid impulse control. This would be overmodulation of impulse, restriction of expressivity, and a going out to the world. Indeed, reflexive compliance that lasts too long is almost a sure sign of overcontrol. In the move toward ego-resiliency, dynamic and resourceful regulation and equilibration of impulses and inhibitions must be achieved.

Certainly, the contribution of impulse control to a child's ability to obey external authority in the light of strong internal presses to act otherwise is not in question. Further, the child's learning of compliance to parental prescriptions, of reflexive, unthinking deference to imposed proscriptions and prescriptions usually does set the stage for developmental advance when it occurs as a replacement for earlier unmodulation. However, such compliance may not necessarily represent an adaptively desirable endpoint. Although compliance is viewed as suggesting the internalization of heretofore external rules and procedures, it may be variously based and represents only a transitory or delimited stage, not a developmental completion.

Compliance, its kinds, and the conditions contributing to and against it are not fully understood; compliance is a noncompliant concept. It is good to know that further thinking and research are being devoted to inquiry regarding its equivocal meaning. (e.g., Emde, 1987; Kochanska & Aksan, 1995; Kochanska, Aksan, & Koenig, 1995; Kochanska et al., 1997; Kochanska, Tjebkes, & Forman, 1998; Vaughn, Kopp, & Krakow, 1984).

Regarding Aggression and Prosocial Behavior

Research on childhood aggression complements studies of prosocial behavior (e.g., Dodge, 1991; McCord et al., 1961; Olweus, 1980; L. Robins, 1995; Rutter, 1997).

The study of aggression may offer clues to understanding conditions leading to the absence of impulse control. However, one should not necessarily equate aggression with impulsivity. The expression of aggression is often immediate and unplanned and thus may indeed be a manifestation of impulsivity, but aggression can also be expressed in more deliberate and planful, nonimpulsive ways. The other side of the coin is that there is nonaggressive impulsivity, for example a spontaneity generously expressing warmth and ease of interpersonal connection.

This point has been brought forward in a study focusing on the differentiation of the antisocial personality pattern from the undercontrolled personality pattern (Block & Gjerde, 1986b). Apparently, antisocial tendencies may be expressed in either or both undercontrolled and overcontrolled ways; the crucial feature of antisociality of either kind being an introspective absence of empathy for the aggressed-against target (see also Pulkkinen & Saastamoinen, 1986). The distinction made between reactive and instrumental aggression has recognized that immediate, impulsive, and unplanned aggression is quite different from aggressive behavior requiring planning, sometimes of an obsessive nature (Feshbach, 1970).

Societally oriented evaluators may often label someone as aggressive, although the errant behavior so classified, when considered psychologically more closely, can be seen to be more a defense or an untargeted reaction to an unstructured situation and the blind frustration it may create. There may be a victim, but fortuitous, not pointed, aggression is involved.

Rising above these distinctions, it is the case that individuals deemed generally aggressive tend generally to lack the ability to inhibit aggressive reactions to evocations—no matter how slight (Feshbach, 1970). As Dodge (1991) has compellingly shown, aggressiveness sometimes is to a fancied provocation. Child rearing that is harsh or nonattentive is related to subsequent aggressive undercontrol (Crittenden & DiLalla, 1988).

Research on prosocial behavior approaches the problem of hurtfulness from the other direction. Conscience development appears to be central, and in its formation, the child's capacity to restrain antisocial or destructive impulses and to behave altruistically traditionally have been emphasized. However, although conscience development and the capacity to refrain from committing transgressions form important components of ego control, especially after the toddler period (Hoffman, 1977; Kochanska, 1993; Kopp, 1982), they cannot serve as stand-ins for the full concept of ego-control.

The key problem is that aspects of conscience and moral behavior, wherein there is a focus on inhibition of aggressive impulses, empirically fail to generalize to other aspects of ego control and conceptually do not accord with the simple behavioral premise of overcontrol. Although sufficient research is lacking in this area, at least conceptually a strong argument can be made that prosocial behavior, empathy, conscience, and thoughtful moral behavior form important aspects of ego resilience (J. Block, 1971) or interpersonal competence (Zahn-Waxler, Radke-Yarrow, Wagner, & Chapman, 1992), not of ego control. In keeping with this hypothesis, at least one study has found no relations between a measure of ego control and measures of moral behavior (Asendorpf & Nunner-Winkler, 1992).

Regarding Imitation–Modeling

The term "internalization" has been shared both by psychoanalytic and social-learning theoretical perspectives. It is viewed as central to the move of behavior from being regulated externally, by others, to being shaped internally, by the consequent individual. However, the summarily descriptive usage of the term has led, more often than not, to conceptual confusion.

The psychoanalytic viewpoint has stressed the motivational bases for the child's adoption of parental attitudes and the parent's moral system. The psychoanalytic emphasis on the development of internal representations of others is a centerpiece of attachment theory. The social-learning perspective, on the other hand, has tended to stress the imitative learning of adult behavior by children. The strength of the social-learning framework has been its ability to empirically support some of its propositions regarding the processes involved.

Learning to delay gratification, to plan for long-term goals, and to inhibit self-involved impulses are learned by children from parents who enforce consistent childrearing. However, are children simply imitating their parents, or are they taking their parents as models? There is an important difference between the two—imitation and modeling.

In imitation, someone is being behaviorally emulated. Emulation, however diverse, provides a quick, unthinking, usually sufficient solution to the individual's behavioral problems. Imitation of others (usually the caregiver) solves the problem of figuring out what to do or how to handle the presenting situation. The individual feels an anxious need for structure ontologically, and assimilation of another's behavioral schema (imitation) provides a convenient, built-in, immediately adaptive way.

In modeling, however, the deep conceptual principles underlying the behaviorally diverse behavior of one's model are slowly discerned. Subsequently, these learned conceptual principles function to shape the individual's own behavior. Modeling behavior is not specifically imitative; it is inductively based and in application necessarily is context-responsive. The modeling individual may behave in ways perhaps quite different from the model but in ways derivative from the model's precepts.

In a sense, imitation may be viewed as a concrete, short-term solution for a specific and immediate behavioral problem, whereas modeling may be viewed as an abstract, long-term, general solution for a host of behavioral problems.

With this definitional distinction in mind, the imitation emphasis of the social learning approach—although in the short term applicable—seems inadequate to account for the full and complex dynamics of individual development. Instead, the psychological taking-in of parents seems to derive from the individual's personality development process of using the structural principles of interpersonal relations to shape his intrapersonal structure (e.g., Loevinger, 1976; Vygotsky, 1960).

How do these internal mental structures come to exist within a person? Much research and contemplation has addressed this question, concerned with how interpersonal transactions (usually between the caregiver and the child) become perceived inductively by the child as patterned, become internal structures in the child, and form the basis of his or her subsequent behavior and ways of perceiving.

Parents provide the child with a framework and a model from which the child organizes his or her own personality system. The child's learnings are filtered through personally evolving assimilative (and therefore accommodative) structures (J. Block, 1982; Grusec & Goodnow, 1994; Loevinger, 1959) and so the effect of parental attitudes and behaviors will depend to a degree on children's cognitive capacities, developmental level, and ongoing concerns and motivations; not on imitation per se.

The modeling of attentive parenting is often linked to "high maturity demands" and increased self-control in children. Parental promotion of autonomy helps development of the cognitive capacities underlying volitional behavior by affording increased opportunities for experimentation and practice. Further, parental encouragement of autonomy may have the consequence for the child of a sense of "self efficacy." So, the structural aspects of parent–child relations may importantly influence the child's understandings of his or her own relation to impulses and capacity for regulation.

Taking dependence as the opposite of autonomy (Eron & Huesman, 1984), it becomes relevant to mention Pulkkinen's (1982) finding of a relation between dependence and subsequent overcontrol. She suggested a parental intrusiveness and excessive control of the child may lead to overdependence on parents and a caution and conservatism. Further, by imitation of parental solutions and mores, identity foreclosure may be intimated (Marcia, 1966).

The degree of model internalization has sometimes been taken as the (easily measurable) degree of similarity between child values and parent values. However, much more may be internalized by children than simply the content of parental values. For instance, youthful protesters adopted their parents' value of commitment to principled action despite disagreeing with their parents' exact political views (Block, 1972; see also Grusec & Goodnow, 1994). It is likely that these highly committed parents employed democratic principles in their childrearing, and that these philosophy-based conceptual modes of relating to their children subsequently were internalized—but not their specific content. It was, then, the formal structure of the parental message, rather than its actual content, that served as guiding principles for the moral development of these children.

Following the modeling principle outlined earlier, rather than the label of internalization, it may be preferable to speak of structuralization: the use by children of earlier experienced interpersonal structures to create structures of intrapersonal schemas.

The structuralization conceptualization leads to a consideration of parents' relation to their own impulses and to their children's impulses. There is some evidence that capricious or uninvolved parents discipline their children in ways that are themselves impulsive, serving the gratification of their own unconstrained needs. Such inattention and inconsistency will impede, by exemplification, their children's development of impulse control (Block, 1971; Loevinger, 1959; McCord et al., 1961). In contrast, parental use of principles to guide their childrearing long has been found associated with higher levels of impulse-control in children (Baumrind, 1971; McCord et al., 1961). This style of parenting is used by authoritative parents, who often follow democratic, egalitarian principles (and by some authoritarian parents) and is linked both to the consistency by which parents enforce rules and to the degree to which parents can delay and modulate the expression of their own impulses.

As Loevinger (1959) concisely remarked regarding so much of what parents try to communicate in rearing their child,

> The chief value of a parental learning theory [about what the child gleans from parents] may well be in providing a model for the child of curbing one's own impulses out of regard for the future welfare of another. The very oversimplification of parental theories may serve to make accessible to the child that his parent is acting on principle rather than on impulse." (p. 150)

References

Achenbach, T. M., & Edelbrock, C. (1989). Diagnostic, taxonomic, and assessment issues. In T. M. Ollendick & M. Hersen (Eds.), *Handbook of child psychopathology* (2nd ed., pp. 53–69). New York: Plenum.

Ahadi, S., & Diener, E. (1989). Multiple determinants and effect size. *Journal of Personality and Social Psychology, 56*, 398–406.

Ahadi, S. A., & Rothbart, M. K. (1994). Temperament, development, and the Big Five. In C. F. Halverson & G. A. Kohnstamm (Eds.), *The developing structure of temperament and personality from infancy to adulthood* (pp. 189–207). Hillsdale, NJ: Lawrence Erlbaum Associates.

Ainslie, G., & Haslam, N. (1992). Hyperbolic discounting. In G. Loewenstein & J. Elster (Eds.), *Choice over time* (pp. 57–92). New York: Russell Sage Foundation.

Allport, F. H. (1955). *Theories of perception and the concept of structure*. New York: Wiley.

Allport, G. W. (1937). *Personality: A psychological interpretation*. New York: Holt.

Allport, G. W. (1961). *Pattern and growth in personality*. New York: Holt, Rinehart & Winston.

Allport, G. W., & Postman, L. (1947). *The psychology of rumor*. New York: Holt.

American Psychiatric Association. (1994). *Diagnostic and statistical manual of mental disorders* (4th ed.). Washington, D.C.: Author.

Ames, A. (1951). Visual perception and the rotating trapezoidal window. *Psychological Monographs, 65*(7), 32.

Angyal, A. (1941). *Foundations for a science of personality*. New York: The Commonwealth Fund.

Anthony, E. J. (1974). The syndrome of the psychologically invulnerable child. In E. J. Anthony & C. Koupernik (Eds.), *Children at psychiatric risk* (pp. 19–37). New York: Wiley.

Arsenian, J., & Arsenian, J. M. (1948). Tough and easy cultures: A conceptual analysis. *Psychiatry, 11,* 377–385.

Asch, S. E. (1956). Studies of independence and conformity: I. A minority of one against a unanimous majority. *Psychological Monographs, 70*(9), 70.

Asendorpf, J. B., Borkenau, P., Ostendorf, F., & van Aken, M. A. G. (2001). Carving nature at its joints: Confirmation of three replicable personality prototypes for both children and adults. *European Journal of Personality, 15,* 169–198.

Asendorpf, J. B., & Nunner-Winkler, G. (1992). Children's moral motive strength and temperamental inhibition reduce their immoral behavior in real moral conflicts. *Child Development, 63,* 1223–1235.

Ashby, W. R. (1960). *Design for a brain: The origin of adaptive behavior.* London: Chapman & Hall.

Ashton, M. C., Jackson, D. N., Helmes, E., & Paunonen, S. V. (1998). Joint factor analysis of the Personality Research Form and the Jackson Personality Inventory: Comparisons with the Big Five. *Journal of Research in Personality, 32,* 243–250.

Atkinson, J. W. (1964). *An introduction to motivation.* Princeton, NJ: Van Nostrand.

Attneave, F., & Arnoult, M. D. (1956). The quantitative study of shape and pattern perception. *Psychological Bulletin, 53,* 452–471.

Bacon, S. J. (1974). Arousal and the range of cue utilization. *Journal of Experimental Psychology, 102,* 81–87.

Baddeley, A. (1986). *Working memory.* Oxford, England: Clarendon Press.

Bakan, D. (1966). *The duality of human existence: An essay on psychology and religion.* Chicago: Rand McNally.

Barkley, R. A. (1997). *ADHD and the nature of self-control.* New York: Guilford Press.

Barlow, D. H. (1988). *Anxiety and its disorders: The nature and treatment of anxiety and panic.* New York: Guilford Press.

Barlow, G. W. (1977). Modal action patterns. In T. A. Sebeok (Ed.), *How animals communicate* (pp. 94–125). Bloomington, IN: University of Indiana Press.

Barratt, E. S. (1965). Factor analysis of some psychometric measures of impulsivenesss and anxiety. *Psychological Reports, 16,* 547–554.

Bartlett, F. C. (1932). *Remembering.* Cambridge, England: Cambridge University Press.

Bateson, G. (1942, April). *Social planning and the concept of "deutero-learning".* Paper presented at the Conference on Science, Philosophy, and Religion (Second Symposium), New York.

Bateson, G. (1951). Conventions of communication: Where validity depends upon belief. In J. Ruesch & G. Bateson (Eds.), *Communication: The social matrix of psychiatry* (pp. 212–227). New York: Norton.

Baumeister, R. F., & Heatherton, T. F. (1996). Self-regulation failure: An overview. *Psychological Inquiry, 7,* 1–15.

Baumeister, R. F., Heatherton, T. F., & Tice, D. M. (1994). *Losing control: How and why people fail at self-regulation.* San Diego, CA: Academic Press.

Baumrind, D. (1971). Current patterns of parental authority. *Developmental Psychology, 4*, 1–103.

Beck, A. T., & Emery, G. (1985). *Anxiety disorders and phobias: A cognitive perspective*. New York: Basic.

Becker, W. C. (1954). Perceptual rigidity as measured by aniseikonic lenses. *Journal of Abnormal and Social Psychology, 49*, 419–422.

Benet-Martinez, V., & Waller, N. (1997). Further evidence for the cross-cultural generality of the Big Seven Model: Indigenous and imported Spanish personality constructs. *Journal of Personality, 65*, 567–598.

Berlinski, D. (1995). *A tour of the calculus*. New York: Pantheon Books.

Berlyne, D. E. (1965). *Structure and direction in thinking*. New York: Wiley.

Bertalanffy, L. v. (1950). *General systems theory*. New York: Braziller.

Bischof, N. (1975). A systems approach toward the functional connections of attachment and fear. *Child Development, 46*, 801–817.

Block, J. (1950). *An experimental investigation of the construct of ego-control*. Unpublished doctoral dissertation, Stanford University, Stanford, CA.

Block, J. (1957). A study of affective responsiveness in a lie-detection situation. *Journal of Abnormal and Social Psychology, 55*, 11–15.

Block, J. (1965). *The challenge of response sets: Unconfounding meaning, acquiescence, and social desirability in the MMPI*. New York: Appleton-Century-Crofts.

Block, J. (1968). Some reasons for the apparent inconsistency of personality. *Psychological Bulletin, 70*, 210–212.

Block, J. (1971). *Lives through time*. Berkeley, CA: Bancroft Books.

Block, J. (1977). Advancing the psychology of personality: Paradigmatic shift or improving the quality of research? In D. Magnusson & N. S. Endler (Eds.), *Psychology at the crossroads: Current issues in interactional psychology* (pp. 37–63). Hillsdale, NJ: Lawrence Erlbaum Associates.

Block, J. (1982). Assimilation, accommodation, and the dynamics of development. *Child Development, 53*, 283–295.

Block, J. (1993). Studying personality the long way. In D. C. Funder, R. D. Parke, C. Tomlinson-Keasy, & K. Widaman (Eds.), *Studying lives through time* (pp. 9–41). Washington, DC: American Psychological Association.

Block, J. (1995a). A contrarian view of the five-factor approach to personality description. *Psychological Bulletin, 117*, 187–215.

Block, J. (1995b). On the relation between IQ, impulsivity, and delinquency: Remarks on the Lynam, Moffitt, and Stouthamer-Loeber (1993) interpretation. *Journal of Abnormal Psychology, 104*, 395–398.

Block, J., & Bennett, L. (1955). The assessment of communication. III. Perceptions and transmission as a function of the social situation. *Human Relations, 8*, 317–325.

Block, J., & Block, J. H. (1951). An investigation of the relationship between intolerance of ambiguity and ethnocentrism. *Journal of Personality, 19*, 303–311.

Block, J., & Block, J. H. (1952). An interpersonal experiment on reactions to authority. *Human Relations, 5*, 91–98.

Block, J., & Block, J. H. (1981). Studying situational dimensions: A grand perspective and some limited empiricism. In D. M. Magnusson (Ed.), *Toward a psychology of situations: An interactional perspective* (pp. 85–103). Hillsdale, NJ: Lawrence Erlbaum Associates.

Block, J., Block, J. H., & Keyes, S. (1988). Longitudinally foretelling drug usage in adolescence: Early childhood personality and environmental factors. *Child Development, 59,* 336–355.

Block, J., & Gjerde, P. F. (1986a). Continuity and transformation in the psychological meaning of category breadth. *Developmental Psychology, 22,* 832–840.

Block, J., & Gjerde, P. F. (1986b). Distinguishing between antisocial behavior and undercontrol. In D. Olweus, J. Block, & M. Radke-Yarrow (Eds.), *Development of antisocial and prosocial behavior: Research, theories, and issues* (pp. 177–206). New York: Academic Press.

Block, J., Gjerde, P. F., & Block, J. H. (1991). Personality antecedents of depressive tendencies in 18-year-olds. *Journal of Personality and Social Psychology, 60,* 726–738.

Block, J., & Kremen, A. M. (1996). IQ and ego-resiliency: Conceptual and empirical connections and separateness. *Journal of Personality and Social Psychology, 70,* 349–361.

Block, J., & Turula, E. (1963). Identification, ego control, and adjustment. *Child Development, 34,* 945–954.

Block, J. H. (1951). *An experimental study of a topological representation of ego-structure.* Unpublished doctoral dissertation, Stanford University, Stanford, CA.

Block, J. H. (1972). Generational continuity and discontinuity in the understanding of societal rejection. *Journal of Personality and Social Psychology, 22,* 333–345.

Block, J. H. (1973). Conceptions of sex role: Some cross-cultural and longitudinal perspectives. *American Psychologist, 28,* 512–526.

Block, J. H. (1983). Differential premises arising from differential socialization of the sexes: Some conjectures. *Child Development, 54,* 1335–1354.

Block, J. H. (1984). How gender differences affect children's orientations to the world. In J. H. Block (Ed.), *Sex role identity and ego development* (pp. 182–206). San Francisco: Jossey-Bass.

Block, J. H., & Block, J. (1972). Parental antecedents of ego-control and ego-resiliency in young children. Unpublished report. Berkeley, CA.

Block, J. H., & Block, J. (1980). The role of ego-control and ego-resiliency in the organization of behavior. In W. A. Collins (Ed.), *Development of cognition, affect, and social relations* (Vol. 13, pp. 39–101). Hillsdale, NJ: Lawrence Erlbaum Associates.

Block, J. H., Block, J., & Morrison, A. (1981). Parental agreement–disagreement on child rearing orientations and gender-related personality correlates in children. *Child Development, 52,* 965–974.

Bock, G. R. (1998). *The limits of reductionism in biology.* New York: Wiley.

Bowlby, J. (1970). Reasonable fear and natural fear. *International Journal of Psychistory, 9,* 79–88.

Bowlby, J. (1973). *Attachment and loss: Separation: Attachment and anger* (Vol. 2). New York: Basic Books.

Bowlby, J. (1986). The nature of the child's tie to his mother. In P. Buckley (Ed.), *Essential papers on object relations* (pp. 153–199). New York: New York University Press.

Broadbent, D. E. (1971). *Decision and stress.* London: Academic Press.

Broadbent, D. E. (1977). The hidden preattentive processes. *American Psychologist, 32,* 109–118.

Brody, G. H., & Shaffer, D. R. (1982). Contributions of parents and peers to children's moral internalization. *Developmental Review, 2,* 31–75.

Bronson, G. (1968). The fear of novelty. *Psychological Bulletin, 69,* 350–358.

Brown, A. L. (1978). Knowing when, where, and how to remember: A problem of metacognition. In R. Glaser (Ed.), *Advances in instructional psychology* (Vol. 1, pp. 77–165). Hillsdale, NJ: Lawrence Erlbaum Associates.

Bruner, J. S. (1957). On perceptual readiness. *Psychological Review, 64,* 123–152.

Bruner, J. S., Goodnow, J. J., & Austin, G. A. (1956). *A study of thinking.* New York: Wiley.

Brunswik, E. (1956). *Perception and the representative design of psychological experiments.* Berkeley, CA: University of California Press.

Brush, F. R., Brush, E. S., & Solomon, R. L. (1955). Traumatic avoidance learning: The effects of CS–US interval with a delayed-conditioning procedure. *Journal of Comparative and Physiological Psychology, 48,* 285–293.

Burton, R. V. (1963). Generality of honesty reconsidered. *Psychological Review, 70,* 481–499.

Butcher, J. N., & Rouse, S. V. (1996). Personality: Individual differences and clinical assessment. *Annual Review of Psychology, 47,* 87–111.

Cacioppo, J. T., & Gardner, W. L. (1999). Emotion. *Annual Review of Psychology, 50,* 191–214.

Cacioppo, J. T., Gardner, W. L., & Berntson, G. G. (1999). The affect system has parallel and integrative processing components: Form follows function. *Journal of Personality and Social Psychology, 76,* 839–855.

Cameron, N. (1951). Perceptual organization and behavior pathology. In R. R. Blake & G. V. Ramsey (Eds.), *Perception: An approach to personality* (pp. 283–306). New York: Ronald Press.

Campos, J. J., Campos, R. G., & Barrett, K. C. (1989). Emergent themes in the study of emotional development and emotion regulation. *Developmental Psychology, 25,* 394–402.

Cantor, N., & Kihlstrom, J. F. (1987). *Personality and social intelligence.* Englewood Cliffs, NJ: Prentice Hall.

Caprara, G. V., Barbaranelli, C., & Comrey, A. L. (1995). Factor analyses of the NEO–PI Inventory and the Comrey Personality Scales in an Italian sample. *Personality and Individual Differences, 18,* 193–200.

Carroll, J. B. (1961). The nature of the data, or how to choose a correlation coefficient. *Psychometrika, 26,* 347–372.

Carroll, J. B. (in press). The five-factor personality model: How complete and satisfactory is it? In H. Braun, D. Wiley, & D. Jackson (Eds.), *The role of constructs in psychological and educational measurement.* Mahwah, NJ: Lawrence Erlbaum Associates.

Carver, C. C., & Scheier, M. F. (1998). *On the self-regulation of behavior.* New York: Cambridge University Press.

Caspi, A., & Silva, P. A. (1995). Temperamental qualities at age 3 predict personality traits in young adulthood: Longitudinal evidence from a birth cohort. *Child Development, 66,* 486–498.

Cattell, R. B. (1941). Some theoretical issues in adult intelligence testing. *Psychological Bulletin, 38,* 392.

Cattell, R. B. (1957). *Personality and motivation structure and measurement.* Yonkers, NY: World Book Company.

Ceci, S. J. (1991). How much does schooling influence general intelligence and its cognitive components? A reassessment of the evidence. *Developmental Psychology, 27,* 703–722.

Cervone, D., & Shoda, Y. (1999). Social–cognitive theories and the coherence of personality. In D. Cervone & Y. Shoda (Eds.), *The coherence of personality: Social–cognitive bases of consistency, variability, and organization* (pp. 3–33). New York: Guilford Press.

Chein, I. (1954). The environment as a determinant of behavior. *Journal of Social Psychology, 39,* 115–127.

Chorpita, B. F. (1998). The development of anxiety: The role of control in the early environment. *Psychological Bulletin, 124,* 3–21.

Church, T. A., & Burke, P. J. (1994). Exploratory and confirmatory tests of the Big Five and Tellegen's three- and four-dimensional models. *Journal of Personality and Social Psychology, 66,* 93–114.

Cloninger, C. R. (1986). A unified biosocial theory of personality and its role in the development of anxiety states. *Psychiatric Developments, 3,* 167–226.

Cloninger, C. R., Surakic, D. M., & Przybeck, T. R. (1993). A psychobiological model of temperament and character. *Archives of General Psychiatry, 50,* 975–990.

Cooley, C. H. (1902). *Human nature and the social order.* New York: Scribner.

Coolidge, F. L., Becker, L. A., DiRito, D. C., Durham, R. L., Kinlaw, M. M., & Philbrick, P. B. (1994). On the relationship of the five-factor model of personality to personality disorders: Four reservations. *Psychological Reports, 75,* 11–21.

Cosmides, L., & Tooby, J. (1987). From evolution to behavior: Evolutionary psychology as the missing link. In J. Dupre (Ed.), *The latest on the best: Essays on evolution and optimality* (pp. 276–306). Cambrdge, MA: MIT Press.

Costa, P. T., & McCrae, R. R. (1980). Still stable after all these years: Personality as a key to some issues in adulthood and old age. In P. B. Baltes & O. G. Brim (Eds.), *Life span development and behaviors* (Vol. 3, pp. 65–102). New York: Academic Press.

Costa, P. T., & McCrae, R. R. (1992a). The five-factor model of personality and its relevance to personality disorders. *Journal of Personality Disorders, 6,* 343–359.

Costa, P. T. J., & McCrae, R. R. (1992b). Four ways five factors are basic. *Personality and Individual Differences, 13,* 653–665.

Costa, P. T., & McCrae, R. R. (1995). Domains and facets: Hierarchical personality assessment using the Revised NEO Personality Inventory. *Journal of Personality Assessment, 29,* 21–50.

Costa, P. T., & McCrae, R. R. (1997). Stability and change in personality assessment: The Revised NEO Personality Inventory in the Year 2000. *Journal of Personality Assessment, 68*, 86–94.

Cowan, P. A., Cowan, C. P., & Schulz, M. S. (1996). Thinking about risk and resilience in families. In E. M. Hetherington & E. A. Blechman (Eds.), *Stress, coping, and resiliency in children and families* (pp. 1–38). Mahwah, NJ: Lawrence Erlbaum Associates.

Crittenden, P. M., & DiLalla, D. L. (1988). Compulsive compliance: The development of an inhibitory coping strategy in infancy. *Journal of Abnormal Child Psychology, 16*, 585–599.

Cronbach, L. J. (1957). The two disciplines of scientific psychology. *American Psychologist, 12*, 671–684.

Crutchfield, R. S. (1955). Conformity and character. *American Psychologist, 10*, 191–198.

Csikszentmihalyi, M. (1990). *Flow: The psychology of optimal experience*. New York: Harper & Row.

Dabady, M., Bell, M., & Kihlstrom, J. F. (1999). Person memory: Organization of behaviors by traits. *Journal of Research in Personality, 33*, 369–377.

Damasio, A. R. (1994). *Descartes' error: Emotion, reason, and the human brain*. New York: Putnam.

Davis, R. C. (1953). Physical psychology. *Psychological Review, 60*, 7–14.

De Raad, B. (1998). Five big, Big Five issues: Rationale, content, structure, status, and crosscultural assessment. *European Psychologist, 3*, 113–124.

Dember, W. N., & Earl, R. (1957). Analysis of exploratory, manipulatory, and curiosity behavior. *Psychological Review, 64*, 91–96.

Depue, R. A., Collins, P. F., & Luciana, M. (1996). A model of neurobiology–environment interaction in developmental psychopathology. In M. F. Lenzenweger & J. J. Haugaard (Eds.), *Frontiers of developmental psychopathology* (pp. 44–77). New York: Oxford University Press.

Dewey, J. (1965). *Philosophy, psychology, and social practice*. New York: Capricorn.

Dickman, S. J. (1990). Functional and dysfunctional impulsivity: Personality and cognitive correlates. *Journal of Personality and Social Psychology, 58*, 95–102.

Digman, J. M. (1997). Higher-order factors of the Big Five. *Journal of Personality and Social Psychology, 73*, 1246–1256.

Digman, J. M., & Inouye, J. (1986). Further specification of five robust factors of personality. *Journal of Personality and Social Psychology, 50*, 116–123.

Digman, J. M., & Takemoto-Chock, N. K. (1981). Factors in the natural language of personality: Re-analysis, comparison, and interpretation of six major studies. *Multivariate Behavioral Research, 16*, 149–170.

Dion, K. L., & Dion, K. K. (1976). The Honi phenomenon revisited: Factors underlying the resistance to perceptual distortion of one's partner. *Journal of Personality and Social Psychology, 33*, 170–177.

Dodge, K. A. (1991). The structure and function of reactive and proactive aggression. In D. J. Pepler & K. Rubin (Eds.), *The development and treatment of childhood aggression* (pp. 201–218). Toronto, Ontario, Canada: Lawrence Erlbaum Associates.

Doob, L. W. (1990). *Hesitation: Impulsivity and reflection*. Westport, CN: Greenwood Press.

Duffy, E. (1951). The concept of energy mobilization. *Psychological Review, 58*, 30–40.

Easterbrook, J. A. (1959). The effect of emotion on cue utilization and the organization of behavior. *Psychological Review, 66*, 183–201.

Ebstein, R. P., Gritsenko, I., & Nemanov, L. (1997). No association between the serotonin transporter gene regulatory region polymorphism and the tridimensional personality questionnaire (TPQ) temperament of harm avoidance. *Molecular Psychiatry, 2*, 224–226.

Eisenberg, N., & Fabes, R. A. (1992). Emotion, regulation, and the development of social competencies. In M. S. Clark (Ed.), *Emotion and social behavior* (pp. 119–150). Newbury Park, CA: Sage.

Emde, R. H., Biringen, Z., Clyman, R. B., & Oppenheim, D. (1991). The moral self of infancy: Affective core and procedural knowledge. *Developmental Review, 11*, 251–270.

Emde, R. N. (1987). The do's and don'ts of early moral development: Psychoanalytic tradition and current research. In J. Kagan & S. Lamb (Eds.), *The emergence of morality in young children* (pp. 245–276). Chicago: University of Chicago Press.

Endler, N. S. (1982). Interactionism: A personality model, but not yet a theory. In M. R. Jones (Ed.), *Nebraska Symposium on Motivation* (pp. 155–200). Lincoln, NE: Nebraska University Press.

Epstein, S. (1979). The stability of behavior: I. On predicting most of the people much of the time. *Journal of Personality and Social Psychology, 37*, 1097–1126.

Epstein, S. (1993). Implications of cognitive–experiential self-theory for personality and developmental psychology. In D. C. Funder, R. D. Parke, C. Tomlinson-Keasy, & K. Widaman (Eds.), *Studying lives through time* (pp. 399–438). Washington, DC: American Psychological Association.

Epstein, S. (1994). An integration of the cognitive and the psychodynamic unconscious. *American Psychologist, 49*, 709–724.

Epstein, S. (1998). Personal control from the perspective of cognitive–experiential self-theory. In M. Kofta & G. Weary (Eds.), *Personal control in action: Cognitive and motivational mechanisms* (pp. 5–26). New York: Plenum.

Epstein, S., & Meier, P. (1989). Constructive thinking: A broad coping variable with specific components. *Journal of Personality and Social Psychology, 57*, 332–350.

Erikson, E. H. (1950). *Childhood and society*. New York, NY: Norton.

Eron, L. D., & Huesman, L. R. (1984). The relation of prosocial behavior to the development of aggression and psychopathology. *Aggressive Behavior, 10*, 201–211.

Eysenck, H. J. (1970). *The structure of human personality*. London: Methuen.

Eysenck, H. J. (1981). *A model for personality*. New York: Springer-Verlag.

Eysenck, H. J. (1998). *Intelligence: A new look*. New Brunswick, NJ: Transaction.

Eysenck, M. W. (1982). *Attention and arousal*. Berlin: Springer-Verlag.

Fabes, R. A., & Eisenberg, N. (1997). Regulatory control and adults' stress-related responses to daily life. *Journal of Personality and Social psychology, 73,* 1107–1117.

Fabrigar, L. R., Wegener, D. T., MacCallum, R. C., & Strahan, E. (1999). Evaluating the use of exploratory factor analysis in psychological research. *Psychological Methods, 4,* 272–299.

Farley, F. (1986). The Big T in personality. *Psychology Today, 20,* 44–52.

Fenichel, O. (1945). *The psychoanalytic theory of neurosis.* New York: Norton.

Feshbach, S. (1970). Aggression. In P. H. Mussen (Ed.), *Carmichael's manual of child psychology* (Vol. 2, pp. 159–259). New York: Wiley.

Fisher, J. (1959). The twisted pear and the prediction of behavior. *Journal of Consulting and Clinical Psychology, 23,* 400–405.

Flory, J. D., Manuck, S. B., Ferrell, R. E., Dent, K. M., Peters, D. G., & Muldoon, M. F. (1999). Neuroticism is not associated with the serotonin transporter (5-HTTLPR) polymorphism. *Molecular Psychiatry, 4,* 93–96.

Fowles, D. C. (1994). A motivational theory of psychopathology. In W. D. Spaulding (Ed.), *Integrative views of motivation, cognition, and emotion* (pp. 181–238). Lincoln, NE: University of Nebraska Press.

Frenkel-Brunswik, E. (1949). Intolerance of ambiguity as an emotional and perceptual personality variable. *Journal of Personality, 18,* 108–143.

Frenkel-Brunswik, E. (1951). Personality theory and perception. In R. R. Blake & G. V. Ramsey (Eds.), *Perception: An approach to personality.* New York: Ronald.

Freud, S. (1936). *The problem of anxiety.* New York: Norton.

Freud, S. (1950). *Beyond the pleasure principle.* New York: Liveright.

Freud, S. (Ed.). (1952). *Papers on metapsychology* (Vol. 14). London: Hogarth Press.

Freud, S. (Ed.). (1961a). *Civilization and its discontents* (Vol. 21). London: Hogarth Press.

Freud, S. (1961b). *The ego and the id.* In J. Strachey (Ed. and Trans.), *The standard edition of the complete psychological works of Sigmund Freud* (Vol. 19, pp. 1–60). London: Hogarth Press. (Original work published 1923.)

Freud, S. (1963). *Introductory lectures on psychoanalysis: Lecture 25. Anxiety.* In J. Strachey (Ed. and Trans.), *The standard edition of the complete psychological works of Sigmund Freud* (Vol. 16, pp. 392–411). London: Hogarth Press. (Original work published 1916–1917.)

Frosch, J. (1977). The relation between acting out and disorders of impulse control. *Psychiatry, 40,* 295–314.

Fuller, J. L. (1950). Situational analysis: A classification of organism–field interactions. *Psychological Review, 57,* 3–18.

Funder, D. C. (1991). Global traits: A neo-Allportian approach to personality. *Psychological Science, 2,* 31–39.

Funder, D. C. (2001). Personality. *Annual Review of Psychology, 52,* 197–221.

Funder, D. C., & Ozer, D. J. (1983). Behavior as a function of the situation. *Journal of Personality and Social Psychology, 44,* 107–112.

Gardner, R. P., Holzman, P., & Klein, G. S. (1959). *Cognitive control: A study of individual consistencies in cognitive behavior* (Vol. 1). New York: International Universities Press.

Garmezy, N. (1983). Stressors of childhood. In N. Garmezy & M. Rutter (Eds.), *Stress, coping, and development in children* (pp. 43–84). Baltimore: Johns Hopkins University Press.

Garmezy, N. (1993). Children in poverty: Resilience despite risk. *Psychiatry: Interpersonal & Biological Processes, 56*, 127–136.

Gazzaniga, M. S. (1989). Organization of the human brain. *Science, 245*, 947–952.

Gelernter, J., Kranzler, H., Coccaro, E. F., Siever, L. J., & New, A. S. (1998). Serotonin transporter gene polymorphism and personality measures in African American and European American subjects. *American Journal of Psychiatry, 155*, 1332–1338.

Gibson, J. J. (1960). The concept of the stimulus in psychology. *American Psychologist, 15*, 694–703.

Gibson, J. J., & Gibson, E. J. (1955a). Perceptual learning: Differentiation or enrichment? *Psychological Review, 62*, 32–41.

Gibson, J. J., & Gibson, E. J. (1955b). What is learned in perceptual learning? A reply to Professor Postman. *Psychological Review, 62*, 447–450.

Gill, M. (1959). The present status of psychoanalytic theory. *Journal of Abnormal and Social Psychology, 58*, 1–8.

Goldberg, L. R. (1993). The structure of phenotypic traits. *American Psychologist, 48*, 26–34.

Gottlieb, G. (1996). A systems view of psychological development. In D. Magnusson (Ed.), *The lifespan development of individuals: Behavioral, neurobiological, and psychosocial perspectives* (pp. 76–97). New York: Cambridge University Press.

Gough, H. G. (1954). General Information Survey. Berkeley, CA: Institute of Personality Assessment and Research.

Gough, H. G. (1987). *The California Psychological Inventory administrator's guide.* Palo Alto, CA: Consulting Psychologists Press.

Gray, J. A. (1987). *The psychology of fear and stress (2nd ed.).* Cambridge, England: Cambridge University Press.

Greenberg, B. D., McMahon, F. J., & Murphy, D. L. (1998). Serotonin transporter candidate gene studies in affective disorders and personality: Promises and potential pitfalls. *Molecular Psychiatry, 3*, 186–189.

Gross, J. J. (1999). Emotion and emotion regulation. In L. A. Pervin & O. P. John (Eds.), *Handbook of personality: Theory and research* (2nd ed., pp. 525–552). New York: Guilford Press.

Gross, J. J., & John, O. P. (1997). Revealing feelings: Facets of emotional expressivity in self-reports, personality ratings, and behavior. *Journal of Personality and Social Psychology, 72*, 435–448.

Grusec, J. E., & Goodnow, J. J. (1994). Impact of parental discipline methods in the child's internalization of values: A reconceptualization of current points of view. *Developmental Psychology, 30*, 4–19.

Guilford, J. P. (1959). *Personality.* New York: McGraw-Hill.

Guilford, J. P., & Guilford, R. B. (1939). Personality factors D, R, T, and A. *Journal of Abnormal and Social Psychology, 34*, 21–36.

Harlow, H. F. (1949). The formation of learning sets. *Psychological Review, 56,* 51–65.

Harlow, H. F. (1953). Mice, monkeys, men, and motives. *Psychological Review, 60,* 23–32.

Harman, H. H. (1967). *Modern factor analysis.* Chicago: University of Chicago Press.

Hart, D., Hofman, V., Edelstein, W., & Keller, M. (1997). The relation of childhood personality types to adolescent behavior and development: A longitudinal study of Icelandic children. *Developmental Psychology, 33,* 195–205.

Harter, S. (1983). Developmental perspectives on the self-system. In E. M. Hetherington (Ed.), *Socialization, personality, and social development* (Vol. 4, pp. 275–385). New York: Wiley.

Hartmann, H. (1958). *Ego psychology and the problem of adaptation.* New York: International Universities Press.

Hauser, S. T., Vieyra, M. A. B., Jacobson, A. H., & Wertlieb, D. (1989). Family aspects of vulnerability and resilience in adolescence: A theoretical perspective. In T. F. Dugan & R. Coles (Eds.), *The child in our times: Studies in the development of resiliency.* New York: Brunner/Mazel.

Hilgard, E. R. (1962). Impulsive versus realistic thinking: An examination of the distinction between primary and secondary processes in thought. *Psychological Bulletin, 59,* 477–488.

Hinde, R. A. (1966). *Animal behavior.* London: McGraw-Hill.

Hinde, R. A. (1984). Attachment: Some conceptual and biological issues. In C. M. Parkes & J. Stevenson-Hinde (Eds.), *The place of attachment in human behavior* (pp. 60–76). New York: Basic Books.

Hinshaw, S. P. (1994). *Attention deficits and hyperactivity in children.* Thousand Oaks, CA: Sage.

Hochberg, J. E., & Gleitman, H. (1949). Towards a reformulation of the perception–motivation dichotomy. *Journal of Personality, 18,* 180–191.

Hoeg, P. (1993). *Smilla's sense of snow.* New York, NY: Farrar, Straus, & Giroux.

Hoffman, M. L. (1977). Empathy, its development and prosocial implications. *Nebraska Symposium on Motivation, 25,* 169–217.

Homans, G. C. (1950). *The human group.* New York: Harcourt Brace.

Horn, J. L. (1997). Human cognitive capabilities: Gf-Gc theory. In D. P. Flanagan & J. L. Genshaft (Eds.), *Contemporary intellectual assessment: Theories, tests, and issues* (pp. 53–91). New York: Guilford Press.

Horn, J. L., & Cattell, R. B. (1966). Refinement and test of the theory of fluid and crystallized general intelligences. *Journal of Educational Psychology, 57,* 253–270.

Hubbard, R. (1995). Genomania and health. *American Scientist, 83,* 8–10.

Hunt, J. M., & Cofer, C. N. (1946). Psychological deficit. In J. M. Hunt (Ed.), *Personality and the behavior disorders* (Vol. 1, pp. 971–1032). New York: Ronald Press.

Huxley, A. (1954). *The doors of perception.* New York: Harper.

Hyland, M. (1985). Do person variables exist in different ways? *American Psychologist, 40,* 1003–1010.

Izard, C. E. (1993). Four systems for emotion activation: Cognitive and noncognitive processes. *Psychological Review, 100*, 68–90.

Jackson, D. N., & Paunonen, S. V. (1985). Construct validity and the predictability of behavior. *Journal of Personality and Social Psychology, 49*, 554–570.

Jackson, D. N., Paunonen, S. V., Fraboni, M., & Goffin, R. D. (1996). A five-factor versus a six-factor model of personality structure. *Personality and Individual Differences, 20*, 33–45.

James, W. (1890). *Principles of psychology*. New York: Holt.

James, W. (1892). *Psychology: A briefer course*. New York: Holt.

Jang, K. L., Livesley, W. J., & Vernon, P. A. (1998). A twin study of genetic and environmental contributions to gender differences in traits delineating personality disorder. *European Journal of Personality, 12*, 331–344.

Jessor, R. (1956). Phenomenological personality theories and the data language of psychology. *Psychological Review, 63*, 173–180.

Jessor, R. (1958). The problem of reductionism in psychology. *Psychological Review, 65*, 170–178.

Jessor, R., Costa, F., & Donovan, J. (1983). Time of first intercourse: A prospective study. *Journal of Personality and Social Psychology, 44*, 606–626.

Jessor, R., & Jessor, S. L. (1977). *Problem behavior and psychological development: A longitudinal study of youth*. New York: Academic Press.

John, O. P., & Srivastava, S. (1999). The Big Five trait taxonomy: History, measurement, and theoretical perspective. In L. A. Pervin & O. P. John (Eds.), *Handbook of personality* (pp. 102–138). New York: Guilford Press.

Johnson, J. A. (1997). Units of analysis for the description and explanation of personality. In R. Hogan, J. A. Johnson, & S. R. Briggs (Eds.), *Handbook of personality* (pp. 73–93). San Diego, CA: Academic Press.

Jones, M. C. (1968). Personality correlates and antecedents of drinking patterns in adult males. *Journal of Consulting and Clinical Psychology, 32*, 2–12.

Jones, M. C. (1971). Personality antecedents and correlates of drinking patterns in women. *Journal of Consulting and Clinical Psychology, 36*, 61–69.

Kagan, J. (1966). Reflection–impulsivity: The generality and dynamics of conceptual tempo. *Journal of Abnormal Psychology, 71*, 17–24.

Kagan, J., Snidman, N., & Arcus, D. (1993). On the temperamental categories of inhibited and uninhibited children. In K. Rubin & J. Asendorpf (Eds.), *Social withdrawal, inhibition, and shyness in childhood* (pp. 19–28). Hillsdale, NJ: Lawrence Erlbaum Associates.

Kamin, L. J. (1954). Traumatic avoidance learning: The effects of CS–UCS interval with a trace-conditioning procedure. *Journal of Comparative and Physiological Psychology, 47*, 65–72.

Kanfer, F., & Karoly, P. (1972). Self-control: A behavioristic excursion into the lion's den. *Behavior Therapy, 3*, 389–416.

Keating, D. P. (1978). A search for social intelligence. *Journal of Educational Psychology, 70*, 218–223.

Kelley, T. L. (1927). *Interpretation of psychological measurements*. Yonkers, NY: World.

Kellogg, R. T. (1995). *Cognitive psychology*. Thousand Oaks, CA: Sage.

Kenrick, D. T., & Funder, D. C. (1988). Profiting from controversy: Lessons from the person–situation debate. *American Psychologist, 43*, 23–34.

King, L. A. (1996). Who is regulating what and why? Motivational context of self-regulation. *Psychological Inquiry, 7*, 57–60.

Klein, G. S. (1953). The Menninger foundation research on perception and personality, 1947–1952: A review. *Bulletin of the Menninger Clinic, 17*, 93–99.

Klein, G. S. (1958). Cognitive style and motivation. In G. W. Lindzey (Ed.), *Assessment of human motives* (pp. 117–139). New York: Rhinehart.

Kochanska, G. (1993). Toward a synthesis of parental socialization and child temperament in early development of conscience. *Child Development, 64*, 325–347.

Kochanska, G., & Aksan, N. (1995). Mother–child mutually positive affect, the quality of child compliance to requests and prohibitions, and maternal control as correlates of early internalization. *Child Development, 66*, 236–254.

Kochanska, G., Aksan, N., & Koenig, A. L. (1995). A longitudinal study of the roots of preschoolers' conscience: Committed compliance and emerging internalization. *Child Development, 66*, 1752–1769.

Kochanska, G., Murray, K., & Coy, K. C. (1997). Inhibitory control as a contributor to conscience in childhood: From toddler to early school age. *Child Development, 68*, 263–277.

Kochanska, G., Tjebkes, T. L., & Forman, D. R. (1998). Children's emerging regulation of conduct: Restraint, compliance, and internalization from infancy to the second year. *Child Development, 69*, 1378–1389.

Koffka, K. (1935). *Principles of gestalt psychology.* New York: Harcourt Brace.

Kohler, W. (1940). *Dynamics in psychology.* New York: Liveright.

Kopp, C. B. (1982). Antecedents of self-regulation: A developmental perspective. *Developmental Psychology, 18*, 199–214.

Kopp, C. B. (1989). Regulation of distress and negative emotions: A developmental view. *Developmental Psychology, 25*, 343–354.

Kopp, C. B. (1997). Young children: Emotion management, instrumental control, and plans. In S. L. Friedman & E. K. Scholnick (Eds.), *The developmental psychology of planning: Why, how, and when do we plan?* (pp. 103–124). Mahwah, NJ: Lawrence Erlbaum Associates.

Kosslyn, S. M., & Koenig, O. (1992). *Wet mind: The new cognitive neuroscience.* New York: Free Press.

Kounin, J. S. (1972). Experimental studies of rigidity: I. The measurement of rigidity in normal and feebleminded persons. In E. P. Trapp (Ed.), *Readings in exceptional children: Research and theory* (2nd ed.). New York, NY: Appleton-Century-Crofts.

Kremen, A. M., & Block, J. (1998). The roots of ego control. *Journal of Personality and Social Psychology, 75*, 1062–1075.

Kris, E. (1952). *Psychoanalytic explorations in art.* New York: International Universities Press.

Kuczynski, L., Kochanska, G., Radke-Yarrow, M., & Girnius-Brown, O. (1987). A developmental interpretation of young children's noncompliance. *Developmental Psychology, 23*, 799–806.

Kuhl, J., & Kraska, K. (1989). Self-regulation and metamotivation: Computational mechanisms, development, and assessment. In R. Kanfer, P. L. Ackerman, & R. Cudeck (Eds.), *The Minnesota Symposium on Learning and Individual Differences* (pp. 343–374). Hillsdale, NJ: Lawrence Erlbaum Associates.

Lacey, J. (1959). Physiological approaches to the evaluation of psychotherapeutic process and outcome. In E. A. Rubinstein & M. B. Parloff (Eds.), *Research in psychotherapy: Proceedings of a conference* (pp. 145–171). Washington, DC: American Psychological Association.

Lazarus, R. S. (1991). *Emotion and adaptation*. New York: Oxford University Press.

LeDoux, J. (1996). *The emotional brain: The mysterious underpinnings of emotional life*. New York: Simon & Schuster.

Leeper, R. (1943). *Lewin's topological and vector psychology: A digest and a critique*. Eugene, OR: University of Oregon.

Lesch, K., Bengel, D., Heils, A., Sabol, S. Z., Greenberg, B. D., Petri, S., Benjamin, J., Muller, C. R., Hamer, D., & Murphy, D. L. (1996). Association of anxiety-related traits with a polymorphism in the serotonin transporter regulatory region. *Science, 274*, 1527–1531.

Lewin, K. (1935). *Dynamic theory of personality*. New York: McGraw-Hill.

Lewin, K. (1946). Behavior and development as a function of the total situation. In L. Carmichael (Ed.), *Manual of child psychology* (pp. 780–832). New York: Wiley.

Lewin, K. (1951). *Field theory in social science*. New York: Harper.

Lewis, M. (1991). Ways of knowing: Objective self-awareness or consciousness. *Developmental Review, 11*, 231–243.

Lezak, M. D. (1983). *Neuropsychological assessment*. New York: Oxford University Press.

Linville, P. W. (1987). Self-complexity as a cognitive buffer against stress-related illness and depression. *Journal of Personality and Social Psychology, 52*, 663–676.

Livesley, W. J., Jackson, D. N., & Schroeder, M. L. (1989). A study of the factorial structure of personality pathology. *Journal of Personality Disorders, 3*, 292–306.

Livesley, W. J., Jackson, D. N., & Schroeder, M. L. (1992). Factorial structure of traits delineating personality disorders in clinical and general population samples. *Journal of Abnormal Psychology, 101*, 432–440.

Loehlin, J. C. (1998). *Genes and environment in personality development*. Newbury Park, CA: Sage.

Loevinger, J. (1959). Patterns of parenthood as theories of learning. *Journal of Abnormal and Social Psychology, 59*, 148–150.

Loevinger, J. (1976). *Ego development: Conceptions and theories*. San Francisco: Jossey-Bass.

Loevinger, J. (1978). *Scientific ways in the study of ego development*. Worcester, MA: Clark University Press.

Loevinger, J. (1994). Has psychology lost its conscience? *Journal of Personality Assessment, 62*, 2–8.

Logan, G. D., & Cowan, W. B. (1984). On the ability to inhibit thought and action: A theory of an act of control. *Psychological Review, 91*, 295–327.

Londerville, S., & Main, M. (1981). Security of attachment, compliance, and maternal training methods in the second year of life. *Developmental Psychology, 17*, 289–299.

Luthar, S. S., & Zigler, E. (1991). Vulnerability and competence: A review of research on resilience in childhood. *American Journal of Orthopsychiatry, 61*, 6–22.

Lynam, D., Moffitt, T., & Stouthamer-Loeber, M. (1993). Explaining the relation between IQ and delinquency. *Journal of Abnormal Psychology, 102*, 187–196.

Lytton, H. (1977). Correlates of compliance and the rudiments of conscience in two-year-old boys. *Canadian Journal of Behavioural Science, 9*, 242–251.

MacLeod, R. B. (1947). The phenomenological approach in social psychology. *Psychological Review, 54*, 193–210.

Macmillan, M. (2000). *An odd kind of fame: Stories of Phineas Gage*. Cambridge, MA: MIT Press.

Malatesta, C. Z. (1988). The role of emotions in the development and organization of personality. *Nebraska Symposium on Motivation, 36*, 1–56.

Maller, J. B. (1934). General and specific factors in character. *Journal of Social Psychology, 5*, 97–102.

Mandler, G. (1980). The generation of emotion. In R. Plutchik & H. Kellerman (Eds.), *Emotion: Theory, research, and experience*. New York: Academic Press.

Mann, L. (1956). The relation of Rorschach indices of extratension and introversion to a measure of responsiveness to the immediate environment. *Journal of Consulting Psychology, 20*, 114–118.

Marcia, J. E. (1966). Development and validation of ego-identity status. *Journal of Personality and Social Psychology, 3*, 551–558.

Marks, I. M. (1987). *Fears, phobias, and rituals: Panic, anxiety, and their disorders*. New York: Oxford University Press.

Marks, I. M., & Nesse, R. M. (1994). Fear and fitness: An evolutionary analysis of anxiety disorders. *Ethology and Sociobiology, 15*, 247–261.

Marr, D. (1982). *Vision: A computational investigation into the human representation and processing of visual information*. San Francisco: Freeman.

Martin, B. (1954). Intolerance of ambiguity in interpersonal and perceptual behavior. *Journal of Personality, 22*, 494–503.

Martindale, C. (1990). *The clockwork muse: The predictability of artistic change*. New York: Basic Books.

Maslow, A. (1962). *Toward a psychology of being*. Princeton, NJ: Van Nostrand.

Masten, A. S., Best, K. M., & Garmezy, N. (1990). Resilience and development: Contributions from the study of children who overcome adversity. *Development and Psychopathology, 2*, 425–444.

Matas, L., Arend, R. A., & Sroufe, L. A. (1978). Continuity of adaptation in the second year: The relationship between quality of attachment and later competence. *Child Development, 49*, 547–556.

May, M. A., & Hartshorne, H. (1926). First steps toward a scale for measuring attitudes. *Journal of Educational Psychology, 17*, 145–162.

McAdams, D. P. (1989). *Intimacy: The need to be close*. New York: Doubleday.

McAdams, D. P. (1992). The five-factor model in personality: A critical appraisal. *Journal of Personality, 60*, 329–361.

McCann, D., & Endler, N. S. (2000). Editorial: Personality and cognition. *European Journal of Personality, 14*, 371–375.

McCartney, K., Harris, M. J., & Bernieri, F. (1990). Growing up and growing apart: A developmental meta-analysis of twin studies. *Psychological Bulletin, 107*, 226–237.

McClelland, D., Atkinson, J. W., Clark, R. A., & Lowell, E. A. (1976). *The achievement motive*. New York: Irvington.

McCord, W., McCord, J., & Howard, A. (1961). Familial correlates of aggression in nondelinquent male children. *Journal of Abnormal and Social Psychology, 62*, 79–93.

McCrae, R. R., & Costa, P. T. (1986). Clinical assessment can benefit from recent advances in personality psychology. *American Psychologist, 41*, 1001–1003.

McCrae, R. R., & Costa, P. T. (1989). Rotation to maximize the construct validity of factors in the NEO Personality Inventory. *Multivariate Behavioral Research, 24*, 107–124.

McCrae, R. R., & Costa, P. T. (1999). A five-factor theory of personality. In I. A. Pervin & O. P. John (Eds.), *Handbook of Personality* (pp. 139–153). New York: Guilford Press.

McCrae, R. R. (1993). Openness to experience as a basic dimension of personality. *Imagination, Cognition, & Personality, 13*, 39–55.

McCrae, R. R., Costa, P. T. J., & Busch, C. M. (1986). Evaluating comprehensiveness in personality systems: The California Q-Set and the five-factor model. *Journal of Personality, 54*, 430–446.

McCrae, R. R., & John, O. P. (1992). An introduction to the Five Factor Model and its applications. *Journal of Personality, 60*, 175–215.

McNemar, Q. (1964). Lost: Our intelligence? Why? *American Psychologist, 19*, 871–882.

McReynolds, P. (1956). A restricted conceptualization of human anxiety and motivation. *Psychological Reports, 2*, 293–312.

Mead, G. H. (1934). *Mind, self, and society*. Chicago: University of Chicago.

Mednick, S. A. (1958). A learning theory approach to research in schizophrenia. *Psychological Bulletin, 55*, 316–327.

Meehl, P. (1992). Factors and taxa, traits and types, differences of degree and differences of kind. *Journal of Personality, 60*, 117–174.

Meehl, P. E. (1978). Theoretical risks and tabular asterisks: Sir Karl, Sir Ronald, and the slow progress of soft psychology. *Journal of Consulting and Clinical Psychology, 46*, 806–834.

Meehl, P. E. (1990). Schizotaxia as an open concept. In A. I. Rabin & R. A. Zucker (Eds.), *Studying persons and lives* (pp. 248–302). New York: Springer.

Mendelsohn, G. A. (1993). It's time to put theories of personality in their place, or, Allport and Stagner got it right, why can't we? In K. H. Craik, R. Hogan, & R. N. Wolfe (Eds.), *Fifty years of personality psychology: Perspectives on individual differences* (pp. 103–115). New York: Plenum.

Metcalfe, J., & Mischel, W. (1999). A hot–cool-system analysis of delay of gratification: Dynamics of willpower. *Psychological Review, 106*, 3–19.

Milgram, N. A., & Palti, G. (1993). Psychosocial characteristics of resilient children. *Journal of Research in Personality, 27*, 207–221.

Millon, T. (1957). Authoritarianism, intolerance of ambiguity, and rigidity under ego- and task-involving conditions. *Journal of Abnormal and Social Psychology, 55*, 29–33.

Mischel, W. (1968). *Personality assessment*. New York: Wiley.

Mischel, W. (1973). Toward a cognitive social learning reconceptualization of personality. *Psychological Review, 80*, 252–283.

Mischel, W. (1999). Personality coherence and dispositions in a cognitive–affective personality system (CAPS) approach. In D. Cervone & Y. Shoda (Eds.), *The coherence of personality* (pp. 37–60). New York: Guilford Press.

Mischel, W., & Shoda, Y. (1999). Integrating dispositions and processing dynamics within a unified theory of personality: The cognitive–affective personality system. In L. A. Pervin & O. P. John (Eds.), *Handbook of personality* (pp. 197–218). New York: Guilford Press.

Mischel, W., Shoda, Y., & Peake, P. K. (1988). The nature of adolescent competencies predicted by preschool delay of gratification. *Journal of Personality and Social Psychology, 54*, 687–696.

Mischel, W., Shoda, Y., & Rodriguez, M. L. (1989). Delay of gratification in children. *Science, 244*, 933–938.

Mosteller, F., & Tukey, J. W. (1977). *Data analysis and regression*. Reading, MA: Addison-Wesley.

Mowrer, O. H. (1950). *Learning theory and personality dynamics: selected papers*. New York: Ronald Press.

Mroczek, D. K., Ozer, D. J., Spiro, A., & Kaiser, R. T. (1998). Evaluating a measure of the five-factor model of personality. *Assessment, 5*, 287–301.

Murdock, P., & Van Bruggen, Y. O. (1970). Stability, generality, and change of category width. *Journal of Personality, 38*, 117–133.

Murray, H. A. (1938). *Explorations in personality*. New York: Oxford University Press.

Neiman, L. (1988). A critical review of resiliency literature and its relevance to homeless children. *Children's Environments Quarterly, 5*, 17–25.

Nigg, J. (2000). On inhibition/disinhibition in developmental psychopathology: Views from cognitive and personality psychology and a working inhibition taxonomy. *Psychological Bulletin, 126*, 220–246.

Nisbett, R. E., & Ross, L. D. (1980). *Human inference: Strategies and shortcomings of social judgment*. Englewood Cliffs, NJ: Prentice-Hall.

Oehman, A., Hamm, A., & Hugdahl, K. (2000). Cognition and the autonomic nervous system: Orienting, anticipation, and conditioning. In J. T. Cacioppo, L. G. Tassinary, & G. G. Berntson (Eds.), *Handbook of psychophysiology* (2nd ed., pp. 533–575). New York: Cambridge University Press.

Olweus, D. (1979). Stability of aggressive reaction patterns in males: A review. *Psychological Bulletin, 86*, 852–875.

Olweus, D. (1980). Familial and temperamental determinants of aggressive behavior in adolescent boys: A causal analysis. *Developmental Psychology, 16,* 644–660.

Ozer, D. J. (1985). Correlation and the coefficient of determination. *Psychological Bulletin, 97,* 307–315.

Patterson, C. M., & Newman, J. P. (1993). Reflectivity and learning from aversive events: Toward a psychological mechanism for the syndromes of disinhibition. *Psychological Review, 100,* 716–736.

Patterson, G. R., DeBaryshe, B. G., & Ramsey, E. (1989). A developmental perspective on antisocial behavior. *American Psychologist, 44,* 329–335.

Patterson, G. R., & Reid, J. B. (1984). Social interactional processes within the family: The study of the moment-to-moment family transactions in which human social development is embedded. *Journal of Applied Developmental Psychology, 5,* 237–262.

Paunonen, S. V., & Jackson, D. N. (1996). The Jackson Personality Inventory and the five-factor model of personality. *Journal of Research in Personality, 30,* 42–59.

Pedersen, N. L., & Reynolds, C. A. (1998). Stability and change in adult personality: Genetic and environmental components. *European Journal of Personality, 12,* 365–386.

Peloquin, L. J., & Klorman, R. (1986). Effects of methylphenidate on normal children's mood, event-related potentials, and performance in memory-scanning and vigilance. *Journal of Abnormal Psychology, 95,* 88–98.

Piaget, J. (1928). *Judgment and reasoning in the child.* New York: Harcourt Brace.

Piaget, J. (1967). *Six psychological studies.* New York: Random House.

Piaget, J. (1970). Piaget's theory. In P. H. Mussen (Ed.), *Carmichael's manual of child psychology* (Vol. 1, pp. 703–732). New York: Wiley.

Pickering, A. D., & Gray, J. A. (1999). The neuroscience of personality. In L. A. Pervin & O. P. John (Eds.), *Handbook of personality: Theory and research.* New York: Guilford Press.

Plomin, R., & Caspi, A. (1998). DNA and personality. *European Journal of Personality, 12,* 387–407.

Plomin, R., & Caspi, A. (1999). Behavioral genetics and personality. In L. A. Pervin & O. P. John (Eds.), *Handbook of personality: Theory and research* (pp. 251–276). New York: Guilford Press.

Plomin, R., Corley, R., Caspi, A., & Fulker, D. W. (1998). Adoption results for self-reported personality: Evidence for nonadditive genetic effects? *Journal of Personality and Social Psychology, 75,* 211–218.

Polivy, J. (1998). The effects of behavioral inhibition: Integrating internal cues, cognition, behavior, and affect. *Psychological Inquiry, 9,* 181–204.

Porges, S. W. (1991). Vagal tone: An autonomic mediator of affect. In J. Garber & K. A. Dodge (Eds.), *The development of emotion regulation and dysregulation* (pp. 111–128). New York: Cambridge University Press.

Posner, M. I., & Rothbart, M. K. (1992). Attentional mechanisms and conscious experience. In A. D. Milner & M. D. Rugg (Eds.), *The neuropsychology of consciousness* (pp. 91–111). London, England: Academic Press.

Postman, L. J. (1955). Association theory and perceptual theory. *Psychological Review, 62,* 438–446.

Postman, L. J., & Bruner, J. S. (1948). Perception under stress. *Psychological Review, 55,* 314–323.

Pulkkinen, L. (1982). Self-control and continuity from childhood to adolescence. In B. P. Baltes & J. O. G. Brim (Eds.), *Life-span development and behavior* (Vol. 4, pp. 63–105). New York: Academic Press.

Pulkkinen, L. (1988). A two-dimensional model as a framework for interindividual differences in social behavior. In D. H. Saklofske & S. B. G. Eysenck (Eds.), *Individual differences in children and adolescents* (pp. 27–37). New Brunswick, NJ: Transaction.

Pulkkinen, L., & Saastamoinen, M. (1986). Cross-cultural perspectives on youth violence. In S. J. Apter & A. Goldstein (Eds.), *Youth violence: Programs and prospects* (pp. 262–281). Oxford, England: Pergamon Press.

Rachlin, H., & Raineri, A. (1992). Irrationality, impulsiveness, and selfishness as discount reversal effect. In G. Loewenstein & J. Elster (Eds.), *Choice over time* (pp. 93–118). New York: Russell Sage Foundation.

Rapaport, D. (1958). The theory of ego autonomy: A generalization. *Bulletin of the Menninger Clinic, 22,* 13–35.

Revelle, W. (1987). Personality and motivation: Sources of inefficiency in cognitive performance. *Journal of Research in Personality, 21,* 436–452.

Richmond, J. B., & Beardslee, W. R. (1988). Resiliency: Research and practical implications for pediatricians. *Journal of Developmental and Behavioral Pediatrics, 9,* 157–163.

Richters, J. E., & Waters, E. (1991). Attachment and socialization. In M. Lewis & S. Feinman (Eds.), *Social influences and socialization in infancy: The positive side of social influence* (pp. 185–213). New York: Plenum.

Robins, L. (1995). The epidemiology of aggression. In E. Hollander & D. J. Stein (Eds.), *Impulsivity and aggression* (pp. 43–55). Chichester, England: Wiley.

Robins, R. W., John, O. P., Caspi, A., Moffitt, T. E., & Stouthamer-Loeber, M. (1996). Resilient, overcontrolled, and under controlled boys: Three replicabled personality types. *Journal of Personality and Social Psychology, 70,* 157–171.

Roger, D., & Najarian, B. (1989). The construction and validation of a new scale for measuring emotion control. *Personality and Individual Differences, 10,* 845–853.

Rogers, C. R. (1959). A theory of therapy, personality, and interpersonal relationships, as developed in the client-centered framework. In S. Koch (Ed.), *Psychology: A study of a science* (Vol. 3, pp. 312–362). New York, NY: McGraw-Hill.

Rogers, C. R. (1963). The concept of the fully functioning person. *Psychotherapy: Theory, Research, and Practice, 1,* 17–26.

Rosch, E. (1978). Principles of categorization. In E. Rosch & B. B. Lloyd (Eds.), *Cognition and categorization* (pp. 27–48). Hillsdale, NJ: Lawrence Erlbaum Associates.

Ross, L., & Nisbett, R. E. (1991). *The person and the situation: Perspectives of Social psychology*. New York: McGraw-Hill.

Rothbart, M. K. (1989). Temperament and development. In G. A. Kohnstamm, J. E. Bates, & M. K. Rothbart (Eds.), *Temperament in childhood* (pp. 187–247). New York: Wiley.

Rotter, J. B. (1955). The role of the psychological situation in determining the direction of human behavior. In M. R. Jones (Ed.), *Nebraska Symposium on Motivation: 1955* (pp. 245–269). University of Nebraska Press, Lincoln.

Rushton, J. P., Brainerd, C. J., & Pressley, M. (1983). Behavioral development and construct validity: The principle of aggregation. *Psychological Bulletin, 94*, 18–38.

Russ, S. W. (1996). Psychoanalytic theory and creativity: Cognition and affect revisited. In J. Masling & R. Bornstein (Eds.), *Psychoanalytic perspectives in developmental psychology* (pp. 69–103). Washington, DC: American Psychological Association.

Rutter, M. (1987). Psychosocial resilience and protective mechanisms. *American Journal of Orthopsychiatry, 57*, 316–331.

Rutter, M. (1997). Antisocial behavior: Developmental psychopathology perspectives. In D. M. Stoff & J. Breiling (Eds.), *Handbook of antisocial behavior* (pp. 115–124). New York: Wiley.

Salovey, P., & Mayer, J. D. (1990). Emotional intelligence. *Imagination, Cognition, and Personality, 9*, 185–211.

Sanford, N., Webster, H., & Friedman, M. (1957). Impulse expression as a variable of personality. *Psychological Monographs, 71*, 1–21.

Schafer, R. (1958). Regression in the service of the ego: The relevance of a psychoanalytic concept for personality assessment. In G. Lindzey (Ed.), *Assessment of human motives* (pp. 119–148). New York: Rinehart.

Schroeder, M. L., Wormworth, J. A., & John, L. W. (1992). Dimensions of personality disorder and their relationship to the Big Five. *Psychological Assessment, 4*, 47–53.

Shapiro, D. (1965). *Neurotic styles*. New York: Basic Books.

Shapiro, D. (1996). The "self-control" muddle. *Psychological Inquiry, 7*, 76–79.

Shedler, J., & Block, J. (1990). Adolescent drug use and psychological health. *American Psychologist, 45*, 612–630.

Sherif, M. (1936). *The psychology of social norms*. New York: Harper.

Shields, A., & Cicchetti, D. (1997). Emotion regulation among school-age children: The development and validation of a new criterion Q-sort scale. *Developmental Psychology, 33*, 906–916.

Shoda, Y., Mischel, W., & Wright, J. C. (1994). Intra-individual stability in the organization and patterning of behavior: Incorporating psychological situations into the idiographic analysis of personality. *Journal of Personality and Social Psychology, 67*, 674–687.

Simon, H. A. (1952). A formal theory of interaction in social groups. *American Sociological Review, 17*, 202–211.

Simon, H. A. (1954). Some strategic considerations for the construction of social science models. In P. F. Lazarsfeld (Ed.), *Mathematical thinking in the social sciences* (pp. 388–417). Glencoe, IL: Free Press.

Simon, H. A. (1992). What is an "explanation" of behavior? *Psychological Science, 3*, 150–161.

Simon, H. A. (1994). The bottleneck of attention: Connecting thought with motivation. In W. D. Spaulding (Ed.), *Integrative views of motivation, cognition, and emotion* (pp. 1–21). Lincoln, NE: University of Nebraska Press.

Sneed, C. D., McCrae, R. R., & Funder, D. C. (1998). Lay conceptions of the five-factor model and its indicators. *Personality and Social Psychology Bulletin, 24*, 115–126.

Snygg, D. (1949). Predicting the behavior of individuals. *Canadian Journal of Psychology, 3*, 19–29.

Sostek, A. J., Buchsbaum, M. S., & Rapoport, J. (1980). Effects of amphetamine on vigilance performance in normal and hyperactive children. *Journal of Abnormal Child Psychology, 8*, 491–500.

Spence, K., & Taylor, J. A. (1964). Relation of eyelid conditioning to manifest anxiety, extraversion, and rigidity. *Journal of Abnormal and Personality Psychology, 68*, 144–149.

Spence, K. W., & Farber, I. E. (1953). Conditioning and extinction as a function of anxiety. *Journal of Experimental Psychology, 45*, 116–119.

Spiegel, D. (1997). Understanding risk assessment by cancer patients. *Journal of Health Psychology, 2*, 170–171.

Sroufe, L. A. (1979). The coherence of individual development: Early care, attachment, and subsequent developmental issues. *American Psychologist, 34*, 834–841.

Sroufe, L. A. (1997). Psychopathology as an outcome of development. *Development and Psychopathology, 9*, 251–268.

Sroufe, L. A., Cooper, R. G., & Marshall, M. E. (1988). *Child development: Its nature and course.* New York: Knopf.

Stagner, R. (1951). Homeostasis as a unifying concept in personality theory. *Psychological Review, 58*, 5–17.

Sterling, P., & Eyer, J. (1988). Allostasis: A new paradigm to explain arousal pathology. In S. Fisher & J. Reason (Eds.), *Handbook of life stress, cognition, and health* (pp. 629–649). New York: Wiley.

Stern, D. N. (1985). *The interpersonal world of the infant.* New York: Basic Books.

Sternberg, R. J. (1985). *Beyond IQ.* New York: Cambridge University Press.

Stuss, D. T., & Benson, D. F. (1984). Neuropsychological studies of the frontal lobes. *Psychological Bulletin, 95*, 3–28.

Sullivan, H. S. (1953). *The interpersonal theory of psychiatry.* New York: Norton.

Taylor, E. (1994). Syndromes of attention deficit and overactivity. In M. Rutter, E. Taylor, & L. Hersov (Eds.), *Child and adolescent psychiatry* (3rd ed.). Oxford, England: Blackwell Science.

Taylor, E. (1998). Clinical foundations of hyperactivity research. *Behavioral Brain Research, 94*, 11–24.

Taylor, J. A. (1951). The relationship of anxiety to the conditioned eyelid response. *Journal of Experimental Psychology, 41*, 81–92.

Tellegen, A. (1985). Structures of mood and personality and their relevance to assessing anxiety, with an emphasis on self-report. In A. H. Tuma & J. D. Maser (Eds.), *Anxiety and the anxiety disorders* (pp. 681–706). Hillsdale, NJ: Lawrence Erlbaum Associates.

Tellegen, A., & Atkinson, G. (1974). Openness to absorbing and self-altering experiences ("absorption"), a trait related to hypnotic susceptibility. *Journal of Abnormal Psychology, 83*, 268–277.

Thelen, E., & Smith, L. B. (1994). *A dynamic systems approach to the development of cognition and action*. Cambridge, MA: MIT Press.

Thomas, A., Chess, S., & Korn, S. J. (1982). The reality of difficult temperament. *Merrill-Palmer Quarterly, 28*, 1–20.

Thorndike, E. L. (1904). *An introduction to the theory of mental and social measurement*. New York: Teachers College, Columbia University.

Tighe, L. S., & Tighe, T. J. (1966). Discrimination learning: two views in historical perspective. *Psychological Review, 66*, 353–370.

Tinbergen, N. (1951). *The study of instinct*. Oxford, England: Oxford University Press.

Turkheimer, E. (1998). Heritability and biological explanation. *Psychological Review, 105*, 782–791.

Turkheimer, E., & Waldron, M. (2000). Nonshared environment: A theoretical, methodological, and quantitative review. *Psychological Bulletin, 126*, 78–108.

Tversky, A., & Kahneman, D. (1974). Judgment under uncertainty: Heuristics and biases. *Science, 185*, 1124–1131.

Underwood, B. J. (1957). *Psychological research*. New York: Appleton-Century-Crofts.

Underwood, B. J. (1975). Individual differences as a crucible in theory construction. *American Psychologist, 30*, 128–134.

Vallacher, R. R., & Nowak, A. (Eds.). (1994). *Dynamical systems in social psychology*. San Diego, CA: Academic Press.

van Aken, M. A. G., van Lieshout, C. F. M., Scholte, R. H. J., & Haselager, G. J. T. (in press). Personality types in childhood and adolescence: Main effects and person–relationship transactions. In L. Pulkkinen & A. Caspi (Eds.), *Personality in the life course: Paths to a successful development*. New York: Cambridge University Press.

Vaughn, B. E., Kopp, C. B., & Krakow, J. B. (1984). The emergence and consolidation of self-control from eighteen to thirty months of age: Normative trends and individual differences. *Child Development, 55*, 990–1004.

Visweswaran, C., & Ones, D. S. (1999). Meta-analyses of fakability estimates: Implications for personality measurement. *Educational and Psychological Measurement, 59*, 197–210.

von Neuman, J. (1958). *The computer and the brain*. New Haven, CT: Yale University Press.

Vygotsky, L. S. (1960). The genesis of higher mental functions. In J. V. Wertsch (Ed.), *The concept of activity in Soviet psychology* (pp. 144–188). New York: Sharpe.

Wachtel, P. L. (1968). Anxiety, attention, and coping with threat. *Journal of Abnormal Psychology, 73*, 137–143.

Wallace, J. (1966). An abilities conception of personality: Some implications for personality measurement. *American Psychologist, 21*, 132–138.

Waller, N. G., & Zavala, J. (1993). Evaluating the Big Five. *Psychological Inquiry, 4*, 131–134.

Watson, D., & Clark, L. A. (1993). Behavioral disinhibition versus constraint: A dispositional perspective. In D. M. Wegner & J. W. Pennebaker (Eds.), *Handbook of mental control* (pp. 506–527). Englewood Cliffs, NJ: Prentice Hall.

Watson, D., & Tellegen, A. (1985). Toward a consensual structure of mood. *Psychological Bulletin, 98*, 219–235.

Webb, E. J., Campbell, D. T., Schwartz, R. D., & Sechrest, L. (1966). *Unobtrusive measures: Nonreactive research in the social sciences.* Chicago: Rand McNally.

Weinberger, D. A., & Schwartz, G. A. (1990). Distress and restraint as superordinate dimensions of self-reported adjustment: A typological perspective. *Journal of Personality, 58*, 381–417.

Werner, E. E., & Smith, R. S. (1982). *Vulnerable, but invincible: A longitudinal study of resilient children and youth.* New York: McGraw-Hill.

Wertheimer, M. (1945). *Productive thinking.* New York: Harper.

White, R. W. (1959). Motivation reconsidered: The concept of competence. *Psychological Review, 66*, 297–333.

White, R. W. (1973). The concept of healthy personality: What do we really mean? *The Counseling Psychologist, 4*, 3–12.

Wiggins, J. A. (1992). Have model, will travel. *Journal of Personality, 60*, 527–532.

Witkin, H. A., Lewis, H. B., Hertzman, M., & Machover, K. (1954). *Personality through perception: An experimental and clinical study.* New York: Harper.

Wohlwill, J. F. (1958). The definition and analysis of perceptual learning. *Psychological Review, 65*, 283–295.

Wold, H. (1956). Causal inference from observational data. *Journal of the Royal Statistical Society, 119*, 18–32.

Woodworth, R. S. (1958). *Dynamics of behavior.* New York: Holt.

Wright, J. C., & Zakriski, A. L. (in press). A contextualizing analysis of external and mixed syndrome boys: When syndromal similarity obscures functional dissimilarity. *Journal of Consulting and Clinical Psychology, 69.*

Wright, J. C., Zakriski, A. L., & Drinkwater, M. (1999). Developmental psychopathology and the reciprocal patterning of behavior and environment: Distinctive situational and behavioral signatures of internalizing, externalizing, and mixed-syndrome children. *Journal of Consulting and Clinical Psychology, 67*, 95–107.

Yerkes, R. M., & Dodson, J. D. (1908). The relation of strength of stimulus to rapidity of habit-formation. *Journal of Comparative Neurology of Psychology, 18*, 459–482.

Yik, M. S. M., & Bond, M. H. (1993). Exploring the dimensions of Chinese person perception with indigenous and imported constructs: Creating a culturally balanced scale. *International Journal of Psychology, 28*, 75–95.

Zahn, T. P., Rapoport, J. L., & Thompson, C. L. (1980). Autonomic and behavioral effects of dextroamphetamne and placebo in normal and hyperactive prepubertal boys. *Journal of Abnormal Child Psychology, 8*, 145–160.

Zahn-Waxler, C., Radke-Yarrow, M., Wagner, E., & Chapman, M. (1992). Development of concern for others. *Developmental Psychology, 28*, 126–136.

Zajonc, R. B. (1980). Feeling and thinking: Preferences need no inferences. *American Psychologist, 35*, 151–175.

Zajonc, R. B. (1984). On the primacy of affect. *American Psychologist, 39*, 117–123.

Zimbardo, P. G. (1977). *Shyness: What it is, what to do about it*. Reading, MA: Addison-Wesley.

Zubek, J. P. (1974). Sensory isolation: Fifteen years of research at the University of Manitoba. *Studia Psychologica, 16*, 265–274.

Zuckerman, M., Kuhlman, D. M., Joireman, J. P. T., & Kraft, M. (1994). A comparison of three structural models for personality: The Big Three, the Big Five, and the Alternative Five. *Journal of Personality and Social Psychology, 65*, 757–768.

Author Index

Subject Index

A

AA, *see* Autochthonous assimilability
Abreaction, 137
Absorption, 113
Acting-out *vs.* acting-up, 155, 187*n*
Adaptability, 10–11
Adaptive mechanisms, 50
Adaptive modulation, *see* Regulation
Adaptive orientations, 142–147
Adaptive *vs.* maladaptive behavior, 3–4
Adjustment, 9–11, 17
Affect-motivational structure of structures, 186
Affect-processing system, personality as, 174, 191, *see also specific topics*
   condensed statement of, 124–125
   phenomena stimulating the theory, 2–13
Agent, self as, 26, 27, *see also* Autonomy
Aggression, 196–197
Alcohol use, 153
Allostasis, 131
Ambiguity, intolerance of, 3, 78, 82, 121
Amphetamines, 152, 153
Antisocial disorder, 150–152
Antisocial personality pattern, 196–197, *see also* Psychopathy

Anxiety, 2–3, 57
   causes, 63, 66–67, 80–81, *see also* Anxiety arousal; Anxiety reduction
   definitions and conceptions of, 61–64
   insufficient, 129
   levels of, 81
      massive/maximum *vs.* minimum, 66–67, 81
   primary/state *vs.* secondary/trait, 63, 129–130
   psychoanalytic writers on, 75
   rational *vs.* irrational, 64
   role of, 129–130
   as sensed indicator of system instability, 61–64
Anxiety arousal, causes of
   insufficient processing of percepts, 77–80
   insufficient reduction of drive, 75–77, 79, *see also under* Drive reduction
Anxiety management, suppressive and expressive modes of, 133
Anxiety-reduction, 57, 58
   direct *vs.* indirect, 81
   as preemptive basis for behavior, 64–66
   psychotherapy and, 136–139
   two basic modes of, 79–81

233

Development, psychological molding, 189–193
Developmental processes, 24, 25, *see also specific topics*
Developmental psychology, 38
Diagnostic and Statistical Manual of Mental Disorders-IV (DSM-IV), 23
Differentiation, 89
  conceptual property of, 134–135
  evolution and, 123
Discrimination, stimulus and response, 5
Disinhibition, 187*n*
Dispositional approach to personality, 169, 176
Dissocial individuals, 154–155
Drive-reduction, 49–53, 59
  anxiety-reducing function, 66, 70–71, 75–77, 79
"Drive slavery," 154
Drive(s), 68–71
  composition, 84
    concept of control apparatus, 84, 87–96
    concept of tension, 84–87
  cumulativeness, 118–119
  definitions and conceptions of, 67–69, 76, 84
  integrating attentional influences with, 49–53
  psychological, 76
  secondary, 69–70
Drugs
  changing ego structures via, 152–154
  hallucinogenic, 74–75, 152–154
DSM-IV, 23
Dynamic systems, 39

E

Effectance, 61
Effectance motivation, 50
"Effort after meaning," 3
Ego, 28, 88–89, 107
  defined, 28
Ego control, 9, 92, 132, 197, *see also* Impulse control
  gender differences in, 188–189
Ego development, basic dilemma of, 183–184
Ego functioning, 88
Ego functioning structures, 184–185

Ego permeability, 123, *see also* Permeability
Ego-resiliency, 12, 25, 118, 123–124, 150, 197, *see also* Resiliency
  gender differences in, 188–189
Ego structures, 184–185
Elasticity, 143, 144, *see also* Resiliency
Emotional expression, 137, 140, 142
Emotional regulation, *see also* Regulation; Self-control
  antecedent- *vs.* response-focused, 141
  efforts at, 141–142
Emotions, summating the effects of, 5–6
Empiricism, 37, 38
Energy, life, 60
Environment-centered view, 42–44
Environment(s), 46, 99, 101
  average expectable, 59
  distinctions and relations between person and, 17, *see also* Societal dimensions of personality
  objective and subjective psychological, 46–49, 99–102, 175
Evolutionary principle of reproductive fitness, 123
Executive (functioning), 88–89, 107
Experimental action, 184
Exploration-attachment balance, 4
Extraversion scale, 158, 160

F

Factor analysis, 158, *see also* Five-factor model
Family environment, structure and predictability experienced in, 192–193
Five-factor model/approach of Costa and McCrae
  evaluative remarks regarding, 163–164
  factor analysis of, 158–159
  higher-order, 161–163
  as the five-factor theory, 163
  history, 156–158
  literature and research on, 157–158
  recent findings, 159–161
  unresolved issues, 158–159
"Flow," 67, 71